Student Resource Manual to Accompany Dudley/Faricy/Rice

THE HUMANITIES

Sixth Edition

Student Resource Manual to Accompany Dudley/Faricy/Rice

THE HUMANITIES

Sixth Edition

Supplemental Exercises, Examples, Illustrations and Readings

James G. Rice
Department of Humanities
Stephens College

McGraw-Hill Book Company
New York St. Louis San Francisco Auckland Bogotá Düsseldorf
Johannesburg London Madrid México Montreal New Delhi Panama
Paris São Paulo Singapore Sydney Tokyo Toronto

Student Resource Manual
to Accompany
Dudley, Faricy, and Rice:
THE HUMANITIES

ISBN 0-07-017973-5

1 2 3 4 5 6 7 8 9 0 WHWH 7 8 3 2 1 0 9 8

The editor was Robert P. Rainier.
The Whitlock Press, Inc., was printer and binder.

See Index of Readings and Acknowledgements on pages 351-352.

CONTENTS

PART THREE ORGANIZATION

PART FOUR STYLE

APPENDIX

PREFACE

This illustrated <u>Student Resource Manual</u> has been written to accompany the Dudley, Faricy, Rice: The <u>Humanities</u>, Sixth Edition. The materials are organized chapter by chapter to correlate with the text.

At the beginning of each chapter there is a section of short-answer questions on the important concepts in it. The purpose of these is to help fix clearly in mind the terms and concepts of the material covered. Knowing a term for a concept not only clarifies its meaning but sensitizes us to occurrences of it in various contexts and situations. Studies have shown that hearing concepts stated in different ways, writing them, or engaging in choices among them reinforces mastery of them.

A second section in each chapter includes exercises in applying the concepts to a variety of materials, sometimes in the text, sometimes in the <u>Student Resource Manual</u>, and sometimes in the environment.

The self-tests in painting, music, and literature are exercises in how one uses the concepts learned in approaching the arts and should be understood as such. The choice of "correct" answers to particular questions is, therefore, not as important as the experience in considering alternative possibilities.

Included in most chapters is a section of Discussion Questions. Many of the True-False questions are not questions of fact but of judgment and are therefore appropriate for discussion.

There are other materials, too: Guides for organizing information learned; pieces which extent the content of the text (for example, the section on Domestic Architecture in the United States); suggestions for further readings; outlines for conducting a study of art; and suggestions for exploring the riches which become available to us as we become aware of how the arts "work" and of what we can learn to hear, see, and enjoy.

Throughout the <u>Student Resource Manual</u> we have tried to direct the reader beyond the text and the course to examine the arts in his or her daily experiences and environment.

James G. Rice

1 INTRODUCTION

ANALYTICAL PRINCIPLES COMMON TO ALL THE ARTS

CONCEPTS

Match the following:

____1. Subject

____2. Function

____3. Medium

____4. Elements

____5. Organization

____6. Style

____7. Judgment

(1) The practical, utilitarian purpose of the work of art.
(2) Differences in mood or personality of art works.
(3) The biography of the artist.
(4) The basic components of an art work which can be talked about separately although we encounter them as integrated combinations.
(5) The monetary value of the art work.
(6) The means of achieving unity and coherence in art.
(7) The beauty of the object represented.
(8) Discriminating evaluation of the art work.
(9) The material of which the work is made.
(10) That which the work of art represents.

One of the numbered items in the summary to this chapter is neither a direct quotation nor a summary of material which is in the chapter. It is, however, an inference or conclusion drawn from what is said there. Can you identify it? Be prepared to explain in a few sentences why you think it is true <u>or</u> untrue.

Mark the following as True or False:

_____ 1. A beautiful waterfall framed naturally by trees proves that nature and art are sometimes the same.

_____ 2. We all see and hear the same things but we sometimes feel differently about them.

_____ 3. Art appears to rank rather low in importance among the activities of primitive peoples.

_____ 4. Literature cannot be taught, but music can.

_____ 5. We usually see and hear only what we have been taught to see and hear.

_____ 6. The conventions of art such as "rail-road perspective" are one language of the arts.

_____ 7. According to Susan Sontag the real function of criticism is to show us what a work of art means.

_____ 8. Because it uses drama, music, and sometimes dance, opera is called a "Combined Art".

_____ 9. Our chances of hearing the works of Mozart are greater than were those of his contemporaries.

_____10. According to Kenneth Clark technology has destroyed our belief in our own immortality.

_____11. The artist's first concern is to create something beautiful.

_____12. Whenever you explain or define art, you substitute the explanation for the experience.

_____13. A work of art is not entirely the product of conscious effort.

_____14. An artist's interpretation of his own work is the most complete and accurate information we have about it.

_____15. Disorder in a painting may be as expressive as order.

_____16. All people at all times at all places of which we have knowledge have created art.

Several of the above statements are related. Consider the pairs below and tell how they are related. Example: Nos. 11 and 15 are related because if disorder is expressive, the artist cannot be concerned with beauty alone.

Nos. 13 and 14 are related because ____________________

____

Nos. 2 and 5 are related because ____________________

____

Nos. 7 and 12 are related because ____________________

____

Nos. 3 and 16 are related because ____________________

____

Name the country in which the following works originated:

1. Queen Nefertiti ____________________
2. Galloping Wild Boar ____________________
3. Odyssey ____________________
4. Saffo's poetry ____________________
5. Rubaiyat of Omar Khayyam ____________________
6. Aesop's Fables ____________________

APPLICATION OF CONCEPTS

Place the NUMBERS of the following items in the MOST correct space on the chart below. The numbers in parentheses after the items indicate that the number should be placed in two spaces.

Example requiring one answer:

A trombone is a MEDIUM of MUSIC.

Example requiring two answers:

A cathedral is an ORGANIZATION in ARCHITECTURE for a particular FUNCTION.

1. Leaping and running in rhythm
2. A flute
3. A classical symphony (2)
4. Harmony
5. A romantic opera (2)
6. A fountain
7. A polka (2)
8. An apartment house
9. Bronze
10. _Carmen_ is still the greatest opera ever written
11. Words
12. A memorial chapel
13. The "Mona Lisa" is Da Vinci's greatest art work
14. Bodies moving in space
15. A realistic statue (2)
16. An arch
17. "Flight of the Bumble Bee" for violin and piano (2)
18. A Cookbook (2)
19. A football stadium (2)
20. Vowel sounds
21. A portrait
22. A march
23. A photograph of a dog
24. A sonnet
25. A tragedy (2)
26. Color
27. Watercolor
28. Brick
29. A poem about spring
30. A novel

	VISUAL ARTS	MUSIC	LITERATURE	ARCHITECTURE	COMBINED ARTS
SUBJECT					
FUNCTION					
MEDIUM					
ELEMENTS					
ORGANIZATION					
STYLE					
JUDGMENT					

THE UNIVERSAL LANGUAGE OF ART

Gyorgy Kepes' Language of Vision (1944) was a pioneering work in the field of art and perception. The quotation from his book The New Landscape (1956) deals with the primary language of the arts discussed on pages 12 and 13 of this chapter. The passage should be read closely for its wide-ranging implications.

There are in it at least four words which you should look up if they are unfamiliar to you. Write the definitions here for ready reference:

1. morphological
2. space-geometry
3. archetypes
4. matrices

Now consider these questions.

1. List four characteristics of each of the "two morphological archetypes" which are the polarities of the language of art.

______________________	______________________
______________________	______________________
______________________	______________________
______________________	______________________

2. According to Kepes, art has a universal language in the sense that particular patterns of elements (lines, colors, shapes) always express the same meaning wherever they are found. Decide whether you agree or disagree with this statement and give two examples to support your position.

3. "Without even recognizing the subject matter, we still respond to form itself, to the configuration, from whatever "thing" it may be derived." Compare Kandinsky's Light Picture #188 (Color Plate 8, following page 56) and Improvisation #30 (Warlike Theme) (Color Plate 9, following page 56). Do these differ in the morphological types toward which they tend? Which is the more ordered?

4. Read the two statements by Henry Moore on pages 33 and 40. Does he seem to be saying the same thing as Kepes about forms and the universal feelings particular forms evoke? Explain. How do Kepes' remarks apply to Moore's Two Forms (page 34).

THE UNIVERSAL LANGUAGE OF ART

Art, in a sense, has a universal language; its variations are no more than its dialects: we can grasp the essential meaning contained in a work of art regardless of whether we possess any key to the cultural climate in which it grew. A prehistoric drawing may tell us as much as a work of our own century. Without even recognizing the subject matter, we still respond to form itself, to the configuration, from whatever "thing" it may be derived. The patterns of action which are apparent in the modulating of lines and in the tectonics of shape and colors cannot fail to give us the expressive meaning. The phrases of this visual language can be formulated neither with words nor with space-geometry, but we can find, nevertheless, a basic vocabulary and grammar for communicating important ideas. We feel common meanings in the most diverse artistic expressions.

There are two basic morphological archetypes among these meanings: expression of order, coherence, discipline, stability on the one hand; expression of chaos, movement, vitality, change on the other. Common to the morphology of outer and inner processes, these are basic polarities recurring in physical phenomena, in the organic world and in human experience. As Emerson has put it, they are "the dynamic substance of our universe, written in every corner of nature." Felt in artistic forms, they can be discerned in the processes of creative scientific thought. They are basic phases of our physiology as well as of our feelings. They are keys to the understanding of social phenomena. They constitute the pulsations of the history of our culture. They are matrices which mold into significance and direction the new impacts which our nervous systems receive from the outside. To find meaning in the world of forms of such expanded scope, we must evaluate each new pattern in these fundamental terms.

-- Gyorgy Kepes

THE EYES CREATE

There is no more dramatic way of illustrating how our eyes "create" from what is presented them than optical illusions. They do so partly because of their physical make up, partly because of our cultural conditioning in "reading" visual images, and partly because of expectancies we bring to our "looking". We have in the text demonstrated how our expectancies can lead us to misread or "underread" de Kooning's Woman I (Color Plate 4, following page 56). Here are some instances of how artists can make us "see" what is physically not there.

Above and on the following pages are three examples of optical illusions. Albers in Homage to the Square: Broad Call (Color Plate 27, following page 260) uses color for his optical effects. These use only black and white.

In the example above, because the white lines and black lines are of the same intensity and are the same thickness, the eye is confused as to which is the background and which the design and a shimmering effect results. Bridget Riley's Shih-li (Figure 10-2, page 240) achieves its effects in the same way.

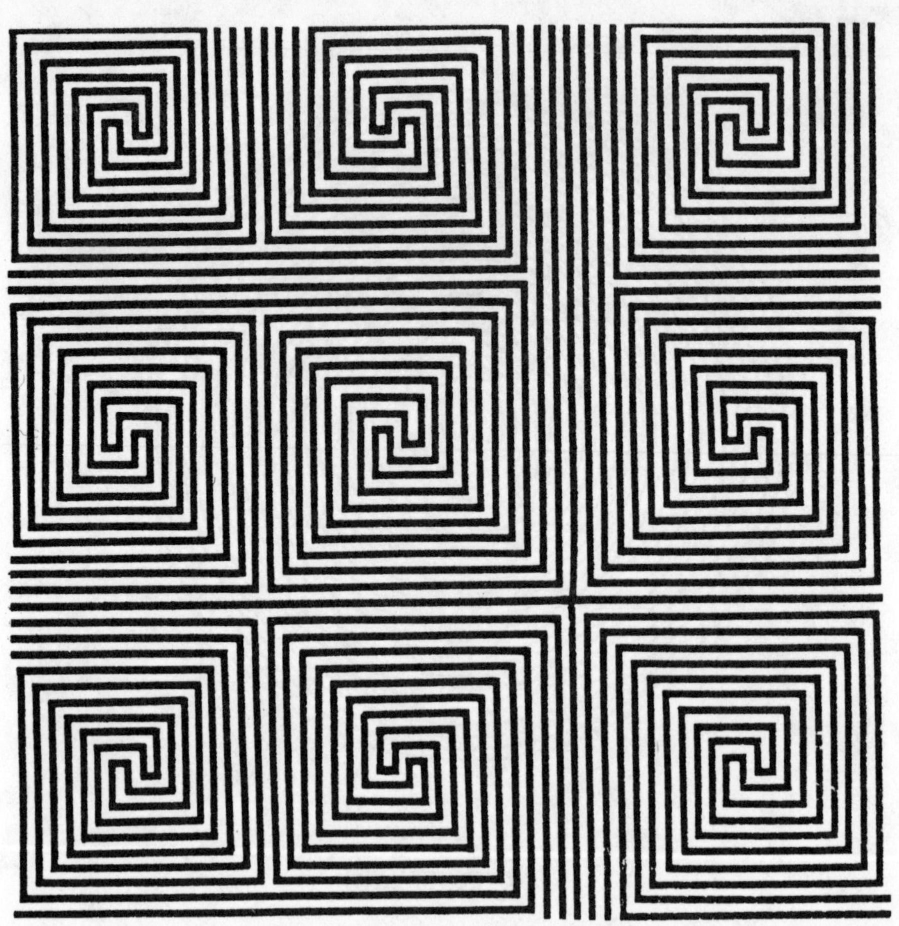

In the example above the eyes are confused even more; they keep shifting focus to determine which is foreground and which is background and they keep searching for a pattern which at first glance looks like a simple repetition and are confused when it is not. A As the page is shifted or the focus is changed either the squares with verticals or the squares with horizontals become grey from the afterimage of the black. In Alber's Aquarium (Figure 2-4, page 39) there is a similar optical illusion; the white areas and black areas keep changing place as foreground and background, creating a sense of movement.

In the last example on the next page the afterimage of the black lines create grey or purple squares at the intersection of the white lines. In Vasarely's Vega (Figure 10-1, page 239), a regular pattern of squares is warped systematically, - - playing with our conditioning that things become smaller as they move away from us and larger as they approach - - to create the illusion of convex or concave areas on a two dimensional surface. The equal distribution of black and white areas create afterimages which produce a shimmering effect. Vasarley is one of the artists responsible for the "Op Art" movement of the 1960's. See the optical effects in his Casiopée (Color Plate 36 following page 312). Can you from the explanations above and your study of Alber's Homage to the Square: Broad Call explain what he has done to get the effects he does?

If you would like to explore other types of illusions used by artists, you will find many interesting books about them. One is that by M. Luckiesh, Visual Illusions: Their Causes, Characteristics and Applications. New York: Dover Publications, Inc., 1965.

DISCUSSION QUESTIONS:

-1-

Rudolf Arnheim believes that we in America are "a generation that has lost touch with its senses." He believes that the value placed on skills to manipulate our sophisticated machinery and to practice our multitude of technologies has been responsible. The consequent emphasis in our education system on training people to do these things has produced a generation that no longer experiences the real world. Reread the quotation on pages 3 and 4 of the text and be prepared to discuss Arnheim's thesis.

Was it this single-purposed emphasis on production, on conquering and controlling nature that led to our ecological crisis? Had we been more sensitive, more observant, more open to our feelings, might the critical phase of our ecological problems have been avoided?

We are currently in a rash of consciousness-expanding activities. They run the gamut from consciousness-expanding drugs to meditation groups, to consciousness raising weekends to an involved interest in eastern religions and religious practices. Might these relate to a hunger for sensory experiences, a revolt of the senses driven underground by our value system, a strictly rationalistic education and a machine-technology dominated culture?

Do you see evidences that we are trying to recover the wholeness of our humanity, to correct the imbalance Arnheim hints at?

Reflect on your own experiences and education. What forces were brought to bear on your thinking about your own education, your own life goals as a person, the choice of a profession? Did your own conditioning come from your education, the culture, the mass media?

-2-

A thought to ponder: Abraham Lincoln is said to have learned most of his statesmanship from reading the history plays of William Shakespeare; who is educating today's political leaders? It is evident that it is not the playwrights, neither past nor present. - - Edward L. Kamarck, "A Deeper and Surer Rooting in Life," Arts in Society, Vol. 8, No. 3, (Fall/Winter, 1971) p. 606.

AIDS TO THE STUDY OF THE HUMANITIES

The materials which follow will be important to you throughout the reading of the text. It will be helpful if you refer to the Table of Contents of the text as you read through each of them. They consist of the following:

AN OVERVIEW OF THE HUMANITIES

This chart puts into graphic form the questions we will be asking about each of the arts we will be discussing. (The Combined Arts are the arts which use more than one medium - - i.e., opera, theater, dance, film.) As you progress through the text you will be able to discuss in some depth the materials needed to complete each of the blocks on the chart. You should make a mental note that the chart is here for ready reference.

REFERENCE MAP OF THE TEXT

This chart indicates the numbers of the chapters in the text in which you will find a discussion of the topics on the left as they apply to specific arts listed across the top. Take, for example, the column headed MUSIC.

Chapters 2 and 3 contain comments on SUBJECT in Music.
Chapter 4 discusses FUNCTION in MUSIC.
Chapters 5 and 7 discuss the MEDIUMS of MUSIC.
Chapter 10 discusses the ELEMENTS in MUSIC.
Chapter 15 explains the ORGANIZATIONS characteristic of MUSIC.
Chapter 17 discusses MUSICAL STYLES.

The chapters on Medium, Elements and Organization in each of the arts are devoted entirely to that art and are therefore, the most substantive.

Should your teacher decide to cover one art in detail before going on to another art rather than follow the outline of the book which takes up the topics in the order in which they are listed in the left hand column this chart will be particularly helpful.

QUESTIONS WE ASK OF WORKS OF ART

This outline is an elaboration of the questions which constitute the order of chapters in the text. You will find it useful as you begin to study specific works in any of the arts and will want to refer to it from time to time throughout the course.

OVERVIEW OF THE HUMANITIES

	VISUAL ARTS	MUSIC	LITERATURE	ARCHITECTURE	COMBINED ARTS
SUBJECT What is the work about? Are there explicit images or ideas? A theme? Is it non-representational?					
FUNCTION Does it have a utilitarian purpose? How effectively does it fulfill the purpose?					
MEDIUM What is the work made of? Techniques used in manipulating the materials? How did choice of medium affect the style of the work? What are the natural affective potentials of the medium?					
ELEMENTS Elements are aspects which can be talked about separately; they are the sensuous units with which the artist works. How have they been used? For what purposes?					
ORGANIZATION Structure is the form into which the elements have been organized. What is the organization? Is it a traditional form? How does it contribute to the significance of the work?					
STYLE What is its mood, temper, personality? Style is usually associated with pervasive characteristics of an individual, a period or movement, or a medium or instrument. Are there recurrent, distinctive features within the work or which relate it to other works?					
JUDGMENT Is the work significant? Why? Does it suggest, reflect, evoke, express particular values, questions? What are they? Are they personal or cultural? Do you like it? Why?					

REFERENCE MAP OF TEXT

	VISUAL ARTS CHAPTERS	MUSIC CHAPTERS	LITERATURE CHAPTERS	ARCHITECTURE CHAPTERS	COMBINED ARTS CHAPTERS
SUBJECT	2, 3	2, 3	2, 3	2, 3	2, 3
FUNCTION	4	4	4	4	4
MEDIUM	5, 6	5, 7	5, 8	4, 14	5, 8
ELEMENTS	9	10	11, 12	14	9, 10, 11, 12
ORGANIZATION	13	15	16	14	16
STYLE	17	17	17	14, 17	17
JUDGMENT	18, 19	18, 19	18, 19	18, 19	18, 19

QUESTIONS WE ASK OF WORKS OF ART

Whatever has been put into a work of art has been put there for some kind of human satisfaction: it is our purpose to learn the range of those satisfactions and how to attain them.

The outline below is an expansion of the questions on pages 23-24 of the text. These constitute the outline of the text. (Question 4 in the text has been divided into two questions here: one having to do with the elements and the other with how they are organized.)

These expanded questions will enable you to begin to engage art in dialogue immediately. When you have completed the text and are able to answer the questions in greater depth and detail the result will constitute a critical analysis of the art work studied.

I. SUBJECT

Does the work have a subject?

Is the subject of primary or secondary importance?
Is it an end or a means to an end?

What was the source of the subject? Is the choice of the subject original, or were there other treatments of the subject known to the artist? Why did the artist choose this subject?

An artist or author can never include every aspect of his subject; he must choose the details which he will represent. What has he included? What are some omissions? What do they imply? Do you understand his inclusions? Can you explain them in terms of attitudes, meanings, patterns?

II. FUNCTION

Does the work perform some service to mankind in a mechanical way? Does it hold up, contain, hold together, carry, protect?

III. MEDIUM

What is the medium? What are the limitations of this medium and how have they affected the results? Why do you think the medium was chosen? Is it suited to the subject? Are there connotations or meanings inherent in the medium which the artist has had to take advantage of or deny?

Any evidence of tools with which medium was worked (brush strokes, chisel marks, and the like)? Do these contribute to the emotional impact of the finished piece?

Has the medium been handled honestly? Has respect been shown the inherent qualities of the medium (texture, strength, coloring, instrumentation, size, choice of words, and the like)?

Is the medium a traditional one or an experimental one?

IV. ELEMENTS

Which of the elements predominate?

Enumerate the elements which seem to be most important to the total meaning and explain how each makes its individual contribution to this meaning.

Is any element or combination of elements used in an unusual or original manner?

V. ORGANIZATION

What structural organization is used?
Do you recognize any traditional form of organization (e.g., sonnet, symphony, pyramidal)? How has the tradition been dealt with? Has it been followed closely, or used as a point of departure?

What is the center of interest, climax?

Is there unity of treatment (same degree of abstraction throughout, e.g.)? Do all elements work together within the organization for unity of effect?

How do the principles of order function in the work - - unity, dominance, variety, balance, continuity, symmetry, proportion, rhythm?

VI. STYLE

Is the intellectual, rational, formal approach revealed in the style or are expressive, subjective, emotional qualities stressed? Give specific examples to show that this is true.

Are there any mannerisms of style in the work which you have come to associate with any artists, school, "ism", or period? List them and, if you can, explain them.

Can you think of another work in the same art which is similar in style to the one you are considering? Can you think of a work in another art which seems to you to be similar in style? Explain these similarities in as much detail as possible.

VII. JUDGMENT

How do you feel about the work? Do you like, enjoy or respect it?

Can you explain your attitude logically, citing specific instances? That is, what seem to you to be the reasons for the attitude you have taken toward the work?

In how many of the following ways are you interested in the work? Which of these ways seems to you to be of most importance in your evaluation of the work?

1. You like the subject. You are interested in what the work is about.

2. You like the work because of the craftmanship and technical skill revealed in producing it.

3. You like the pattern. You are interested in such things as texture, scale, design, and organization. You are interested in the way the principles of order are applied in the work.

4. You like the work as biography. You know the biographical facts in connection with the work or the general circumstances of its composition and you enjoy the work in connection with these.

5. You like the work as history. You think of it in terms of what it shows about the culture and period which produced it.

6. You like the philosophic content. You are interested in the ultimate values and meanings which the work reveals to you. You tend to think of the work in terms of its morals or its message.

2 SUBJECT

CONCEPTS

Match the following:

____1. Representational art	(1) The interaction of the nominal or recognizable subject and the sensuous and formal elements in art.
____2. Abstract art	(2) Art with clearly recognizable objects.
____3. Non objective art	(3) Has no direct reference to objects.
____4. Subject in art	(4) Art with a basis in objects, though they may not be recognizable.
____5. Content in art	(5) Recognizable objects or situations in works of art.

Match the following:

____1. Program Music	(1) Something which in a given context represents or suggests something other than itself.
____2. Absolute Music	(2) Something, which when associated with a person or thing identifies it.
____3. Distortion	(3) Something which stands independently for something other than itself without representing it.
____4. Attribute	(4) Music which has no subject.
____5. Symbol	(5) Music which tells a story.
____6. Sign	(6) Change in a natural form exaggerating some particular characteristics.

Complete these sentences by inserting the appropriate words from the definitions above:

1. If we take the title of Mondrian's Composition in Blue and White literally we would accurately call it ______________ art.

2. If we take the title of Broadway Boogie-Woogie literally we could classify it as ________________ art.

3. Artists and critics could easily disagree as to whether a particular painting is ______________ or ________________ since only the artist can know whether he got his composition from ________________ or invented it.

4. Starting with representing natural objects the artist may ________________ little or much from them for a composition, so there are degrees of abstraction.

5. Since no art can include everything in a scene, nor all the details in an object, all art is to some degree __________.

6. If in addition to simplfying and leaving out details in a representational painting, the artist exaggerates particular aspects and details for expressive purposes, we say that he uses ______________________.

7. Choose 6 illustrations (excluding those by Picasso) from the chapter on Subject and list them in decreasing order of abstraction - - that is, list the most realistic painting first and the most abstract last:

Title	Figure No.	Artist
1.		
2.		
3.		
4.		
5.		
6.		

Mark the following <u>True</u> or <u>False</u>:

____ 1. The only fit subjects for art are the beautiful, the lovely, the noble.

____ 2. All art is partial, incomplete in its presentation of life.

____ 3. The more like life art is, the better art it is.

____ 4. Modern artists would not draw distorted figures if they knew how to draw lifelike ones.

____ 5. Art is good if it has a great subject and poor if it has an ignoble subject.

____ 6. All art is imitative.

____ 7. An oil painting is greater as a work of art than a watercolor.

____ 8. Art can present life only as it is interpreted by an artist.

____ 9. A building is greater as a work of art than a statue.

____10. All paintings have subject.

____11. Music which is programmatic is better than music which does not tell a story.

____12. The more noble the subject, the greater the work of art will be.

____13. No art is really lifelike.

____14. When music does have a story, it is necessary to know that story in order to enjoy it.

____15. The value of a work of art depends upon the artist, not the subject.

SUBJECT IN MUSIC

Only program music has subject. Several pieces of program music are mentioned in the text, including Moussorgsky's Pictures at an Exhibition. We suggest that you listen to this in the Ravel transcription for orchestra and have included the program to enable you to follow it in your listening. Note especially how Ravel has chosen instruments with timbre which suggest the mood and subject matter of the various pictures, especially instruments chosen to suggest the various persons in the pictures.

Beethoven's Symphony No. 6, the Pastoral Symphony is also program music. On page 386 of the text, in the chapter on Form in Music, we have quoted Beethoven's program from it. We think you will want to listen to this also. Either now or when you come to the chapter in which it is included.

Smetena, too, provided a program for one of his most popular orchestral pieces, The Moldau (from My Fatherland, a cycle of six symphonic poems). Its program is a musical description of Bohemia's largest river, following it from its source to the point where it flows past Vysehrad, the ancient castle of Bohemian kings. The music suggests the scenes along the river bank.

To guide your listening we paraphrase here the program which Smetena provided. We have divided it into short numbered paragraphs which correspond to the changes we think you will be able to hear in the music, especially on a second listening.

1. Two springs gush forth in the shade of the Bohemian forest, the one warm and spouting, the other cold and tranquil.

2. Their ripples, gaily flowing over rocky beds, unite and glisten in the morning sun. The forest brook, rushing on, becomes the River Moldau, which, hurrying through Bohemia's valleys, grows into a mighty stream.

3. It flows through dense woods, where the joyous noise of the hunt and the tones of the hunter's horns sound nearer and nearer.

4. It flows through verdant meadows where a wedding feast is celebrated with song and dance.

5. At night the wood nymphs and water sprites revel in its glistening waves...

6. ...which reflect many fortresses and castles--witnesses of the past splendor of chivalry and the vanished martial frame of bygone days.

7. At the rapids of St. John the stream speeds on, winding its way over cataracts and cutting a channel with its foaming waters through the rocky chasm...

8. ...into the broad river bed in which it flows on in majestic calm...

9. ...toward Prague, welcomed by the time-honored Vysehrad (famous Bohemian castle, citadel of the ancient kings).

10. It then disappears in the far distance from the poet's gaze.

PICTURES AT AN EXHIBITION
Modest Moussorgsky

The music was composed for piano by Moussorgsky in 1874 after viewing an exhibition of works by painter Victor Hartmann. It is best known in transcriptions for orchestra, especially that by Maurice Ravel (1923). The composition consists of the following sections:

Promenade - Gnomus
Promenade - Il Vecchio Castello
Promenade - Tuileries
Bydlo
Promenade - Ballet of Chicks in their Shells
Two Polish Jews, One Rich, the Other Poor
Promenade
Limoges: The Market Place
Catacombae, Sepulcrum Romanum
Con Mortuis in Lingua Mortua
The Hut on Fowl's Legs
The Great Gate of Kiev

The Promenade, which is heard several times, is intended to suggest the composer, himself, wandering about from picture to picture in the gallery. Each time we hear it, its character is altered according to the mood induced in the composer by the picture he has just seen. In its first brisk appearance, the Promenade creates a curiously awkward, waddly effect because of the alternation of rhythmic design. Here, Moussorgsky is turning his realistic guns upon his own far from sylph-like figure.

The Gnome. Here, the artist, who was Victor Hartmann, created a drawing for a carved wooden nutcracker with a wizened face that cracked nuts in its mouth. Moussorgsky uses this as a springboard for a musical sketch which suggests a jumping, twitching gnome.

The Old Castle. Hartmann made numerous watercolors of buildings in Western Europe, often adorning these with human figures engaged in some appropriate activity. The painting which Moussorgsky reflects in this music is of an old Italian castle with a troubadour singing a serenade.

Tuileries. Hartmann's painting is of a walk in the famous Parisian park, with a group of children and nursemaids. Moussorgsky's fast, breezy musical picture is subtitled "Dispute of the Children After Play."

Bydlo. This is a Polish word meaning cattle, and Hartmann's watercolor represented a Polish ox-cart which he had seen in a village street. The music suggests the lumbering progress of this crude vehicle.

Ballet of Chicks in Their Shells. The music is a little scherzo in the peeping, chirping tradition of Rameau's La Poule.

Two Polish Jews, One Rich, the Other Poor. This was a pen-and-ink sketch which Hartmann had made in the ghetto of a Polish village. It starts with a heavy, pompous theme to suggest the well-dressed member of the pair, while a wheedling, whining theme suggests the beggar. The rich man tries to fulminate a reply, but the beggar goes on chattering almost to the end.

Limoges: The Market Place. Hartmann painted more than 150 watercolors at Limoges, one of them representing market women in spirited conversation over their pushcarts. Moussorgsky reconstructs their conversation in his music. He also scratched some prose suggestions as to the subjects of their conversations on a margin of his original manuscript, but he erased these. Nevertheless, we can easily sense the varied moods and spirited "gossipy" content of the conversations through the music. There is no pause between this movement and the next one.

The Catacombs. Hartmann's watercolor showed the artist, himself, and a friend going through the catacombs of Paris with a guide holding a lamp. Moussorgsky's movement is brief, solemn and climactic, and leads without pause to the next movement.

Con Mortuis in Lingua Mortua. The Latin may not be above reproach, but the sentiment is. The movement is an extremely sad restatement of the Promenade theme, as if Hartmann's picture of a burial place had brought a special pang of grief to the composer. Moussorgsky wrote, as a footnote to the title, "A Latin text: 'With the dead in a dead language.' Well may it be in Latin! The creative spirit of the departed Hartmann leads me to the skulls, calls out to them, and the skulls begin to glow dimly from within."

The Hut on Fowl's Legs. Baba Yaga is a Russian witch who eats human bones which she grinds to a paste in a mortar and pestle. She also uses the mortar to ride through the sky, and she lives in a hut supported on fowl's legs. Hartmann's picture is a design for a clock in the form of Baba Yaga's hut. Moussorgsky's piece, however, suggests the witch and her ride through the air rather than Hartmann's clock. Baba Yaga rides up and into . . . .

The Great Gate of Kiev. Hartmann's design for a solemn ceremonial gateway at Kiev called forth a piece of music which evokes a great procession, with much military pageantry and the chanting of priests. Moussorgsky puts himself into the procession too, by quoting the Promenade before the end.

FIVE ROCKING CHAIRS

The article which follows is by Russell Green, a contemporary artist. We have included it here to illustrate how a single subject can be handled in various ways and styles to produce quite different paintings. We think that you will be interested in the way an artist thinks and writes about his work. In some of the paintings you will probably recognize a similarity in style to those of certain well-established modern artists. If you do not recognize all of the prototypes in style at this stage in your study you probably will later on.

Five Rocking Chairs

By Russell Green

An adventure in creativity as related by a living, working artist

FEW situations are as dismal to the professional art critic as the sight of a painter seizing a pen, not to make a sketch, but to write about his own work in progress. They may justifiably point to horrible examples, articles on art by famous artists of the past and present, to prove their point. In the first place, any artist who isn't dead and buried is liable to change his style, go exploring, try to find the headwaters of some river or other. This is endlessly troublesome to the art critic and art historian because it involves leg work, gallery going, and even thinking. A living artist can't see himself in retrospect, and any right-minded critic would agree with his brother critics that a writing artist, alive and kicking, should be tried but not hung.

The present case is particularly ominous for it is an effort to tell the story of a moment of seeing, the recording of a motif, and of the five diverging paths that grew out of this split second of intensified vision. None of the paintings in the Rocking Chair series are three months old, and even a year old painting is, for me, a young painting. When one is actively engaged in painting a subject there are so many choices to make, so many subtractions and additions to juggle, that even when the work is judged to be done as far as the eye and one's capabilities can judge, it is almost impossible to see what visually remains on the surface of the picture planes. The inner eye retains a synthesis of the whole. It is not until the memory of earlier choices and decisions have faded that it is possible to see what is left.

Bodily removing the painting from the studio is a way to speed up the maturation process. Once a painting has been hanging on loan in the house of a friend or has been shipped out to an exhibition it almost always returns home displaying either a self-possessed vitality or an inscrutable lifelessness. The Rocking Chairs will settle down, jelled, in the future; it is more important now to trace where the idea came from and to suggest some directions it took.

The season is early fall, the day is grey, the hour is about five o'clock. I have glanced at the evening paper and have turned to look at my wife who is peeling fruit. She sits in a webbed chair and near her on a small table is a bowl of apples. Between us the old black rocking chair makes a pattern against the part-wall, part-window background. I pick up my fountain pen and draw what I see on an envelope.

I have sat in the same chair and have seen the things in my drawing many times. Only now has this familiar corner of the living room linked itself into a harmonious design. I begin to see relationships between the curved rocking chair, the square table, the figure, and the background that suggest a painting.

Here is an idea to develop. I must decide on style, how I will gain unity through repetition and gain interest through variation of direction, size, shape, color, value, and texture. All these elements can be planned and carried out through the help of the less controllable quality, enthusiasm. Enthusiasm seems to come from underneath. It is identifiable only through a feeling that everything is all right.

My first effort is usually in a realistic direction; chairs look like chairs, people like people, a window like a window. The relationship between the objects is close to the distances observed in nature. The color, too, is often similar to natural color. I have a sketch to take into the studio, a blank white space waiting to be filled, dry color, brushes, and medium (gum arabic in solution).

In direct painted lines I draw shapes similar in position and size relation to the original subject (lower left). Within these shapes, once the proportions are established, I draw not only the outlines of the objects but the complexity of interweaving lines that defines arms and legs of both the rocking chair and the figure. I repeat the fleur-de-lis pattern in the chair arm, in the leaf pattern in the window, in the hair of the figure, and in the table. I repeat ovals, circles, and rectangles over the entire surface.

Have I a variety of sizes? Are there resting spots? Have I used vertical and horizontal lines for stability? Have I enough linear movements in curves and diagonals to relieve the stabilizing straight lines and shapes? Now, Paint!

I scrub on areas of color as quickly as I can mix and decide. Only when the whole surface is covered will I be able to see if it works—whether each area stays in its place. I see the yellow background at the upper right is too intense in color; it jumps ahead of the figure. The choice is to grey the yellow or brighten the caning in the rocking chair to push the drapery back. Once the areas fall into position I can delineate smaller patterns, emphasize directions, straighten bent lines, place shadows to tie objects to the floor. The landscape seen through the window draws the eye too far out; by flattening the landscape the attention remains in the room.

I do these things and it does not work. I put the painting aside for a day. The next afternoon I go into the studio, walk quickly toward the painting, trying for a fresh impression. The edge of the back of the chair needs sharpening. Once that is done the lines that define the window need muffling. The background pattern can be reduced by half. What else? The caning in the chair . . . heighten the value. Look again. It works.

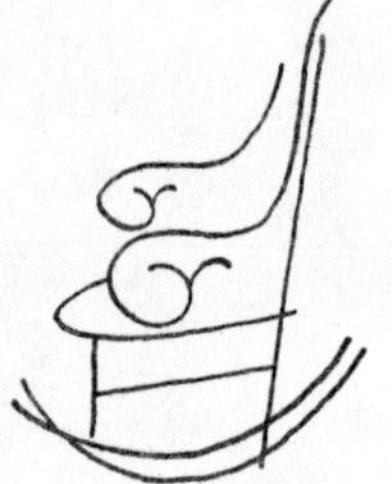

Why is it that an artist, having once painted a subject, paints it again? For me it grows out of studying the first painting. If the motif is an interesting one, a new attack on the same material suggests itself. Ideas attach themselves to the motif similar to the way particles of fat combine in buttermaking. Half automatically the "old" painting is removed from my mind and a fresh white surface for a fresh idea takes its place.

In rocking chair number two (upper left) there is intentional distortion. The drawing is controlled by placing the pencil on the paper and not lifting it until the whole design is finished. I have to think about every direction, size, and shape while filling the entire area. This way of drawing forces one to work directly, slowly. The edges which cross and recross are thickened black lines, and the distortion of the shapes they create is reminiscent of a reflection in a funhouse mirror.

Because of the direct line technique which is active in itself, my whole body moves as I draw. Emphasis on curves and diagonals causes the objects to move in the painting. The chair seems to rock, the figure wants to cook dinner, the wind blows the hanging basket outside. This more dramatic painting relies on arbitrary lights and darks with bold color definitions for its mood. When I looked at the painting later I got a feeling of mystery or witchery as in a fairy tale.

I like reds. I like all kinds of reds together. The gum tree in the back yard shows many bright reds and yellows like fall on fire. It has been a week since I painted and the sketch of the rocking chair remains pinned to the painting table. I pick it up, mix a brilliant red and put a spot in the upper right of the paper, then a smaller one in the lower right, then a stripe in the middle left. Why not try an experiment in color and line? (lower left) I use orange-red, violet, cold red, pink, and dirty yellows. I scrub on these colors in sizes and shapes which approximate the positions of objects in the sketch. A full scale of reds and half tones of yellow weave over the surface in varying sizes, shapes, and intensities. Then directly, with a brush loaded with black, I identify the object, careful to show a variation of thickness and thinness of line moving through and around my colors.

Here again is activity; the rocking chair rocks faster, my wife sits in the chair as if she will leave the next moment, and the temper of the entire surface seems fleeting. There is stability, and I'm conscious that the vertical and horizontal directions keep the melting mass of color intact. Again there is a recurring rectangular shape in the window, the moon, the flower box, the table, and the wall spaces. The fleur-de-lis repeats in the top and arms of the chair, in the leaves of plants, and in the bowl on the small table at the right. There is a planned variation of edges, both crisp and crusty. So here is freedom in color and line and shape; another distortion but with all objects somewhat recognizable.

Since a circle can be a head or a balloon or a wheel, or a square can be a box or a table, I can now turn my interest to building a picture of shapes which need not be recognizable as things; an abstraction (upper right). I'll turn the objects in my sketch into varied shapes. Now I must depend on design and order to give a sense of unity, and all the areas should be consistent; if a bowl is a circle, the table must be a square and not look like a table. I start with the fleur-de-lis by drawing it large, small, twisted, curved, and straightened. Now it has no subject quality. By taking many of the objects of the original sketch and simplifying them, I manipulate the shapes in the painting into variations on a circle and a square. Sometimes I can start with a delineating square and end with a part of a circle. The pattern is completely drawn with pencil on the paper, and I fill the shapes with a green-black for the darks, red-orange and blue for the medium tones, and pale blue and tan for the light areas. The white of the paper is left as the very light pattern. All of the parts are essential to the unity of the composition. Remove one spot and the whole crumbles.

Number five (lower right) is delight and fun and seriousness. The medium is pen and ink and transparent water color. This colored drawing is an inside-outside idea. It is packed with funny and serious symbols, some vague, some obvious. I'm not sure this is art; it is graphic and cartoon-like. It has literary implications in its graphic reference to Jane Austen and to the manuscript rolling out of the head, as well as hidden references. It tells a story, if you like, and the relationships are personal. It is not a psychological portrait of the person but possibly of the cat. An attempt to control line directions and motifs and color is made. I laughed aloud while working on it. You may laugh.

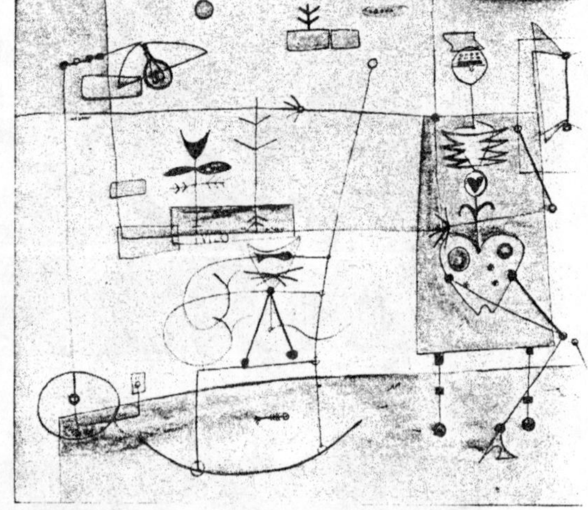

Those are my five Rocking Chairs. My paintings depend on color for much of their structure, so seeing them in black and white reproduction is like looking at five peeled apples with part of the core showing.

The figure in the background has stepped out of the frame with a reminder that in the attic there is another tangible rocking chair in need of caning. It would look fine on the other side of the fireplace.

The author Russell Green (1910-   ) was for many years Chairman of the Art Department of Stephens College, Columbia, Missouri. He has had many one-man shows, and has been represented in numerous national and international exhibits. Mr. Green is currently giving full time to his painting.

"Five Rocking Chairs" appeared in the Stephens College Bulletin, January, 1958. It is reprinted here by permission of Mr. Green and Stephens College.

3 SOURCES OF ART SUBJECTS

CONCEPTS

The paragraph on the first page of this chapter makes two important points about subject in the arts. Write them here:

1.____

2.____

The remainder of the chapter is about which of these points?____

Sources of subject matter for art are grouped under the six headings at the left below. Under each write the titles of two art works: 1. an example in the text (in this chapter or in other chapters) and 2. an example not in the text.

NATURE:

1.____

2.____

HISTORY (legend, folklore, current events):

1.____

2.____

GREEK AND ROMAN MYTHOLOGY:

1.____

2.____

THE JUDAEO-CHRISTIAN TRADITION:

1. ______________________________

2. ______________________________

ORIENTAL SACRED TEXTS:

1. ______________________________

2. ______________________________

OTHER WORKS OF ART:

1. ______________________________

2. ______________________________

APPLICATION OF CONCEPTS

Underline the correct answer to complete the following statements:

1. The subject source of "The Persistence of Memory" is--religion, mythology, another work of art, the artist's imagination.

2. The subject source for Cezanne's "Well and Grinding Wheel..." is--history, nature, religion.

3. When music is said to have subject, it is called--absolute music, expressionist music, program music.

4. Jackson Pollock's *No. 1, 1948*, has its source in--a broken bag of marbles, the physical act of painting, a grassy field in summer.

5. Ruben's *Judgement of Paris* has its subject source in--Greek mythology, French history, a walk through a meadow.

6. Anne Sexton's "Starry Night" (Page 83 in the text) has its subject source in--a personal experience, a painting, a song by Don Mclean.

7. Modigliani's *Anna Zborowska* (Page 11 in the text) has its subject source in--a person, an Egyptian sculpture of Nefertiti(Color Plate 1), a fashion illustration.

8. Alber's *Homage to the Square: Broad Call* (Color Plate 27)

has its subject source in--his experiments, Renaissance perspective, a loud noise.

9. Poulenc's *Mass in G* has its subject source in--plainsong, a ritual of the church, Bach's *Air for the G String*.

10. Picasso's *Guernica* has its subject source in--a mural in a Spanish cathedral, the bombing of a Spanish town, memories of his childhood in Spain.

There are many common symbols with which we are all familiar. Can you match the following?

____ 1. the dove	1. Christ
____ 2. the palm leaf	2. victory or triumph
____ 3. the olive branch	3. temptation
____ 4. the anchor	4. the Church (cf. nave)
____ 5. the peacock	5. faith or hope
____ 6. the phoenix	6. peace
____ 7. the ship	7. peace
____ 8. the serpent (snake)	8. Satan, the sly one
____ 9. the fish	9. rising after being burned
____10. the apple	10. immortality

Can you elaborate and explain this statement: *Astrology and its lore involve both signs and symbols*.

Examine a one dollar bill: find all the symbols you can on it and search out the meanings in an encyclopedia or other source.

GREEK MYTHOLOGY AND LEGEND IN ART

What follows is a list of fifteen important gods and goddesses frequently represented in art. You will find much more about them and the stories associated with them in books on Greek mythology. In this list the Roman name is given first, then the Greek.

Jupiter, Jove - Zeus: Supreme ruler of the Gods, frequently represented with a thunderbolt in his hands.

Juno - Hera: Wife of Jupiter represented in art with a peacock or a cow.

Minerva - Athene or Athena: Goddess of Wisdom and Science, including the Science of War. Frequently represented with a shield, spear, and aegis (a shield on which there was engraved the head of Medusa which turned all to stone who looked upon it), or with an owl.

Mars - Ares: God of War identified by weapons and war-like dress.

Vulcan - Hephaestaus: God of Fire, associated with blacksmithing and metal work.

Apollo - Apollo: God of light, music poetry, identified with the sun, serenity, reason, ideal male beauty.

Diana - Artemis: Goddess of the Moon, huntress. Usually carries a bow; often represented with a crescent moon in her hair.

Venus - Aphrodite: Goddess of love and beauty often represented with a swan, a sparrow, or a dove, mother of Cupid.

Mercury - Hermes: Messenger of the Gods and a healer, identified in art by a caduceus (a staff entwined with snakes), a petasus (winged hat), and wings on his ankles.

Cupid - Eros: God of Love, son of Venus, represented with bow and arrows, sometimes as blind, and sometimes with wings.

Ceres - Demeter: Goddess of Agriculture, the fruitful earth, and social order, represented by sheaves of corn and poppies.

Bacchus - Dionysus: God of wine and ecstasy associated with wild orgiastic beauty, identified in art with wine, the tiger, grape leaves and grapes.

Pluto - Hades: King of the Underworld.

Proserpina - Proserpine - Persephone: Wife of Pluto, daughter of Ceres.

Neptune - Poseidon: God of the sea. Usually identifiable by his trident (a three-pronged fishing spear.)

BIBLICAL SUBJECTS IN ART

The biblical incidents usually given the names below are common subjects of works in all the arts. If you need to look up sources in order to identify or understand a work with one of these titles or a variant on it the references on the right will be useful.

Annunciation.	Luke	1:26-31
Visitation.	Luke	1:39-45
Magnificat.	Luke	1:46-48
Presentation in the Temple.	Luke	2:21-24
Benedictus.	Matthew	21:9
Nunc dimittis.	Luke	2:29-33
Nativity	Luke	2:4-7
Gloria in excelsis.	Luke	2:14-16
Shepherds.	Luke	2:13-16
Magi.	Matthew	2:11-12
Flight into Egypt.	Matthew	2:13-15
Boy Jesus in the Temple.	Luke	2:41-47
Massacre of the Innocents.	Matthew	2:16
Temptation.	Luke	4:1-14
Death of John the Baptist.	Mark	6:25-28
Woman at the well.	John	4:7-10
Pool of Bethesda.	John	5:5-8
Good Samaritan.	Luke	10:30-33
Prodigal son.	Luke	15:13-16
Rich man and Lazarus.	Luke	16:19-25
Raising of Lazarus.	John	11:34-38
Entry into Jerusalem.	Matthew	21:8-11
Transfiguration.	Matthew	17:1-7
Last Supper.	Matthew	26:20-23
Pieta.	Luke	23:53-56
Resurrection.	Mark	16:1-6
Supper at Emmaus.	Luke	24:28-31
Ascension.	Acts	1:1-3
Pentecost.	Acts	2:1-6

ORIGINS OF WORDS IN MYTH AND LEGEND

Using a dictionary, book on mythology, or other source (1) define the following words and (2) explain the origin of the words in mythology.

	MEANING OF THE WORD	MYTHOLOGICAL REFERENCE
1. chaotic		
2. saturnine		
3. narcissistic		
4. Promethean		
5. jovial		
6. elysian		
7. martial		
8. vulcanize		
9. volcano		
10. venereal		
11. mercurial		
12. cereal		
13. titanic		
14. bacchanal		

15. Phoenix-like		
16. panic		
17. plutonium		
18. protean		
19. Atlantic		
20. erotic		
21. Olympic		
22. apollonian		
23. dionysian		
24. odyssey		
25. herculean		
26. mercury (the metal)		
27. siren		
28. atlas		
29. aphrodisiac		
30. aegis		

SYMBOLS AND ATTRIBUTES

When the subject of a visual art is not immediately self-evident, we are sometimes helped to understand what it is about by symbols and attributes. Look at the Artemision sculpture, Figure 5-1, on page 113. A controversy still wages over whether the sculptor intended this figure to be Zeus as we have labeled it or whether it was intended to be Poseidon, God of the Sea. The controversy exists because the attribute which would have identified the subject of the sculpture has been broken off.

If the Artemision sculpture held a ________________________ in his right hand, the figure would unquestionably be _______________. If it was a ____________________ it would be __________________.

Four attributes of Buddha by which we recognize representations of him are the ____________________ usually covered with hair; the tuft of hair between his eyes, called __________________________; the _________________________ symbolical of ______________________; and his ________________________.

The symbolic objects which Siva holds in his two upper hands are a ______________________ representing control over ________________; and _________________________ representing _____________________. The ring of fire in which he dances represents ________________. The dwarf on which he stands is __________________________________.

Look again at <u>The Birth of Venus</u> (Color Plate 12). How has Botticelli told us which of the seasons is waiting to receive her? ____

SELF TEST ON PAINTING

Rubens, The Judgment of Paris
(Figure 2-16, page 53)

A story from Greek Mythology is the subject of this painting. The story goes that at the marriage of Peleus and Thetis all the gods had been invited with the exception of Eris, the goddess of discord. Enraged at her exclusion, she threw a golden apple among the guests with an inscription, "For the fairest." Juno, Venus, and Minerva claimed it. Jupiter sensing that such a decision was frought with danger sent the goddesses to Mount Ida with instructions that Paris, son of Priam, king of Troy, who was tending his flocks there should make the choice. Rubens has painted the scene on Mount Ida. Complete these sentences.

1. The shepherd boy is easy to identify by his ____________________ and ____________________.

2. The god holding in one hand the apple he has brought Paris to award to the fairest goddess is ____________________. We know this because of the ____________________ in his hand and because of ____________________.

3. The goddess on the left is ____________________. We know this because of ____________________ and ____________________.

4. The child playing in the lower left hand corner is ____________. He has his usual ____________________ and ____________________.

5. The middle goddess is ____________________, his mother, and it is because of him that we can identify her.

6. The goddess to the right is ____________________ because of her traditional attribute, the ____________________.

7. The shadowy, threatening figure in the sky must be ____________ with a torch in one hand and serpent in the other.

What each of the goddesses offered Paris in an attempt to seduce him into giving her the apple, who was awarded the apple, what the other two goddesses did in revenge and how this brought about the Trojan War you must read elsewhere.

REVIEW OF PAINTINGS

All of the paintings described in this exercise appear in the first three chapters of the text.

Identify the painting described by giving (a) the name of the artist and (b) the name of the painting.

(a)____________________
(b)____________________

1. A rectangular canvas divided into subordinate rectangles of white and pure colors, separated by black bars which are adjusted for proportion and balance.

(a)____________________
(b)____________________

2. A landscape which has both the clarity and irrationality of dreams.

(a)____________________
(b)____________________

3. A painting which has the quality of a stained glass window, with a limited number of areas outlined in black and filled with jewel-like color applied so as to suggest force and strong emotions.

(a)____________________
(b)____________________

4. A landscape with a heaving line of hills, flaming cypress trees, comets, exploding stars, all swirling in a universal rhythm which, of course, the artist did not see but which express his ecstatic sense of cosmic forces in nature.

(a)____________________
(b)____________________

5. A painting which combines several abstracted aspects of a scene viewed at different angles but presented simultaneously.

(a)____________________

(b)____________________

6. A painting in which the painter tells us that a cow is thinking of the little farmer woman who will soon come to milk her, by painting the scene in her head.

(a)____________________

(b)____________________

7. A near-abstract painting in which we can still discern a canon and toppling buildings in a swirl of smoke and explosions.

(a)____________________

(b)____________________

8. A painting in which there are several figures, some of them painted almost realistically and some of them showing the influence of cubism and African masks in presenting more than one view of the subject simultaneously.

(a)____________________

(b)____________________

9. A twentieth-century portrait in which the elongated neck of the subject recalls a statue of an Egyptian princess.

(a)____________________

(b)____________________

10. A painting which resembles a collage in which scraps of photographs, as though from a news magazine, are organized to catch the spirit of a period.

Which of the paintings described might be said to be in the styles below?

___________________________________ 1. surrealistic

___________________________________ 2. abstract

___________________________________ 3. expressionistic (2)

____

COLOR YOUR OWN MONDRIAN

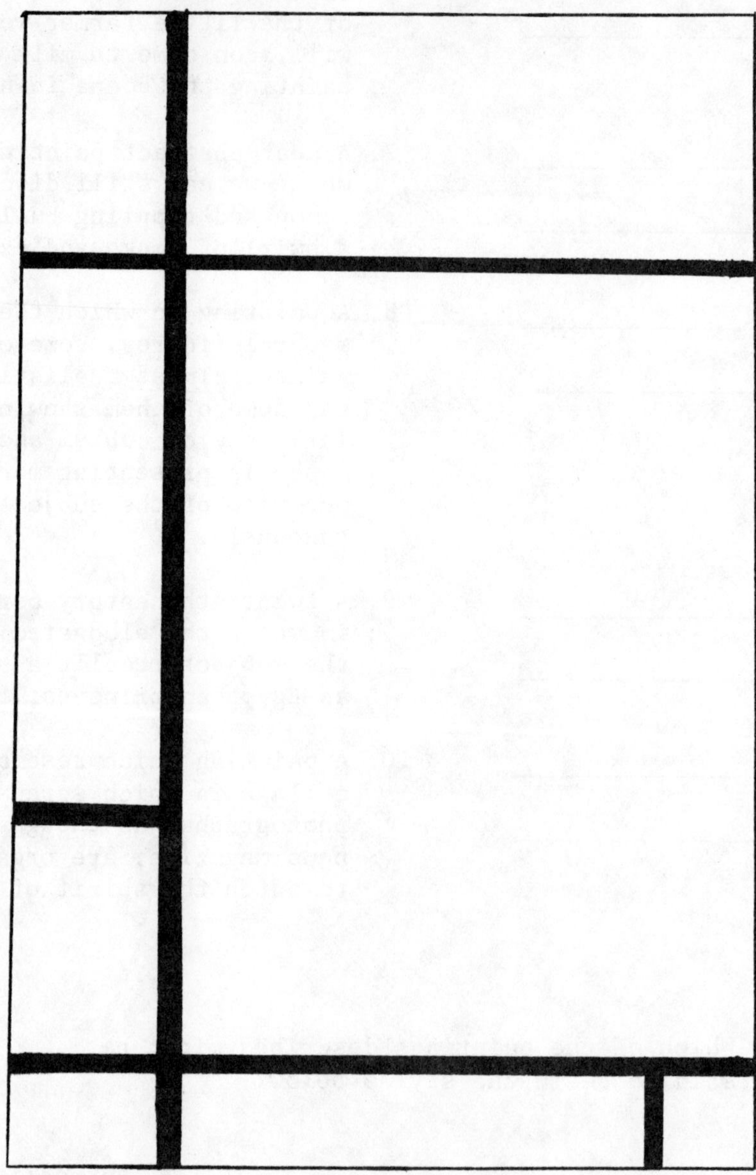

There are two reproductions of works by Piet Mondrian in the text (Color Plates 3 and 5, following page 56). The sketch above reproduces exactly the shapes, the proportions, and line widths of another painting by Mondrian, entitled Composition, Paris, 1927. But in the sketch all the colors, even the values of the colors, have been omitted. Try coloring the areas yourself (1) to distribute interest, (2) to maintain balance and (3) to produce a pleasing effect.

4 FUNCTION

CONCEPTS

Mark the following True or False and for each sentence you mark False explain the reason why on the line following the sentence.

_____ 1. Literature and painting are usually not functional.

____

_____ 2. Ghiberti's "Gates of Paradise" were hung on stonehenges.

____

_____ 3. Music and dance were functional in their origins.

____

_____ 4. Cylix and kithara are Greek words.

____

_____ 5. Altamira did primitive drawings on the walls of a cave in Spain.

____

_____ 6. "The Volga Boatman" is another name for Execias' *Dionysus Sailing the Sea.*

____

_____ 7. Sculpture is more functional than painting or literature.

____

_____ 8. Advertisements are always functional.

____

_____ 9. Architecture and applied arts are the least functional of the arts.

____

_____10. Stained glass windows were frequently functional.

____

_____11. Chopin's waltzes are functional.

____

_____12. The paint which is applied in various colors to wooden structures is an example of non-functional decoration.

____

_____13. Wright's Guggenheim Museum (page 332) seems to have grown from the site and to express structurally its function.

____

_____14. Works which were once functional and are no longer so may still be considered artistic.

____

In keeping with the definition and examples in the text mark the following as Functional or Non-Functional:

_____ 1. music for dance

_____ 2. a hymn tune

_____ 3. a portrait

_____ 4. a love sonnet

_____ 5. pyramids

_____ 6. a cylix

_____ 7. early cave paintings

_____ 8. a symphony

_____ 9. a landscape painting

_____10. the Eiffel tower

Now consider some examples of art works which are less clearly functional or non-functional. State which you think the example is and give your reason for thinking so.

1. Moore's *Two Forms* is __________ because __________.

2. Hex signs on Pennsylvania barns are __________ because __________.

3. Bookplates are __________ because __________.

4. Moore's *Sheep Piece for Kansas City* is __________ because __________.

5. "Auld Lang Syne" sung on New Year's Eve is __________ because __________.

6. An overture to a Broadway musical is __________ because __________.

7. A crown is __________ because __________.

8. Tapestries hung on the walls of a Medieval Castle were __________ because __________.

9. The Japanese flag is __________ because __________.

10. A funeral urn is __________ because __________.

11. Commemorative postage stamps which remind us of great men, important events, and art of the past are __________ because __________.

12. The Eifel Tower which is expressive of the advanced technology of the time of its construction is __________ because __________.

APPLICATION OF CONCEPTS

The following statements are to be marked TRUE or FALSE.

______ 1. The function of the walls of a building is chiefly to hold up the roof.

______ 2. The shape of the roof depends primarily on the amount of rain and snow in the climate.

______ 3. In northern countries there is greater need for many, large windows.

______ 4. The functional reason for the "setback" on modern skyscrapers is to center the weight in the middle of the building.

______ 5. Thick walls are more necessary in extremely hot or cold climates than in temperate climates.

______ 6. The turned up roof common on Chinese buildings is functionally unsound.

______ 7. Le Corbusier's comment that a house is "a machine for living" means that function should follow form in architecture.

______ 8. Modern architecture tends to put more emphasis on the interior of the house than on the exterior.

______ 9. New methods of heating have made possible the use of more partitions in modern houses than were possible before.

______10. The good modern architect is likely to pay little attention to climatic conditions because he knows that up-to-date utilities can easily overcome them.

______11. The John Hancock building with its system of cross-girders would be functional in an area of frequent earthquakes.

______12. That which is truly functional is always beautiful.

______13. Gregorian chant was more functional than Ravel's "Pavane for a Dead Princess".

Mark the following statements as TRUE or FALSE: then list <u>three</u> examples to justify your answer.

_____1. The kind of building material found in an area influences the kind of building in that area.

Examples: 1.______________________________

2.______________________________

3.______________________________

_____2. The climate of an area affects the type of construction used.

Examples: 1.______________________________

2.______________________________

3.______________________________

_____3. The interests, customs, and amusements of people show in their architecture.

Examples: 1.______________________________

2.______________________________

3.______________________________

_____4. All buildings intended for purposes of worship are much the same.

Examples: 1.______________________________

2.______________________________

3.______________________________

_____5. <u>Social conditions</u> is just another term for <u>natural conditions</u>.

Examples: 1.______________________________

2.______________________________

3.______________________________

FUNCTION IN ARCHITECTURE

The "ruler" below may help you in seeing how function combines with aesthetic considerations in producing differences in architectural style.

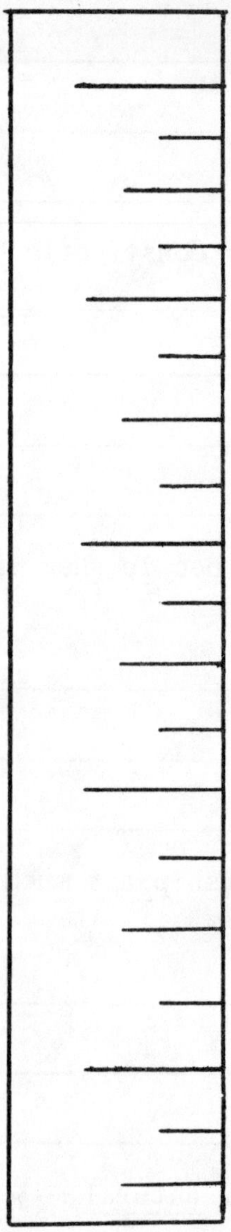

1. Bare utility. Architecture conceived as engineering with no thought of the eye, but only to serviceabileness, economy, and strength.

2. Well-proportioned utility. Between two proportions equally utilitarian, architect chooses the one more pleasing to the eye; thinks of repetition and variety, movement of line, effects of contrast, gradation and climax.

3. Organic design and pattern growing out of structural forms, such as elaboration of capitals, cornices, and frames of doors and windows - - may be highly reserved or profuse and generous.

4. Design and pattern not inconsistent with structure, but not obviously growing out of it; structure thought of as frame for support of design and pattern and when not contradicted by it may be concealed under it - - "painter's architecture".

5. Design and pattern without respect of structure, and even in contradiction to it - - e.g., Gothic surface designs of steel skyscrapers.

Identify in your area one building (with its location) which seems to fit each of these descriptions.

1.______________________ 4.______________________

2.______________________ 5.______________________

3.______________________

A statement by Eero Saarinen on the principles which are important to him in his architecture is reproduced in this chapter. In it he cites three principles which are common in modern architecture. They are:

1. ______________________

2. ______________________

3. ______________________

He states his feelings about each of these as it has affected his own work. Using the same order in which you listed the principles, summarize what he says about each:

1. ______________________

2. ______________________

3. ______________________

In addition to these common principles, Saarinen believes that there are two additional principles which "are equally or more important". They are:

1. ______________________

2. ______________________

Three examples of Saarinen's work are illustrated in the text: (1) The Gateway Arch (page 95); (2) The TWA Terminal, Kennedy Airport (page 360) and (3) The Stephens College Chapel (page 359). Show how the three common principles of modern architecture are or are not present in each of these structures.

1. ______________________

2. ______________________

3. ______________________

QUESTIONS FOR REFLECTION AND DISCUSSION

-1-

The word function is used in the text in a quite specific way - - to refer to the practical usefulness of art objects and music and literature. In the discussion there the word is limited to its sense of utility. It was felt that to use it in its broader sense would have diffused our study of art into areas where speculation, opinion and subjectivity take precedence over accurate observation and response. However, our limitation of the word to this narrow sense in the text should not be interpreted to mean that art which has no utilitarian function in getting work done is for this reason of less importance in human affairs and well-being. As a kind of supplement or complement to the use of "function" in the text and to indicate the directions a broader application of the word might take we suggest that you consider the following and be prepared to discuss them in class.

1. In THE PURPOSES OF ART (New York: Holt, Rinehart and Winston, 1972), Albert E. Elsen states the thesis of his book in this way:

    > Along with providing immeasurable joy to its creators, art's great purposes have been to assist men to come to terms with their environments and to realize self-reproduction and self-liberation. Art takes its place along with science . . . in civilizing of humanity.

    At various points in our text we comment in passing on the role of art in human functioning - - to give form to feelings and emotions which arise spontaneously and threaten to overwhelm our sense of autonomy or individual being until we can gain some control over them, some mastery of them as objective entities. Elsen seems to go beyond this in his statement. Test his thesis from your own knowledge, observations and speculations.

2. In the UNESCO volume on THE ARTS & MAN: A WORLD VIEW OF THE ARTS IN SOCIETY (Englewood Cliffs, N.J.: Prentice Hall, Inc., 1969, p. 11), there are listed ten uses of the arts:

    1. discovery
    2. intensification
    3. expression
    4. record
    5. communication
    6. interpretation
    7. information
    8. enhancement
    9. order
    10. integration

1. Which of these seem to you to be utilitarian in a work-a-day context? Which go beyond physical needs and point to enhancing roles of the arts in our emotional and psychic life? Which hint at something beyond these two?

2. Whether or not you think "uses" is the best term to apply to this list of relationships of the arts and human activity, try to think up at least two examples of each of the relationships listed.

3. Can you think of at least one relationship of art to human life and culture which is not included in the list?

4. It is sometimes said - - for example by John Canaday - - that art which is produced as social criticism is inferior to the best art, that it rarely transcends the place-time-situation which evoked it. Study the art works in the text which were produced as social criticism, or as protest against particular practices or attitudes. Do these works have a significance beyond the events they anathematize? Did any of them contribute to bringing about ameliorative action in the situations they deal with?

-2-

1. Write a paragraph telling how climate has influenced building in your home town.

2. Write a paragraph telling how the particular demands for worship in the church you attend are reflected in the architecture (e.g., baptismal fount, arrangement of choir, altar, etc.).

This chapter deals with art which has two qualities to a greater or lesser degree: being functional in a utilitarian sense and satisfying and expressive in an aesthetic sense. In an overzealous concern for one or another of these, some artists in various periods have failed to produce objects of lasting appeal (except as curiosities, or cultural artifacts). Concern for elaborate decoration on architecture in the Victorian period resulted in buildings which were frequently grotesque in appearance and awkward or impossible functionally. A revolt against this tendency resulted in the early part of this century in International Style - - an unadorned, strictly utilitarian architecture - - which went to extremes in the other direction. At the present we seem to be moving to a better balance in constructing buildings which are functional, expressive, and aesthetically pleasing.

Give the name and location of one building nearby which in your judgment combines these three qualities and explain why you think so.

____
Name of the Building

____
Location

5 MEDIUM—GENERAL CONSIDERATIONS

CONCEPTS

Medium in the arts is (1)______________________________.

On the basis of medium, the arts are classified in three different ways:

as (2)________________ arts and auditory arts; as space arts, (3)________________ arts, and (4)________________ arts; and as (5)________________ arts and (6)______________ arts or applied arts.

Three examples of space arts are (7)________________, (8)________________, and (9)________________. Three examples of time arts are (10)________________, (11)________________, and (12)____________________. The combined arts are so-called because they (13)______________. Three examples of combined arts are: (14)________________, (15)________________, and (16)____________________.

The major arts are (18)________________, (19)______________, (20)____________________, (21)________________, and (22)________________. These five arts are classified as <u>major</u> because (23)________________________.

APPLICATION OF CONCEPTS

Write the word True or False before the following statements depending upon your evaluation of them: For each statement you mark False explain why on the line immediately following the statement.

_____ 1. Reproduction is the only means by which we can preserve the time arts.

_____

_____ 2. There is a closer relationship between the artist and his audience in the auditory arts than in the visual arts.

_____

_____ 3. The best way to get at the meaning of music is through a translation of medium--that is, through a translation of the meaning into words.

_____

_____ 4. A mobile is a sculpture in which the parts are delicately balanced to move in the gentlest breeze or current of warm air.

_____

_____ 5. There is only one limitation to what the artist may express in a medium: he may express what he can express.

_____

_____ 6. The best singer is the one with the widest range and the greatest technical skill.

_____

_____ 7. Poor medium may make poor art.

_____

_____ 8. Good medium makes good art.

_____

_____ 9. Sculpture in relief is more versatile in representing range of subject matter than sculpture in the round.

____

_____ 10. Sculpture of the past has been limited almost entirely to the bodies of animals, especially to the bodies of human beings.

____

Complete these statements:

1. The medium of the parthenon is ____________________.

2. The medium of Calder's mobile, Lobster Trap with Fish Tails is ____________________.

3. The medium of the Artemision Zeus is ____________________.

4. The medium of Moore's Two Forms is ____________________.

5. The medium of Debussy's The Afternoon of a Faun is ____________________.

6. The medium of the Flying Horse of Kansu is ____________________.

7. Some of the newer mediums in sculpture are ____________________.

8. John Cage has developed a new medium in music by ____________________.

9. In a Japanese garden the medium is ____________________.

10. In an igloo the medium is ____________________.

Mark the following True or False and for each statement you mark False, explain why on the line directly below it.

____ 1. The musical notation we use today was developed by the Egyptians.

____

____ 2. We can be more certain that we are hearing a piece as Chopin intended it to sound than we can that we are seeing a Michaelangelo fresco as he intended it to be seen.

____

____ 3. The combined arts are also called applied arts because they are used in performance.

____

____ 4. The artist who translates an old work into a new medium is morally obligated to translate it accurately and precisely.

____

____ 5. Technique is the artist's way of handling his medium.

____

____ 6. The most important criterion in judging a work of art is whether the artist has mastered the technique of his craft.

____

____ 7. Technique is a more legitimate criterion in judging a performance (the recreation) of a musical composition than in judging the work of the composer.

____

____ 8. Medium cannot be translated.

____

____ 9. Labonotation is a system of symbols for preserving dance choreography.

____

_____10. When literature is read it is a visual art, but when it is spoken it becomes an auditory art.

____

_____11. A play such as Romeo and Juliet was written for a particular time and place and should not be adapted to contemporary audiences.

____

_____12. Written words are accurate symbols for preserving the poet's conception of a poem.

____

_____13. Opera is called a combined art because a combination of people are required to perform it.

____

_____14. An artisan is more likely than an artist to make display of technique the purpose of a work.

____

_____15. Great artists try to mask or hide the qualities of the medium in which they work.

____

Name three arts which are preserved through symbols:

1.______________________________

2.______________________________

3.______________________________

Name three arts in which the preservation is a matter of keeping the medium in good condition and safe:

1.______________________________

2.______________________________

3.______________________________

Name three combined arts:

1.______________________________

2.______________________________

3.______________________________

Each of the combined arts involves one time art. Name the time art involved in the three combined arts you have listed above:

1.______________________________

2.______________________________

3.______________________________

DISCUSSION QUESTIONS:

-1-

Mondrian paintings are now copied as designs in commercially produced rugs, linoleum, and scarves. The medium is changed, the perspective from which the paintings were intended to be viewed is changed, and the intended expressive qualities presumably ignored. Be prepared to discuss your feelings about this and similar practices. What motivations seem to be involved in their production <u>and</u> in the fact that they sell? What kind of persons would you conjecture to be buyers?

-2-

What is the relationship between the value of the medium used in an art work and the value of an art work in the medium? Would a poor work of art in gold or other precious metal be more admired for this fact? Should it be? Can you think of examples of great art in mediums which have little intrinsic value? How many examples can you think of in which the intrinsic value of the medium of an art work led to its destruction?

SAME SUBJECT : DIFFERENT MEDIUMS

Compare Marcel Duchamp's painting, Nude Descending a Staircase and X.J. Kennedy's poem, "Nude Descending a Staircase", both on page 122 of the text.

Duchamp's painting inspired by Cubism and Futurism caused a riot in New York when it was shown as the centerpiece of the Armory Show that brought the avant-garde to America in 1913. Kennedy's poem (1950) takes its title from the painting and has the same theme. This presents an opportunity to consider questions about the differences in the mediums of the visual and literary arts, and their distinct imagery.

1. Can you demonstrate analogies in the painting and the poem which justify the use of the same title?

   a. In the poem each stanza alludes to "her" or "she". What is there in the painting that is specifically feminine? What descriptive phrases in the poem show her motion analogous to the feeling of motion in the painting?

   b. What, if anything, is named in the poem that is visually presented in the painting? Can you identify a figure of speech in the poem that could not have an analogy in the painting? Is there a kind of equivalence of effects between the visual and the literary? What feelings elicited in the one are peculiar to its medium and are not elicited in the other?

2. One aspect of Futurism, which derived from Cubism, was an attempt to give painting a new dimension by presenting many points of view or many successive stages of an action simultaneously - - to present a process rather than a posed culmination of the dramatic moment. This effort was probably inspired by multiple exposure and the study of motion photography. Duchamp's Nude Descending a Staircase is explicitly a figure in motion (which may be a nude).

Is the linearity of the poem an asset when movement in time toward a climax is being expressed?

b. Is the poem richer in its imagery in achieving the same effects? Would the painting be as coherent if it included the imagery of the poem explicitly?

c. How have figures of speech and the sounds of words been used to create a sense of rising excitement?

d. Does the poet seem to be commenting on the painting, or on a common subject-matter which inspired both the painting and the poem?

4. Compare Langston Hughes' "African Dance" and Aaron Douglas' mural, both on page 199 in the text.

a. Both have dance as subject matter. Specifically, how has a sense of the rhythm of dance been achieved in each?

b. Is there a kind of equivalency in the symmetry and repetition of forms in the mural and repetition of sounds and rhythm in the poem?

c. Does the word *tom-tom* serve some purpose in the poem beyond identifying a musical instrument?

a. How could the poet have suggested the kinetic effects of the painting? Is he more explicit and less abstract in treating the subject than the painter? Do you or do you not consider the poem as experimental or avant-garde as the painting? Is Kennedy only making explicit what is implicit in the painting? Or is the poem simply a linguistic comment on the painting?

b. Is the poem imitating the painting in any way? If so is it limited by the fact that the subject must be presented linearly whereas the visual effect is simultaneous? If not, what effects can the poet achieve in his medium that the painter could not? Is the poet's linearity inherent in his medium - - i.e., is it inherent in the structure of language?

c. In general, what effects can be expressed in the time arts more easily than in the space arts?

d. When it was first exhibited the painting facetiously was called "an explosion in a shingle factory". Is there more organization and unity in the painting than this kind of criticism would suggest or are we now more ready in the 70's to understand expression in abstraction? Demonstrate in the painting how coherence is achieved.

3. Make a comparison similar to the above between Sargent's <u>El Jaleo</u> (Color Plate 21, following page 152) and Rilke's "Spanish Dancer" in the MacIntyre translation, page 201. (See the comment on the poem on page 185.) The subject is an Andalousian dance in which the spectators encourage the dancer by clapping more and more vociferously.

a. Demonstrate both in the painting and in the poem how this progressive rhythm is built up and sustained to a climax.

d. What sounds contrast with the _low-slow_ combinations? How are analagous contrasts suggested in the painting?

5. In the text (page 200) we have quoted Walter Sorrell on the different conceptions represented in Michelangelo's _Creation_, in fresco and on the Sistine ceiling (Color Plate 15, following page 88) and Rodin's _Creation of Man_, a sculpture in bronze (Figure 8-3, page 200). To what extent do you think the medium used has affected the different conceptions? How might Michelangelo, commissioned to do a fresco on a ceiling, have expressed the conception Sorrell attributes to Rodin? How might Rodin have expressed Michelangelo's conception in his preferred medium, bronze sculpture?

Find an example of a subject which has been treated in several mediums. Be prepared to discuss the different art works which have resulted, demonstrating (1) differences in conception of the subject, (2) differences in treatment forced upon the artist by the chosen medium, and (3) ways in which similar effects have been gained in the different mediums. List the art works and your notes on them below:

d. What sounds contrast with the low-alto combinations? How are analogous contrasts suggested in the painting?

In the text (page 200) we have quoted Walter Sorell on the different conceptions represented in Michelangelo's Creation in fresco and on the Sistine ceiling (Color Plate 15 following page 48) and Rodin's Creation of Man, a sculpture in bronze (Figure 6-8, page 200). To what extent do you think the medium used has affected the different conceptions? How might Michelangelo, commissioned to do a fresco on a ceiling, have expressed the conception credited to Rodin? How might Rodin have expressed Michelangelo's conception in his preferred medium, bronze sculpture?

Find an example of a subject which has been treated in several media. Be prepared to discuss the different art works which have resulted, demonstrating (1) differences in concepts of the subject, (2) differences in treatment forced upon the artist by the chosen medium, and (3) ways in which similar effects have been gained in the different media. List the art works and your notes on them below.

6 MEDIUMS OF THE VISUAL ARTS

CONCEPTS

The visual arts discussed in this chapter are (1) _________, (2) _________, (3) _________, (4) _________, (5) _________, (6) _________, and (7) _________. In architecture, mediums used to be determined by (8) _________, but this is no longer true. The most common mediums in sculpture are (9) _________, (10) _________, and (11) _________. The qualities of the medium can be used in sculpture to contribute to the overall effect (the content). The sculptor can use the (12) _________ of wood or the (13) _________ of bronze for special effects. Paintings, drawings, and prints all use (14) _________ in a (15) _________ applied to a surface. Although the medium is not pigments (16) _________, (17) _________, and (18) _________ are classified as painting. Because pushing a button seems so simple, (19) _________ has been slow in being accepted as a visual art. Even after one is aware of the highly technical and complex developing and printing processes, it is easy to forget the many, many artistic decisions which are made in producing the finished (20) _________.

The Mediums of Painting

A medium in painting consists of two parts: (1)________________ which are the coloring materials and (2)______________________ which enable the painter to control the dry colors as they are applied.

The history of mediums in painting is also the history of a search for ways to achieve freer, easier, and more realistic effects. (3) _________________, in which the vehicle was warm wax, was an early medium used by the (4)______________________, (5)____________________ and (6)________________________.

Egg tempera, another older medium, is usually painted on a panel of (7)____________________, which is grounded with (8)_____________. Because the paint dries almost immediately, no fusing of color shades is possible, so the effect is highly (9)________________. The medium is very detailed and painstaking. Botticelli is one of the masters in this medium. His (10)__________________________ is an example.

Fresco means literally (11)______________________________. It is used to refer to a method of painting on freshly spread (12)______________________. The vehicle is (13)______________. Fresco must be painted boldly, quickly and surely because (14)__________________________. To guide the artist in his necessarily rapid work, a full-scale drawing in complete detail of the finished painting, called a (15)_______________________ is made. The colors in fresco have a tendency to be (16)__________ ____________. Michaelangelo's Sistine Chapel ceiling is done in fresco. A more recent artist who used this medium is (17)____________________. Both fresco and tempera were favorite mediums in the (18)_________________________ and (19)____________________________ periods.

Painting in oil is one of the most popular and versatile of mediums. Oil paints yield colors which are (20_______________ and which dry (21)_________________. Therefore a greater degree of (22)______________________ in depiction of subject matter is possible.

There are several methods of using oils. In the (23)___________ method, several thin layers of color glazes are painted over one another, which show through one another since oil, when thinned with turpentine, is (24)________________. The old masters, of whom (25)__________________ is one, used this slower and more difficult method.

A faster and more spontaneous method, a favorite with the more modern masters, is the (26)________________, in which the paints are applied in a single opaque layer. An example of an artist who uses this method is (27)________________________. It is possible in both techniques to apply oil paint very thickly so that the canvas surface is rough in texture. This method is extensively used by such an artist as (28)___________________. A third method, in which small dots of color are placed close together to form a pattern, is called pointilism and is usually associated with the French painter (29)________________________ and such a painting as (30)________________________. The disadvantage of oil is that with time it (31)________________.

The freest, easiest, and most spontaneous of the painting mediums is <u>watercolor</u>, which may be either (32)________________________ or (33)________________________. The watercolor paint sold as "tempera" or showcard color, usually used for posters and very quick work, is (34)________________________. The colors achieved in the watercolor methods are (35)________________________ but not (36)________________________. An example of watercolor painting is (37)________________________ by the artist (38)__________.

The Mediums of Prints

The history of printmaking shows a constant development of easier methods of printing and of ways of increasing subtleties in shading and details to secure more realistic effects. In the (1)________________________, the design to be inked is left standing out from the surface of the plate which is usually made of (2)________________________. In another type of print (intaglio), the design is cut or eaten out of the plate, which is usually of (3)________________________. The freest and easiest method is to draw directly on the (4)____________________ of the plate, which is of (5)________________________________.

The (6)________________________, the earliest kind of print, is usually quite abstract in depiction of subject matter because (7)______________________________. The (8)__________________, in which the lines are cut directly into the plate, while more naturalistic, still has a tendency to be (9)____________________. The (10)______________________ in which the lines are more easily eaten out of the plate by acid, affords more realistic effects because a greater variety of (11)____________________________ is possible. The (12)______________________, the most recent of the four common types of print, is the most spontaneous and freest of the methods and can be easily identified because it looks like a (13)__________________________ drawing.

The Three Trees, by (14)________________________ is an example of (15)__________________________. St. Jerome In His Cell, by (16)__________________________ is an example of (17)___________. The Rue Transnonain, of (18)______________________, is an example of (19)______________________________. Schmidt Rottluff's (20)________________________ is an example of (21)_____________. Mary Cassett's The Bath is a (22)__________________. George Bellow's (23)__________________ is a (24)____________________. Cezanne's The Bathers is a (25)____________________________. Three types of prints made by relief processes are (26) _________, (27) _________________, and (28) _________________. Three types of prints made by intaglio processes are (29) __________________, (30) _________________, and (31) _________________. An example of the planographic process is the (32) _________________________.

APPLICATION OF CONCEPTS

Below there are series of words. In each series all the words but one belong to one category (have to do with one subject). Write the word which does not belong in the first space below the series and identify the category of the remaining words in the second space.

Example: a) tapestry, b) mosaic, c) sculpture, d) cantata, e) illumination.
Cantata (d) does not belong. The category is visual arts.

1. a) oil, b) watercolor, c) pastel, d) woodcut, e) fresco

   ____________________ does not belong.

   The category is ______________________________.

2. a) terra cotta, b) pigment, c) gilded wood, d) marble, e) bronze

   ____________________ does not belong.

   The category is ______________________________.

3. a) stone, b) wood, c) cantilever, d) steel, e) brick

   ____________________ does not belong.

   The category is ______________________________.

4. a) acid, b) oil, c) wax, d) water, e) acrylic

   ____________________ does not belong.

   The category is ______________________________.

5. a) woodcut, b) linoleum, c) a rubber stamp, d) encaustic

   ____________________ does not belong.

   The category is ______________________________.

6. a) post and lintel, b) skeleton, c) tesserae, d) arch

   ____________________ does not belong.

   The category is ______________________________.

7. a) Zorach, b) Roszak, c) Seurat, d) Praxiteles, e) Moore

____________________ does not belong.

The category is ____.

8. a) Kuan Yin Bodhisattva, b) Two Forms,
c) Christ and S. John, d) The Charioteer

_____________________________________ does not belong.

The category is ____.

9. a) pencil, b) tesserae, c) silverpoint, d) pen, e) charcoal

____________________ does not belong.

The category is ____.

10. a) Edward Weston, b) Mary Cassatt, c) Alfred Stieglitz,
d) Imogene Cunningham

_____________________________________ does not belong.

The category is ____.

DISCUSSION QUESTION:

Igloos are domes built of blocks of ice. The temperature inside can never get above 32 degrees, except as the heat from a small fire or lamp and the heat from the persons in it raise it slightly. As this happens, the ice walls and ceiling slowly melt on the inside, increasing the interior space; but more ice is forming on the outside to increase the thickness of the walls and new snow is increasing the thickness and height of the "buttressing". In a sense, therefore, the igloo grows. What principles will eventually lead to its collapse? You will want to consider the qualities of the medium, the principles in arch construction, and the requirements in post lintel construction in answering this question.

PRINCIPLES OF CONSTRUCTION IN ARCHITECTURE

The questions refer to the sketches on the right with the same number.

1. The principle illustrated is ______________. It is suited for construction in what mediums? ____________________ ____

2. The principle illustrated is ______________. It is suited for construction in what mediums? ____________________ ____

3. The principle illustrated is ______________. It is suited for construction in what mediums? ____________________ ____

4. The principle illustrated is ______________. It is suited for construction in what mediums? ____________________ ____

5. The principle illustrated in the upper portion of the McDonnell Planetarium, St. Louis, is ____________________. This principle is used with what medium? ____________

6. The principle used for the dome of the Religious Center at the Southern Illinois University at Edwardsville is ________ __________. This type of construction was developed by ____.

   The mediums are usually ______________________________ ____

   Buildings in the text using this principle are __________ ________________ and ______________________________

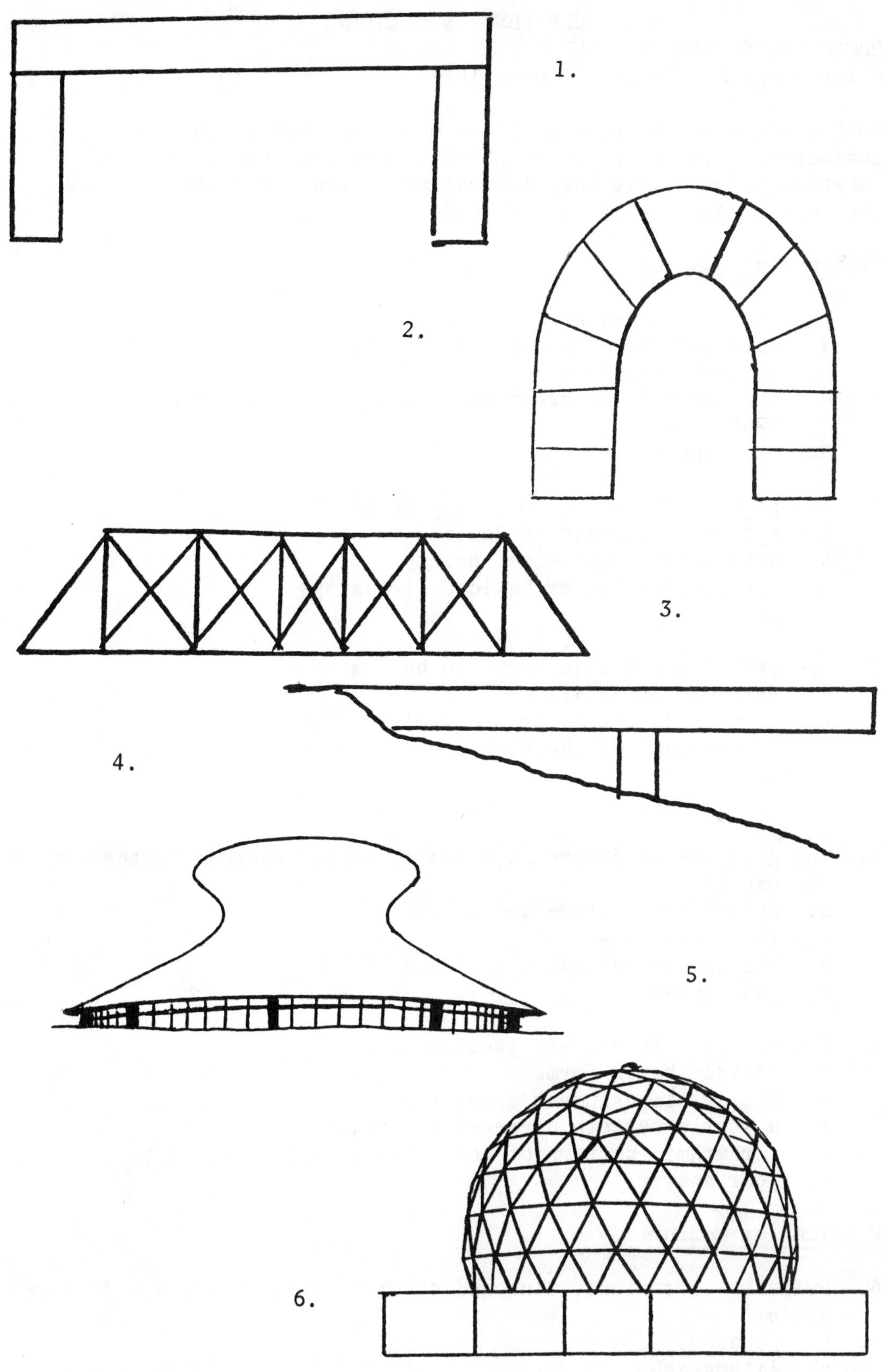
1.
2.
3.
4.
5.
6.

SELF-TEST IN PAINTING

EDGAR DEGAS: BALLET SCENE
Color Plate 20 (following page 152)

Most answers to interesting questions about art are more or less subjective. So, when you think of a more suitable answer to a question below, circle the alternative(s) you think are best and then write your answer in the space provided.

Problems of Subject

1. The picture suggests
   a. carefully posed models in the studio
   b. a candid snapshot
   c. the artist's re-creation of the first performance of Swan Lake
   d. your answer:

2. The gestures of the figures appear to be
   a. natural movements of dancers
   b. attitudes of classical beauty
   c. an illustration of basic ballet steps
   d. your answer:

3. The artist's attitude seems to be one of
   a. detached observation
   b. sympathy with the problems of the dancers
   c. disapproval of the theater
   d. admiration of women
   e. your answer:

4. The grouping of figures appears to be of interest to the artist because of
   a. details of costume and hair
   b. the spectators' response
   c. the accidental pattern formed
   d. your answer:

5. The dancers' skirts are treated as
   a. solidly based forms
   b. breezy, translucent draperies
   c. a static pattern of receeding cones
   d. a rhythmic pattern of hemispheres on tilting axes
   e. your answer:

Problems of Medium

6. Evidence of texture, line and color suggest that the medium is
   a. oil
   b. gouache
   c. lithograph

d. pastel
e. your answer:

7. The use of this medium is
   a. characteristic of the artist
   b. almost unique in his works
   c. your comments:

<u>Problems of Elements</u>

8. The lines created by the arms and legs of the dancers are
   a. measured regular curves
   b. angular and awkward
   c. mostly vertical and horizontal
   d. your answer:

9. The costumes of the two figures on the left form
   a. a cool-warm contrast which causes the far left figure to recede
   b. a light-dark contrast which causes the far left figure to recede
   c. a light silhouette which moves into the foreground
   d. your answer:

10. The palette chosen (colors used) is best described as
    a. monochromatic variations on blue
    b. a complex treatment of red-green complements
    c. intensification of all colors toward pure primaries
    d. your answer:

11. The foreground figures are distinguished by
    a. larger size
    b. a variety of carefully rendered details
    c. intensity of color and value contrasts
    d. more accurate portraiture
    e. your answer:

12. Volumes are
    a. gently modeled in tones of grey
    b. suggested by folds of cloth
    c. in some cases, heavily outlined
    d. your answer:

13. Looking at the line of the floor, which statement is not true ?
    a. it is based upon the laws of perspective
    b. it echos the diagonal placement of the figures
    c. it might remind one of Japanese prints
    d. it is a contrast to the movements of the dancers
    e. your comments:

14. The source of light is
    a. above left
    b. above right
    c. behind the dancers
    d. your answer:

15. Color areas are
    a. small and distinct
    b. large and distinct
    c. well-blended
    d. your answer:

16. The color of the shadows on the legs of the figure on the right
    a. is obviously distorted for emotional impact
    b. is a darker shade of skin color
    c. by its intensity implies light penetrating the fabric of the skirt
    d. suggests that the dancer has injured her leg
    e. your answer:

<u>Problems of Organization</u>

17. The artist's interest is concentrated on
    a. the foreground figures
    b. all the dancers
    c. the background
    d. your answer:

18. Which of the following does not contribute to a feeling of unity ?
    a. gestures of the dancers
    b. line of the floor
    c. bold background colors
    d. your comments:

19. Which contributes most to a feeling of stability ?
    a. gestures of the dancers
    b. lines of the floor and curtains
    c. bold background colors
    d. your answer:

20. Covering the section of the picture occupied by the two figures on the left, your impression is
    a. completion of motion within the remaining section
    b. incomplete motion toward the right
    c. incomplete motion toward the left
    d. the picture seems higher on the page
    e. your answer:

21. Which conveys the mood of the theater?
    a. the dancers' personalities
    b. the backstage setting
    c. the effect of light and motion
    d. your answer:

22. The title "Ballet Scene" relates to the picture in its
    a. theatricality
    b. factuality
    c. classicism
    d. your answer:

23. Which method of modeling is used more often

a. b. c. d. your answer:

24. Which diagram best expresses the main organizing lines of the picture

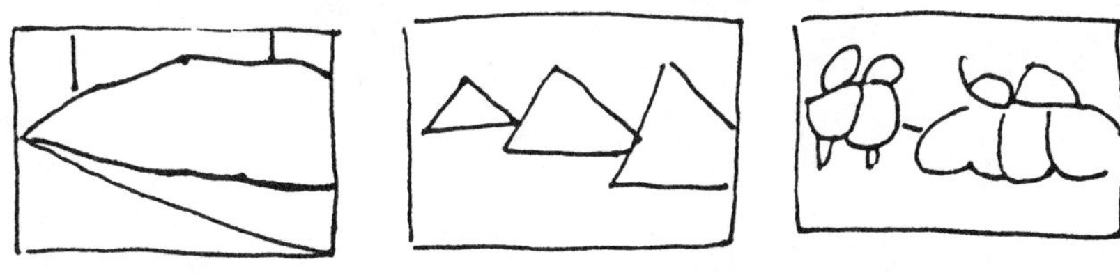

a. b. c.

d. your diagram:

A GUIDE FOR CRITICAL ANALYSIS OF A PAINTING

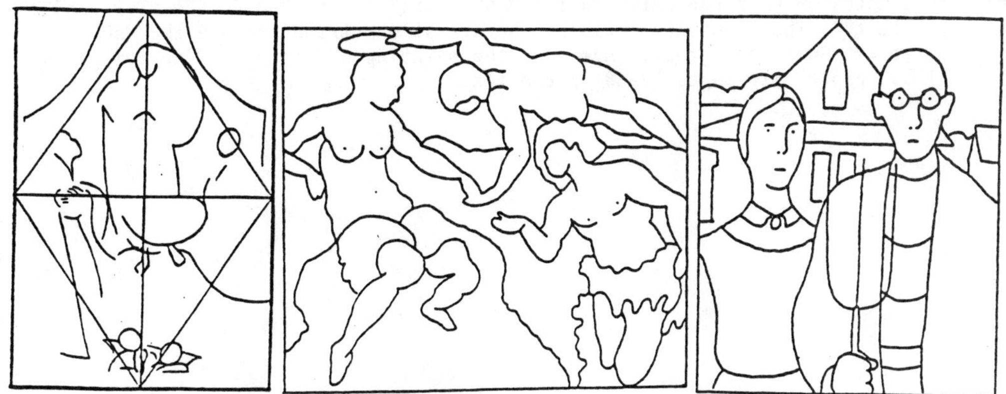

For this analysis you will be assigned or asked to choose on your own a painting to study. It is suggested that you read the Guide through and review the passages in THE HUMANITIES to which you are referred before undertaking the study.

PART ONE

In Part One you will study the painting from several points of view and make informal notes in the spaces provided.

PART TWO

In Part Two you will make a comprehensive statement about the painting and your experiencing of it. This reflective evaluation should be carefully organized as a separate essay. <u>Two thirds of the grade will be based on Part Two</u>.

NAME OF PAINTING____

ARTIST__________________________ DATES______________________

NAME____________________________ CLASS MEETING TIME____________

ADDRESS_________________________ DATE_______________________

PAINTING ANALYSIS NO.________

PART ONE: Informal notes on the painting.

In Part One you are asked to study the painting from several points of view and to make notes in the spaces provided. Formal sentences are not necessary. You may work through the various points of view in any order you choose. There will probably be more things to note under some headings than others, but make your coverage as complete as possible.

1. Make notes on what the painting is about. What is its "subject matter" <u>and</u> "content"? The "content" includes the artist's attitude toward the "subject matter." Comment on this. How does the painting affect you? (Review pages 31-56, especially pages 32-38 in the text.)

2. What seems to have been the feelings the painter wished to communicate? Explain why you think so. Your own emotional response is valid. "Define" it as best you can. Try also to identify what the painter has done to evoke this response (e.g., in handling of the elements of the visual arts.) That is, submit your own subjective feeling to objective analysis. Have any limitations of purpose, function, size, etc., been imposed on the artist? How have these affected the work? (Review pages 213-237 in the text.)

3. What is the medium? What are the potentials of this medium? How fully did the artist exploit these? Make notes on how the medium seems to have affected the methods of expression? (Review pages 133-161 in the text.)

4. Make notes on the use of the elements in the painting - - things which can be considered separately, such as line, color, use of light and dark, shape, volume, etc. Make notes on the artist's general methods of expression (handling of space, distortion, use of light, interest in textures, volumes of the objects represented, etc.) How are these used in the organization of the painting? (Review pages 309-330 in the text.)

5. Draw here two outlines of the frame of the painting. Be careful to approximate the shape of the painting itself. In the first, sketch in the <u>most important</u> organizing lines. (Do not try to copy the painting.) In the second, shade in the value distribution in the painting. Which type of organization described in the text does the organization in this painting resemble most? (Review pages 309-330 in the text.)

6. Do the characteristics of form, use of elements, or content of the painting lead you to believe that it belongs to a particular geographic area, period, trend, "school"? Does this painting seem typical of this artist's work? (Review pages 21-23, 38-40, 48-56, 235-238, 425-436 in the text and see "Abstract art," "Abstract expressionism," "Cubism," "Romanticism," and "Classicism," in the Glossary.

Note here any sources beyond the text which you have used in studying the painting.

PART TWO: Critical analysis and personal perception.

In Part One you have made informal analytical notes on the painting from various points of view. From your review of these and reflections on them, you are asked in this part to articulate your personal coherent perception of the work. Use any of the ideas from Part One that you think are pertinent, plus additional ideas you have from reflecting on the interrelations of these. Your statement should relate personal response to objective analysis and should be more than a mere repetition of the notes you have made. It should be presented as a well-rounded, well-organized essay.

PART ONE: Answers ranked: 0 - no credit 1 - fair 2 - good 3 - excellent Highest possible score-18	PART TWO: Essay ranked: 0 - no credit 1 - fair (and multiplied 2 - good by 12) 3 - excellent Highest possible score-36	PART ONE + PART TWO for Total Score Highest possible total-54
Score	Score	Total

SUBJECT : ELEMENTS : CONTENT

The above is a copy of Christ and S. John (page 68) on which you can experiment. Study the artist's handling of the elements to make a statement about the subject matter represented. Trace the lines of the shawls which cover the outer shoulders, disappear around the necks to drape over the inner shoulders and then follow the arms and meet where the hands touch. Note the line formed by the cloth which picks up the line of Christ's right arm, rises and falls across their knees and connects with John's left arm. These are just a beginning. Study the other lines: repetitions, variations, contrasts of lines and/or patterns. Be prepared to discuss these as they relate to the subject to express its significance, its content.

7 MEDIUMS OF MUSIC

CONCEPTS

The medium of music is _____________. Musical instruments are ways of making and controlling it. To do this they must have a (1)_________________, a (2)________________, and (3)_________________. The (1) is necessary to________________. The (2) is necessary to ________________ and the (3) is necessary to __________________. In the human voice, the vocal chords serve as a (1)____________________; the head and chest serve as (2)___________________; and the control of muscles forcing air through the throat as (3)__________________________.

You can review the material in this chapter by filling in the information called for on the chart on the following page. In the column marked "Range" use simply the four basic pitch ranges: soprano, alto, tenor or bass, adding the adjectives high or low when necessary, or indefinite for percussion of indefinite pitch.

As you fill in the chart, you should put a check by the instruments which are not familiar to you - - in other words, the instruments which force you to go back to the text in order to complete the chart. In the section on Application of Concepts which follows, you can then pay particular attention to the timbre and range of these unfamiliar instruments.

INSTRUMENTS OF THE ORCHESTRA

STRINGS

Instrument	Range	Method of Playing	Vibrator	Resonator	Character of tone
Violin Viola Cello Double Bass					

WOODWINDS

Instrument	Range	Method of Playing	Vibrator	Resonator	Character of tone
Piccolo Flute Oboe English Horn Clarinet Bass Clarinet Bassoon Contra Bassoon					

BRASSES

Instrument	Range	Method of Playing	Vibrator	Resonator	Character of tone
Trumpet Clarinet French Horn Trombone Bass Trombone Tuba					

PERCUSSION

Instrument	Range	Method of Playing	Vibrator	Resonator	Character of tone
Tympani or Kettle Drums Side, Snare, or Military Drum Bass Drum Tambourine Castanets Cymbals Triangle Xylophone Chimes Bells Celesta Piano Harp					

APPLICATION OF CONCEPTS

If this chapter is to be of use to you in understanding music and enjoying it, you must go beyond words to sounds themselves - - the medium of music. The only way to do this is to listen to music played on the various instruments described. Ideally, you will hear and see the instruments at the same time, but this is not always possible. You can, however, learn to recognize the sound of the various instruments and to know their capabilities by guided listening. We suggest that you begin with the three pieces described below. Guides for listening to them are included to help you. You will discover that it is important to listen to the same piece more than once for the musical sounds and the instruments making them to become firmly associated in your mind.

1. Benjamin Britten's _Young Person's Guide to the Orchestra_. This is a set of variations and a fugue on a theme by Henry Purcell (1659-1695) which was composed expressly to display the sounds of the different instruments of the orchestra. You will notice that the piece ends with a short fugue, an interesting musical form discussed later in Chapter 15.

2. _Bolero_ by Maurice Ravel. This is a set of 18 variations on a theme. There is a definite ending of the melody in each variation. The components of the composition are the _melody_, the _accompaniment_ and the _drum rhythms_. The patterns of each of these is given you below the chart. Letters have been inserted in the chart itself to guide your listening as various instruments and combinations of instruments are played in each variation.

3. The Fourth Movement of Franz Schubert's _Piano Quintet in A Major_. The Quintet is usually called "The Trout" because Schubert uses as his basic theme in this fourth movement a song he had written earlier about a trout. The words of the song describe the way the trout was caught, while the accompaniment portrays in realistic style the darting movements of the fish in the water. This set of variations on the air elaborates the accompaniment as we hear the trout leaping and frolicking through the churning water.

There are additional suggestions for your listening at the end of the chapter in your text.

Benjamin Britten, THE YOUNG PERSON'S GUIDE TO THE ORCHESTRA
Variations and Fugue on a Theme of Purcell

The Theme of eight measures quoted above is played in succession by

a. full orchestra
b. woodwinds
c. brasses
d. strings
e. percussions
f. entire orchestra

and is followed immediately by 13 variations and a fugue based on it.

Variation 1: a duet for two flutes (with harp), followed by two flutes and piccolo.

Variation 2: two oboes.

Variation 3: two clarinets in ballet dance. Note the flexible runs and hollow clear tones of the clarinet.

Variation 4: a slightly jazzy dance by bassoons. Note the ponderous movement and pitch of double-reed quality.

Variation 5: polonnaise by first and second violines.

Variation 6: sombre tune by violas, rich, full, alto.

Variation 7: song by cellos.

Variation 8: double bass violins.

Variation 9: harp plays chords and fast runs.

Variation 10: four French horns plus snare druns.

Variation 11: trumpets.

Variation 12: three trombones and tuba.

Variation 13: percussion instruments

a. 3 kettledrums
b. bass drums, cymbals, kettledrums
c. tambourine, triangle, kettledrums
d. snare drum, Chinese wood block, kettledrums
e. xylophone, kettledrums
f. castanets, gong, kettledrums, whip
g. all percussions end with duet for xylophone and triangle

Fugue: the individual instruments of the four sections of the orchestra enter in rapid succession:

1. Woodwinds
   a. Piccolo
   b. Flute
   c. Oboe
   d. Clarinet
   e. Bassoon
2. Strings
   a. Violins
   b. Viola
   c. Cello
   d. Double-basses
   e. Harp
3. Brasses
   a. French Horns
   b. Trumpets
   c. Trombones
4. Percussions

and the piece concludes with the brasses and drum slowly sounding out the original Theme.

FOR DISCUSSION

Examine the photograph of a piano which John Cage has "prepared" for his music, Figure 5-9, page 131. From the information in this chapter on medium in music, what would you expect to happen when he presses two strings apart with an eraser? What would happen when he places a metal bar directly under the strings? Discuss these questions using the correct technical language.

MAURICE RAVEL : BOLERO

Var																			
	Th	1	2	3	4	5	6	7	8	9	10	11	12	13	14	15	16	17	18
Piccolo									M			M	M	M	M	M	D	M	M
Flutes	M	D	D	D		M	A		D		D	M	M	M	M	M	D	M	M
Oboes								A		M		M	M	M	M	M	D	D	D
Ob. d'Am					M			A		M									
Cor Ang.								A		M		M	M	M	M	M			A
E flat Clar				M															
Clarinet		M								M	A	M	M	M	A	M	D	D	D
Bass Clar.									A	A	A	A		A		A	A	A	A
Bassoons			M		D				A	A		A	A	A	A	A	A	A	A
Contra B.											A	A	A	A	A	A	A	A	A
Horns I						D			D	A	D		D	A	D	D	D	D	D
Horns II									M	D		D	A	D	A	D	D	D	D
Trumpets						M	D	D				D			M	A	M	M	M
Trombones											M				A	M	A	M	M
Tuba															A	A	A	A	A
Sop. Sax.								M						A	A	M	M	M	M
Ten. Sax.							M					M		M	A		M	M	M
Harp			A	A					A	A	A			A	A	A	A	A	A
Celesta									A										
Timpani													A	A	A	A	A	A	A
Snare Dr.	D	D	D	D	D	D	D	D	D	D	D	D	D	D	D	D	D	D	D
Percussion																			D
1st violin						A		A		A		A	M	M	M	M	M	M	M
2nd violin					A		A		A	A	A	A	D	A	M	M	D	D	D
Violas	A	A	A	A	A	A	A	A	A	A	D	A	A	A	A	M	D	D	D
Cellos	A	A	A	A	A	A	A	A	A	A	A	A	A	A	A	M	D	D	D
Bass viol					A	A	A	A	A	A	A	A	A	A	A	A	A	A	D
	Th	1	2	3	4	5	6	7	8	9	10	11	12	13	14	15	16	17	18
Var																			

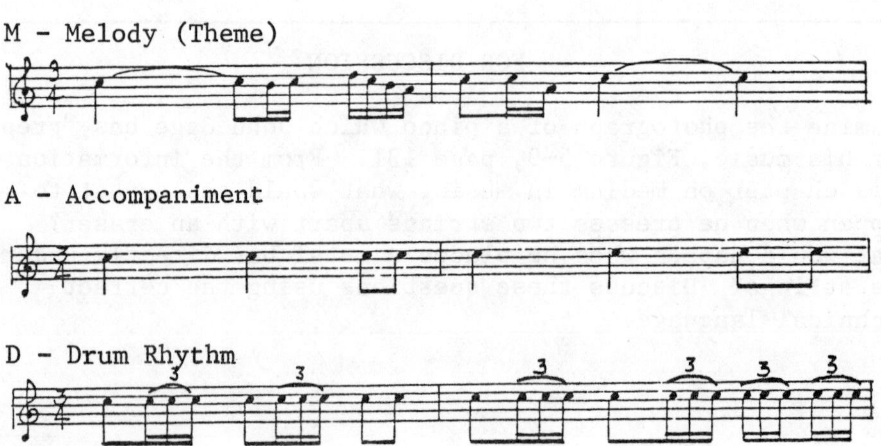

FRANZ SCHUBERT : PIANO QUINTET IN A MAJOR
Fourth Movement

The instrumentation for the Quintet is violin, viola, cello, double bass, and piano. The form of the Fourth Movement is theme and variations. The theme is binary. It is played pp by the strings only. Six variations follow.

Variation 1: The theme is played by the piano in octaves while the strings accompany it with broken triads and high trills.

Variation 2: The viola and piano alternate in playing the theme against a graceful running counterpoint of the violin.

Variation 3: The cello and double bass play the melody accompanied by the piano in a florid counterfigure.

Variation 4: There is first a change of key to D minor in a mock-heroic mood then to F major in the second half of the variation. There are various rhythmic, harmonic, and dynamic modifications of the theme throughout.

Variation 5: This variation is a lyrical flowing solo for cello with occasional commentary by the piano and violin.

Variation 6: There is a final key change to D major. This variation is a kind of finale with the original theme dispersed among various instruments against a florid accompaniment of the piano.

ROUNDS TO SING

Below are two rounds which are probably less familiar to you than "Row, row, row your boat" which is mentioned in the text. You can familiarize your ears with contrapuntal sound by singing them. These will be canon in three voices. The "Alleluia" of Mozart is especially effective.

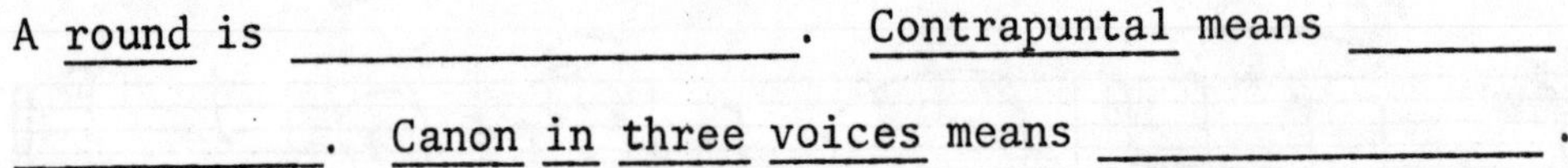

A round is ________________. Contrapuntal means ________________. Canon in three voices means ________________.

MAN'S LIFE'S A VAPOR

Traditional

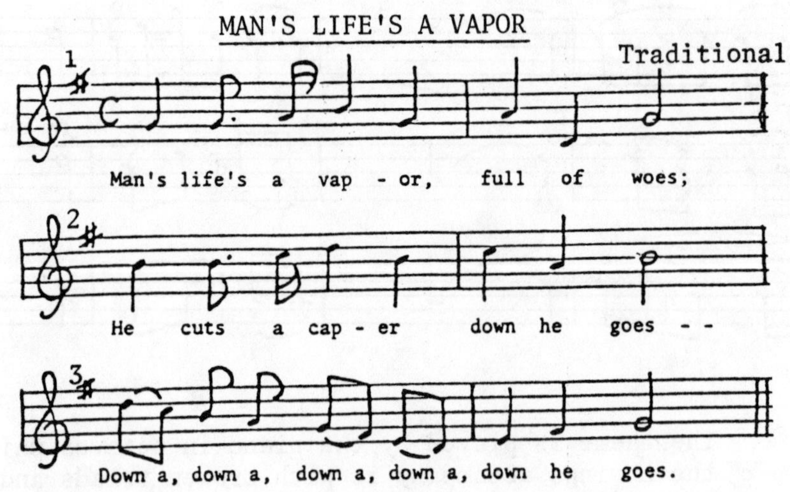
1
Man's life's a vap - or, full of woes;
2
He cuts a cap - er down he goes - -
3
Down a, down a, down a, down a, down he goes.

ALLELUIA

Wolfgang Amadeus Mozart (1756-91)

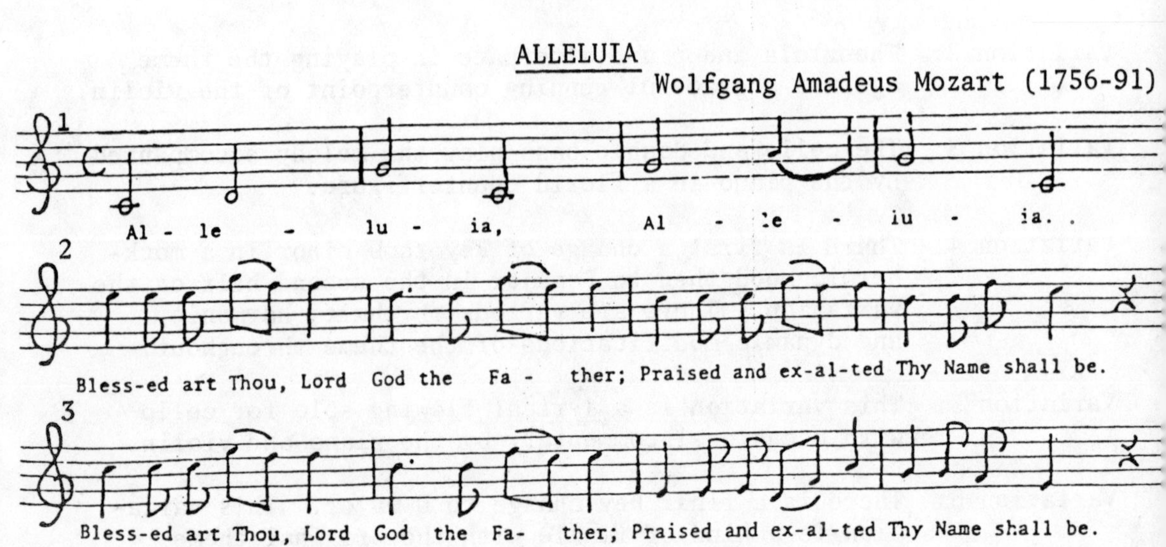
1
Al - le - lu - ia, Al - le - lu - ia.
2
Bless-ed art Thou, Lord God the Fa - ther; Praised and ex-al-ted Thy Name shall be.
3
Bless-ed art Thou, Lord God the Fa- ther; Praised and ex-al-ted Thy Name shall be.

ATTENDING A SYMPHONY REHEARSAL OR CONCERT

One usually thinks of a concert as something to be heard, but there are many things to watch at a concert which will enhance the experience. A good way to learn about the instruments of the orchestra, what they look like, how they are played, what the conductor does, and even about the music being played is to attend a rehearsal. There is a better opportunity to observe how the conductor shapes the performance to his own interpretation of the score; controlling the dynamics in various passages, determining the tempo, ensuring that every instrumentalist is playing the exact notes as written, etc. etc. One has a chance, to become aware of what the different sections of the orchestra contribute to the overall effect.

Here are a few specific things to watch for:

1. Note the seating arrangement of the orchestra. The "typical seating chart of an orchestra" on page 176 in the text will serve as a guide, but it should be remembered that particular conductors vary this seating to their own preference. The first violins are always on the left. The concert master who leads the violin section and acts somewhat as an assistant conductor, is at the head of the first violins on the outside. The second violins may be next to the first violins or they may be at the front of the stage opposite the first violins. Variations in seating of other instruments may be used in different orchestras.

2. During the "tune-up" period before the conductor comes on stage there are many things to observe: Watch the "concert master", who is the first violinist. Note that he or she sounds the "A" to which all other instruments are tuned. Watch the performers as they tune their instruments, adjusting their pitch to that of the "A" sounded by the concert master: the tympani player adjusts the taps on his drums, the violins are tuned with "pegs" which are turned to tighten or loosen a string, the woodwind players moisten the reeds so that they will not be too stiff and adjust the mouthpiece in or out to lengthen or shorten the air column. Watch for the "cue" of the concert master indicating that all instruments are in tune. Note the sudden silence in the orchestra and the "hush" which spreads through the audience just before the conductor makes a dramatic appearance.

3. The conductor bows to the audience and assumes the podium, checks to see that all performers are in readiness and attentive. The baton (or sometimes simply the hand) is raised and held indicating that all must be ready and alert for the piece to start.

4. Watch the conductor with a hand or baton describe in a stylized movement the time pattern of the piece - - the meter represented in the time signature. There are many individual variations in the manner of doing this but they follow a general pattern. A stroke straight down in front of the conductor is used for the first beat of a measure. Normally this is a strong beat in the time pattern and for this reason the first beat of a measure is called the down beat. If the pattern is a two beat pattern, the second beat is a weaker accented one and is indicated by bringing the hand which has been lowered on the down beat directly up on what is called the up beat. If the meter is a three beat pattern the lowered baton is moved to the right on a second beat and then up on a third beat, to enscribe a triangle, where it is in position to begin the next measure on a down beat. The movements for a four beat measure are down, right, left, and up.

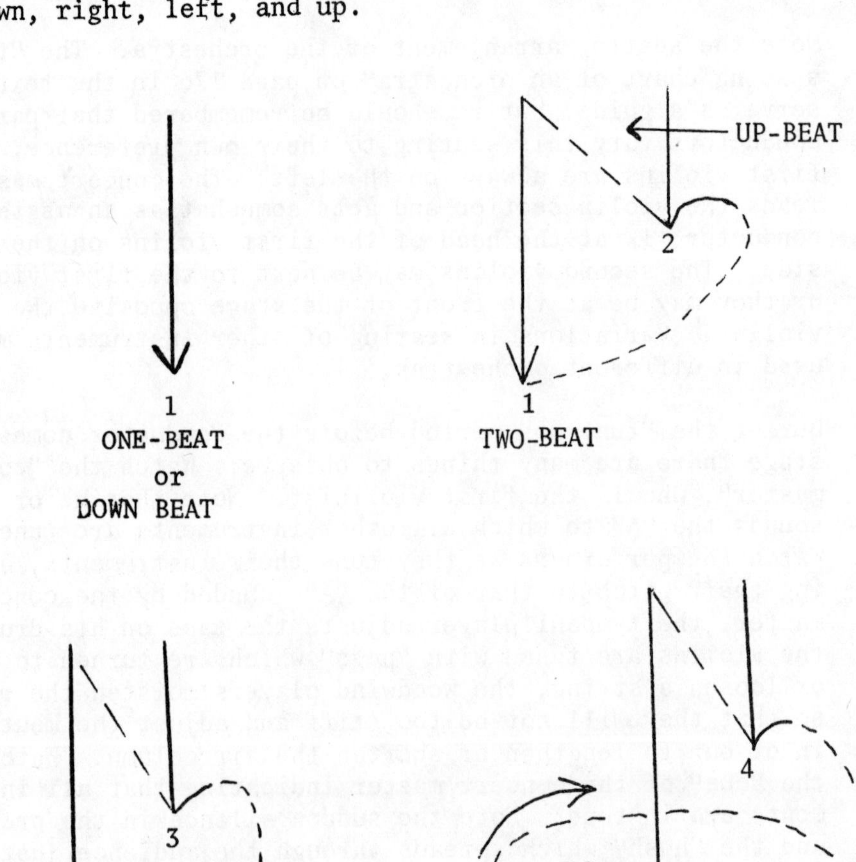

A GUIDE FOR CRITICAL ANALYSIS OF MUSIC

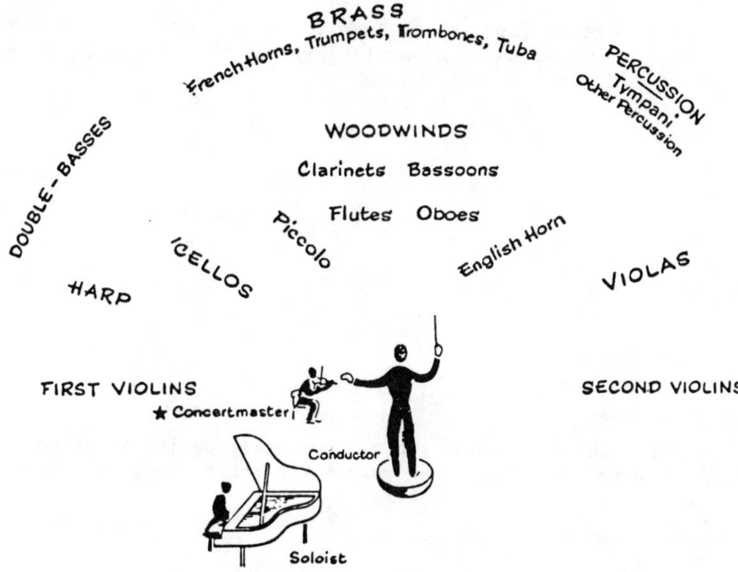

For this analysis you will be assigned or asked to choose on your own a piece of music to listen to and to study. It is suggested that you read the Guide through and review the passages in THE HUMANITIES to which you are referred before undertaking the study.

PART ONE

In Part One you will study the piece from several points of view and make informal notes in the spaces provided.

PART TWO

In Part Two you will make a comprehensive statement about the composition and your experiencing of it. This reflective evaluation should be carefully organized as a separate essay. Two thirds of the grade will be based on Part Two.

NAME OF COMPOSITION ______________________________

COMPOSER ______________________________

DATE OF COMPOSITION, IF KNOWN ______________________________

NAME ____________________ CLASS MEETING TIME __________

ADDRESS ____________________ CLASS MEETING TIME __________

MUSIC ANALYSIS NO. __________

PART ONE: Informal notes on the selection.

In this section you are asked to examine the selection from several points of view and to make notes in the spaces provided. Formal sentences are not necessary, and you may work through the various points of view in any order you choose. There will probably be more things to note under some headings than under others, but you should make your coverage as complete as possible.

1. Make notes on the moods or feelings which seem to be expressed in this work. What musical elements and combinations of elements are used to express them? (Review pages 32-34, 123, and 386 in the text.)

2. Does the piece suggest any particular social, cultural, political or religious values? Does it have any function other than to delight? Explain. (Review pages 91-92 in the text.)

3. What instrument, group of instruments, voice, or combinations of these is used? Make notes on the effect the choice of instruments and/or voices has on the music. (Review pages 162-184 and 389-392 in the text.)

4. Make notes on the elements which can be discussed separately, such as tempo, rhythm, melody, harmony, timbre, dynamics, etc. What relationships or uses of these elements aid in achieving unity and/or variety in the piece? (Review pages 238-271 in the text.)

5. What is the musical form? If it is a traditional form, how strictly does the composer follow it? (Review pages 364-392 in the text.)

6. Are there characteristics of form, use of elements, expressive content which lead you to believe the piece belongs to some particular geographic area, period, trend, school, or composer? (Review pages 430-432 on "classicism" and "romanticism," but see especially pages 429-430 for other suggestions in considering "style."

Note here any sources beyond the text which you have used in studying the piece, e.g., album covers, books, comment by the composer, etc.

PART TWO: Critical analysis and evaluation of your experience in studying the musical selection.

In Part One you have made informal notes on the selection from various points of view. From your reflection on these, you are asked in this part to make a statement about your personal coherent perception of the work. Use any of the ideas from Part One you think are pertinent, plus additional ideas you have from reflection on the interrelation of these. Your statement should relate personal to objective analysis and should be more than a mere repetition of the notes you have made. It should be presented as a well-rounded, well-organized essay.

PART ONE: Answers ranked: 0 - no credit 1 - fair 2 - good 3 - excellent Highest possible score-18	PART TWO: Essay ranked: 0 - no credit 1 - fair (and multiplied 2 - good by 12) 3 - excellent Highest possible score-36	PART ONE + PART TWO for Total Score Highest possible total-54
Score	Score	Total

8 LITERATURE AND THE COMBINED ARTS

CONCEPTS: Literature

The space arts and the time arts are different in the way we experience them: In the space arts the work of art is (1) ________________ but in the time arts, the work of art is (2) ________________. Both literature and music are (3) ________________ arts, but they are different in that literature uses (4) ________________ symbols and music uses (5) ________________ symbols. Since music, therefore, plays on our emotions directly for its meaning and does not depend on assignment of referents or specific meanings to the symbols it uses, it is sometimes said to be a more (6) ________________ language than literature, which not only depends on assignment of specific meanings to its symbols, but the symbols are in a particular language.

Spoken language, or language intended to be spoken, involves both (7) ________________ and (8) ________________. When the author wishes, he may use (9) ________________ to reinforce a meaning or even to convey a meaning. When this happens, as in some poetry, literature can approach music in its method of expression. For example, when we compare the poem by Joseph Albers on page 29 of the text with the poem by Langston Hughes on page 199, it is clear that the poem by (10) ________________ is more dependent on the elements of music for its content than the poem by (11) ________________ in which sense rather than sound is emphasized.

CONCEPTS: Combined Arts

A combined art is one which uses more than one (1) ____________. Three examples of combined arts are (2) ____________________ (3) ________________, and (4) ________________. Since these combine mediums of the other arts, the artist has for use the elements of these arts. For example, the elements of the visual arts and of music are these:

Visual arts	Music
(5) ________________	(12) ________________
(6) ________________	(13) ________________
(7) ________________	(14) ________________
(8) ________________	(15) ________________
(9) ________________	(16) ________________
(10) ________________	(17) ________________
(11) ________________	

Opera and theater, for example, as visual arts use (18) ________ __________, (19) __________________, and (20) __________________ to create designs within the proscenium of a stage which serves as a (21) _________________. In addition, opera uses two mediums of the auditory arts: a story, called the (22) _______________, and (23) ________________. Theater, of course, in addition to being a space art is also an (24) __________________ art, with literature as its primary medium.

Film makes use of the elements of the other arts, but it is able to do things with them which the other arts cannot. For example, it can do such things as (25) _________________________________, (26) _____________________, and (27) ___________________________. Since the images and organized sounds of the other arts are recorded on film, the medium of this art is (28) ______________.

According to Lincoln F. Johnson, whose quotation is reproduced on the cover of the GUIDE FOR CRITICAL ANALYSIS OF FILM included in this section, the ability to see films intelligently is difficult to learn because (29) _____________________________________ _______________________________; and what can be put into words about a film are (30) __________________, (31) _________________, and (32) __________________, which are not the film experience.

More and more the director of a film who has complete responsibility for what is released to the public is also the editor. Two of the editor's functions in film making are (33) __________ and (34) ______________. Three expressive devices in film art which were pioneered by Sergi Eisenstein are (35) ____________, (36) ______________________ and (37) ______________________.

Dance uses as mediums bodies moving in space, creating visual designs, usually to music. Basic dance has its origins in the natural movements and rhythms of all human beings as they respond to inner and outer stimuli in the early stages of life. Universally the language of movement in basic dance is the same: (38) ________________, (39) ________________, and (40) ____ ________________ express excitement, agitation, pleasure; (41) ______________, (42) ______________ and (43) __________ express resignation, serenity and contentment. As these random movements are developed into styles and patterns in different cultures, distinguishing characteristics develop. Below list four characteristics of each of three such developments:

Oriental dance:

(44) ______________________ (46) ______________________

(45) ______________________ (47) ______________________

Spanish dance:

(48) ______________________ (50) ______________________

(49) ______________________ (51) ______________________

African dance:

(52) ______________________ (54) ______________________

(53) ______________________ (55) ______________________

APPLICATION OF CONCEPTS

Mark the following statements True or False. For each statement you mark False state the reason why on the line following it.

_____ 1. A camera is a machine which makes an accurate record of what is presented to it and is therefore incapable of expression and interpretation.

____

_____ 2. D.W. Griffith, credited with developing motion photography into an art, described his endeavors as an effort to make us "hear."

____

_____ 3. Documentary films illustrate the fact that selection and arrangement of images are not enough to make an interesting film; they must be accompanied by words and music.

____

_____ 4. The visual and temporal structure of The Space Odyssey: 2001 are more important than the story to our enjoyment of it.

____

_____ 5. The auteur theory of film making argues that the director as auteur (French for author) is responsible for writing the scenario and script.

____

_____ 6. The lack of much dialogue in The Space Odyssey: 2001 is a basic weakness in the film.

____

_____ 7. The famous Odessa Steps sequence appeared in D.W. Griffith's Birth of a Nation.

____

_____ 8. Sync as used in the expressions "not in sync" and "lip-sync" is an abbreviation for synchronization.

____

_____ 9. The films of Griffith, Welles, and Ford illustrate the fact that greatness in films is more dependent on the technology available than upon the artist.

____

_____10. The purpose of analysis of the elements and structure of film is to impress those you talk to with technical terminology they do not understand.

____

DISCUSSION QUESTIONS:

1. A few years back film producing companies assumed that the public chose to see or not see a film because of the actors in it. Some critics now feel that the "star" system is over, that audiences now pay as much or more attention to who directed a film as to who the actors are. Do you feel that this is true? Be prepared to state your opinion with examples to illustrate it.

   Can you name three directors whose films you have liked and films they have directed?

   (1)____________________ who directed ____________________,

   ____________________, and ____________________.

   (2)____________________ who directed ____________________,

   ____________________, and ____________________.

   (3)____________________ who directed ____________________,

   ____________________, and ____________________.

2. We frequently read - - in both criticism and advertising - - that a film or play is a "box-office success." What are the assumptions underlying these statements? Do you agree or disagree with the assumptions? How do such statements affect your decision to see or not to see a film or a performance? Does your experience with "box-office successes" lead you to value this kind of success in the art you seek out and enjoy? Are the satisfactions in having seen a "box-office success" different from the satisfactions you have had in discovering on your own, a work which pleases you very much? How? May one enjoy knowing about popular art and being able to discuss it with friends without judging it to be good,

significant, or aesthetically rewarding? If your answer is yes, what are the values involved? Where do these rank in your hierarchy of values? Is popular art bad because it is popular or popular because it is bad?

3. It is said that Broadway is killing creativity in theater. What is meant by the statement? The development of an "off Broadway theater" and even an "off off-Broadway theater" are sometimes attributed to the fact that Broadway producers cannot risk producing works which are not "certain successes." What kinds of works are likely to be certain successes? Does the use of known, popular stars add to the likelihood that a play will be a success?

4. "In ordinary conversation one does not know what one is about to say until it is said." You are undoubtedly aware of this phenomenon from experience. Be prepared to discuss it, giving examples or demonstrating it.

5. "Art, including language, is both the creator of the social reality and a commentary on it." Consider this statement. What does it mean? Do you agree or disagree with it. Be prepared to discuss your point of view.

PROJECTS

These projects may be undertaken by you individually or your instructor may wish to make them cooperative projects with the whole class collecting materials to be shared and discussed.

1. Look up at least four, more if possible, writeups of a film you have seen recently. First, decide which of them are reviews - - that is, simply summarize the story brightly or amusingly and advise you to see or not see it - - and those writeups which are critiques of the film - - that is, analyze the way in which the director has used the film medium and their effectiveness.

2. Where do you get the information which helps you decide whether or not to see a film? What is the nature of the information?

List the names of the people who cover films for local newspapers.

1. ______________________

2. ______________________

3. ______________________

Try in a few phrases for each film critic to characterize the kinds of information included.

1. ____

2. ____

3. ____

3. Find out who writes commentary on film for the following magazines.

The New Yorker ______________________

New York Magazine ______________________

Esquire ______________________

Cosmopolitan ______________________

Vogue ______________________

The New York Times ______________________

The Village Voice ______________________

Read one article by each reviewer. Can you deduce from this the kind of audience at which the magazine is aimed?

SOME QUESTIONS TO ASK ABOUT A PLAY

Possibly the most productive way to move toward understanding and fully experiencing any work of art is to begin asking yourself questions about it and about the experience which you have with it. As you answer your own questions, and the additional questions they suggest, you may extend your awareness of all that makes that work function as an experience.

The questions you will ask about a play will have to do with (1) the CHARACTERS AND THE ACTING; (2) the PLOT AND ORGANIZATION; (3) the SETTING AND ALL ASPECTS OF PRODUCTION; (4) the THEMES OR INTENTIONS; and (5) the LANGUAGE OR PECULIARITIES OF MEDIA OF PRESENTATION.

CHARACTERS AND ACTING:

1. Do the characters represent a particular "class" or "types: (such as national types, ethnic types, personality types, etc.)?
2. Is there a protagonist (main character)? An antagonist? What are their traits of strength, weakness, etc.?
3. What are the special functions of various characters in relation to each other and to the play's intent?
4. What means are used by the playwright to characterize? For example, by actions, self-revelation by monologue or conversation, habits of dress, certain eccentricities, manners and patterns of speaking, etc.?
5. Are any characters intended to change during the play? What is the nature of the change? How does this come about?
6. Are the characterizations convincing and sustained throughout the play, or did the actors' own personalities interfere with the depiction of the fictional characters?

PLOT AND ORGANIZATION:

1. What are the main elements of the plot? Are these elements presented in some sort of organized way, such as in separation into scenes, patterns of alternating tension and relaxation, etc.?
2. Is there dramatic conflict? If so, how does it begin and how is it propelled?
3. Is the plot sufficiently interesting to hold your attention? Do the incidents seem plausibly connected and believable?
4. Is the conclusion (*denouement*) sufficiently inevitable or is it brought about by arbitrary coincidence (*deux ex machina*)?

SETTING AND ASPECTS OF PRODUCTION:

1. What is the setting? Indoor? Outdoor? Realistic? Imaginative? Fantasy-like?
2. How is the setting depicted? Furniture? Symbolic aspects? Unusual design plan: Abstract? Realistic? Traditional? Modern?
3. Does the setting change? Why the changes? Is the change necessary and natural?
4. How does the setting contribute to the characterization, the theme content, the ideas, etc.?
5. What devices of production other than setting contribute to the effectiveness of the play? Costuming? Lighting effects? Music or other sound effects? Uses of films, slides, etc.?

THEMES OR INTENTIONS:

1. Is a moral stressed or some human significance exemplified in the play?
2. Does the play deal with social, moral, intellectual, ethical, political, educational or other problems or ideas?
3. Is the play interested in stimulating thought and/or implying answers to problems? Or is it primarily a play to entertain, or a representation of human frivolity for our amusement?
4. Does the play end in a believable way? Does it leave us wholly satisfied with its solution to the plot, or does it conclude in an open-ended manner, leaving us to supply answers or conclusions?
5. In what ways is the theme or intention communicated and reinforced during the play? Through symbols? Costumes? Dialogue? Other ways?

LANGUAGE OR PECULIARITIES OF PRESENTATION:

1. Is the language that of common people in a particular type of social group, ethnic group, or the like? Is the language realistic or elevated? Is there a dialect or regional flavor to the language or the manner of speaking? Are characterizations enhanced by the language?
2. Do the actors and actresses handle the language convincingly and consistently?
3. What special characteristics of language are there (such as verse, short-clipped sentences, long involved sentences, etc.)?

VOCABULARY AID IN DISCUSSING DANCE

When making notes on a dance performance and in writing about it and discussing it you will be reflecting on what you observe and what you experience in observing--sort of watching yourself react and trying to account for your reactions. The following words and phrases may be helpful to you in articulating these.

Remember they are only a sample of the kinds of phrases you can use. They do not exhaust by any means what can be said. And none of them may apply to the work you are studying. Nonetheless reading them through may suggest possibilities for saying what you want to say or may suggest other words and phrases which fit your experience:

SUBJECT:	plotless story, character study, depiction of mood, pantomine, satiric, humorous, abstract, interpretation of music, improvisation.
MEDIUMS:	number of dancers, where, kind of space, costumes, lights, sets, music.
TECHNIQUES:	balancing, turning, elevation, point work, patterning, falling, stretching.
ELEMENTS:	of visual arts: line, color, shape, etc. of music: rhythm, tempo, dynamics, etc.
ORGANIZATION:	narrative, ABA, rondo, variations, contrasts, repetitions, improvisation, symmetrical-asymmetrical designs, forming in circles, lines, groups, movements sustained, stacatto, energetic, graceful, angular.
STYLE:	classical ballet, modern, Grahamesque, ethnic or folk, jazz, gymnastic, etc.

A GUIDE FOR CRITICAL ANALYSIS OF THEATER - DRAMA

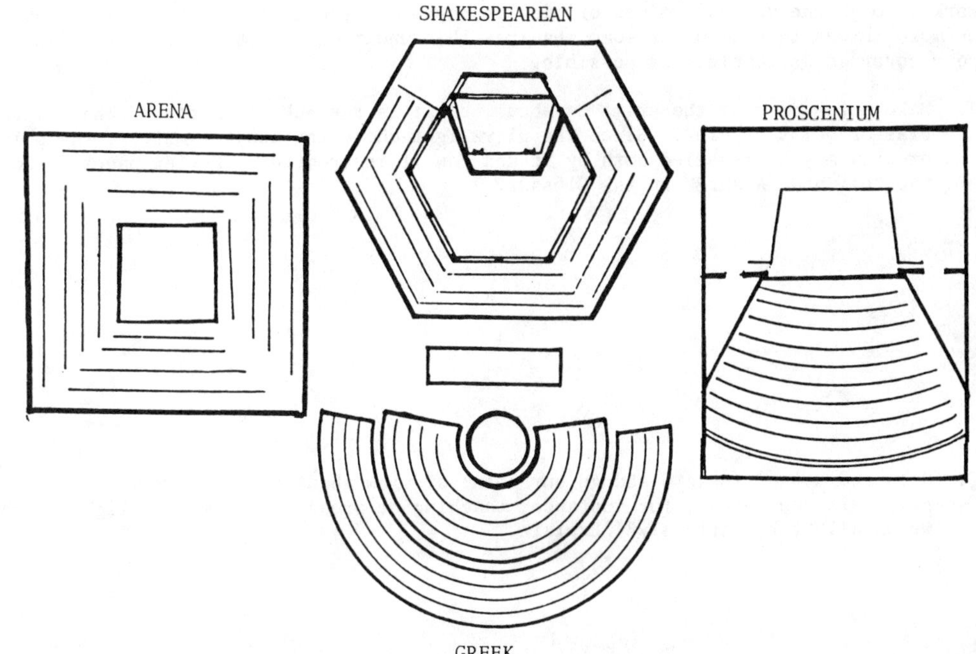

For this analysis you will read a play (drama) and/or see a performance of it (theater) Whichever you do, you are for the analysis to consider drama (the written text) and theater (performed drama) as a combined art, since the playwright is writing for performance and must make the text conform to both the limitations and possibilities of performance. It is suggested that you read this Guide through and review the passages in THE HUMANITIES to which you are referred before undertaking the study.

PART ONE

In Part One you will study the drama and/or production of it from several points of view and make informal notes in the spaces provided.

PART TWO

In Part Two you will be asked to make a comprehensive statement about work and your experiencing of it. This reflective evaluation should be carefully organized as a separate essay. Two thirds of the grade will be based on Part Two.

NAME OF THE PLAY____

AUTHOR__________________ DATES____________ NATIONALITY________________

DATE OF WRITING OF THE PLAY, IF KNOWN________________________________

IF SEEN IN PERFORMANCE: WHEN, BY WHOM?__________ DIRECTOR__________________

ATTACH PROGRAM IF POSSIBLE

NAME______________________________________ CLASS MEETING TIME__________________

ADDRESS____________________________________ DATE______________________________

THEATER - DRAMA ANALYSIS NO.____________

PART ONE: Informal notes on the play as read and/or seen in performance.

In this section you are asked to examine the play from several points of view and to make notes in the spaces provided. Formal sentences are not necessary, and you may work through the various points of view in any order you choose. There will probably be more things to note under some headings than under others, but you should make your coverage as complete as possible.

1. Make notes on what the drama is about. What is the subject matter? What is the bias or point of view? Since the playwright chose the subject matter, the point of view may be revealed both by it and how it is treated. (Review pages 35-36 in the text and "Absurd" in the Glossary.)

2. Does the author seek to change our point of view about the subject matter of the play? Is the author, for instance, teaching or preaching or making light of what we usually take seriously? Explain.

3. Theatre is a combined art. Identify the mediums used: literature, design (staging, makeup, lighting, deployment of actors, costumes), acting (persons dressed in a particular way, speaking in a particular way and moving in a defined space), music, dance. (Review pages 190-194 in the text and "Frame" and "Combined arts" in the Glossary.)

4. Analyze two or three of the mediums mentioned above and comment on how the elements of each are used to contribute to the play's effectivenes. (Review pages 190-194 in the text.)

5. A drama presents a story or narrative or familiarizes us with a group of characters in a particular set of circumstances. What is the narrative unfolded in this play (the actual chronology of events)? Make notes on the real time sequence of events and on the order in which these have become the "plot" of the play. Are they the same? Why do you suppose the playwright chose this particular order of presentation? (Review pages 398-402 and 407-410 in the text and "Plot" in the Glossary.)

6. The essentials of narrative are exposition, conflict, climax, and denoument. Using a simple diagram like the one below indicate roughly how much of the play is given to each. (Review pages 398-400 in the text and "Exposition" in the Glossary.)

7. Make notes on the style of the drama as written or, if seen in performance, as presented. Have changes been made in the written play to update it, to emphasize or modify the "content" or to adapt it to a particular audience or to particular circumstances of presentation? Comment. (Review pages 35-38 and 435 in the text.) Stage settings and costumes tend to duplicate styles in the arts, running the gamut from realism to pure abstraction, from impressionism to abstract expressionism. (Review pages 38-51 in the text and see "Abstract," "Abstract expressionism," "Impressionism," and "Representational art" in the Glossary.)

Note here any sources you have used in studying the work . . . e.g., text notes, program notes, books (other than the text), articles, etc.

PART TWO: Critical analysis and evaluation of your experience in studying this example of theatre-drama.

In Part One you have made informal notes on the play and/or performance from various points of view. From your reflection on these, you are asked in this part to make a statement about your personal coherent perception of the work. Use any of the ideas from Part One you think are pertinent, plus additional ideas you have from reflection on the interrelations of these. Your statement should relate personal response to objective analysis and should be more than a mere repetition of the notes you have made. It should be presented as a well-rounded, well-organized essay.

PART ONE: Answers ranked: 0 - no credit 1 - fair 2 - good 3 - excellent Highest possible score- 21	PART TWO: Essay ranked: 0 - no credit 1 - fair (and multiplied 2 - good by 14) 3 - excellent Highest possible score- 42	PART ONE + PART TWO for Total Score Highest possible total- 63
Score	Score	Total

A GUIDE FOR CRITICAL ANALYSIS OF DANCE

For this analysis you will watch the performance of a dance. It may be on film, on the stage or in some other setting. It is suggested that you read this Guide through and review the passages in the text to which you are referred before undertaking the analysis.

PART ONE

In Part One you will study the dance from several points of view and make informal notes in the spaces provided.

PART TWO

In Part Two you will make a statement on your concluding perception of the dance after analysis and reflection. This comprehensive statement about the dance and your experiencing of it should be carefully organized as a separate essay. Two thirds of the grade given will be based on Part Two.

TITLE OF THE DANCE________________ PERFORMER(S)________________

WHERE OBSERVED________________ CHOREOGRAPHER AND COMPOSER________________

NAME________________ CLASS MEETING TIME ________________

ADDRESS________________ DATE________________

DANCE ANALYSIS NO.________________

PART ONE: Informal notes on the dance.

In Part One you are asked to study and reflect on the dance from several points of view and to make notes in the spaces provided. Formal sentences are not necessary. You may work through the various points of view in any order you choose. There will probably be more things to note under some headings than others, but you should make your coverage as complete as possible.

1. Make notes on the "subject matter" and/or "content-communication" and/or "theme" of the dance (story, depiction of mood, feelings, environment, character study, satiric comment, design in movement, etc.) (Review pages 34 and 194-201 in the text.)

2. Makes notes on the specific use of the separate arts which are combined in dance: music, visual arts (designs in two and three dimensional space), and theater (movement, mime, gesture, costumes.) (Review pages 112, 190, and 416-418 in the text.)

3. Make notes on how the elements of the different arts are used in the dance: lines and volumes in two and three dimensional patterns (for example, bodies in relation to each other, to the frame of the stage, and to the space of the stage), dynamics (tensing-relaxing, falling-recovering, contracting-releasing, strong movements, gentle movements, staccato, etc.), phrasing (even, uneven, improvised, danced as fluid, disconnected, etc.), and rhythm (regular, irregular, strong-weak, simple-complicated, used-ignored, etc.). (Review page 411 in the text.)

4. Make notes on how the elements are used to give form to the piece. Is the form narrative, some musical form, non-repetitive, improvisation, made of contrasting themes, contrapuntal, variations of a theme, or some other? (Organization in dance can be represented in the same way as is organization in music. Review theme and variation (page 368-372), rondo (pages 377-378), suite (page 384), free forms (pages 385-386), contrapuntal (pages 256-261), program music (page 386) in the text.) If the content is narrative, you will want to make notes on how the essential parts of it are handled. (Review pages 398-402 in the text.)

5. Make notes on the general classification of dance to which this dance belongs (ethnic, social, classical ballet, modern, ritualistic, some combination of these.) (Review pages 411-419 in the text.)

6. Make notes on the specific characteristics of this dance within the general category to which it belongs. Do you associate these with some tradition, period, geographic area, choreographer, a particular dancer? (Review pages 194-197 in the text.)

Note here any sources beyond the performance and text which you have used in writing your analysis of the dance.

PART TWO: Critical analysis and personal perception.

In Part One you have made informal analytical notes on the dance from various points of view. From your review of these and reflections on them, you are asked in this part to articulate your personal coherent perception of the work. Use any of the ideas from Part One that you think are pertinent, plus additional ideas you have from reflecting on the interrelations of these. Your statement should relate personal response to objective analysis and should be more than a mere repetition of the notes you have made. It should be presented as a well-rounded, well-organized essay.

PART ONE: Answers ranked: 0 - no credit 1 - fair 2 - good 3 - excellent Highest possible score-18	PART TWO: Essay ranked: 0 - no credit 1 - fair (and multiplied 2 - good by 12) 3 - excellent Highest possible score-36	PART ONE + PART TWO for Total Score Highest possible total-54
Score	Score	Total

A GUIDE FOR CRITICAL ANALYSIS OF MUSICAL THEATER (OPERA, OPERETTA, MUSICAL)

For this analysis you will be assigned or asked to choose on your own an example of musical theater to listen to, to study and perhaps see performed. It is suggested that you read the Guide through and review the passages in THE HUMANITIES to which you are referred before undertaking the study.

PART ONE

In Part One you will study the piece from several points of view and make informal notes in the spaces provided.

PART TWO

In Part Two you will make a comprehensive statement about the composition and your experiencing of it. This reflective evaluation should be carefully organized as a separate essay. Two thirds of the grade will be based on Part Two.

NAME OF WORK ______________________________

COMPOSER ______________ DATES ______________

NATIONALITY ______________

DATE OF COMPOSITION ______________ SOURCE OF THE LIBRETTO ______________

IF SEEN IN PERFORMANCE, WHERE, BY WHOM? ______________

NAME ______________ CLASS MEETING TIME ______________

ADDRESS ______________ DATE ______________

MUSICAL THEATER ANALYSIS NO. ________

PART ONE: Informal notes on the opera, operetta, or musical.

In this section you are asked to examine the work from several points of view and to make notes in the spaces provided. Formal sentences are not necessary, and you may work through the various points of view in any order you choose. There will probably be more things to note under some headings than under others, but you should make your coverage as complete as possible.

1. Early opera used mythological stories as the basis for libretti. Later, nationalistic subject matter was used. Still later, opera was based on literary works, especially those with exotic backgrounds and stories. Some libretti were written expressly for musical dramas. Into which of these categories does the work you are studying fall? Summarize the story briefly and indicate its source. How has the source been modified? (Review pages 124-125, 202-203, and 118-119 in the text.)

2. What values are suggested by or in the work - - e.g., aesthetic, social, cultural, political and/or others? Are there remnants of the aristocratic origins of opera in the work?

3. Operas, operettas, musicals use several mediums, thus are sometimes called "combined arts." In different works the mediums used receive different emphasis and serve different purposes. Make notes on the use of the different mediums in the work you are studying - - the comparative importance of music and story, use of spectacle, inclusion of dance, spoken or sung dialogue, a chorus, etc. Which medium predominates? Explain. (Review pages 389-390 in the text.)

4. Make notes on how the different mediums are used - - i.e., the elements of vocal music, instrumental music, drama, acting, choreography, dancing, scene design and costume design. Are the uses made of different elements characteristic of the period in which the piece was written? How do they contribute to the story? To the total impact of the piece? You may decide the story is a mere vehicle for integrating spectacle, dance, music. If so, the elements of these arts are the important ones to consider. Characterize the music (vocal and instrument), the plot, the setting, design, staging, and the overall result as they are integrated. (Review pages 389-390 in the text.) Make notes on the effect the choice of instruments and/or voices has on the work.

5. Make notes on the organization of the composition. Is narrative the only structural feature? Is it straight forward, sequential, or presented in some other order? How are the other arts used to contribute to the structural unity of the work? Is it through-composed or a compilation of "set pieces" held together by dialogue or recitative? (Review pages 419-420 in the text.)

6. Choose a particular sequence or episode in the work you think effective and explain how the elements of each of the arts used contribute (or do not contribute significantly) to the total effect.

7. In the various periods of history different sets of conventions have characterized operatic style. Note explicitly the conventions in the piece being studied and relate them to the period in which it was written. Some composers developed highly individual conventions of their own which have become hallmarks of their works. Are the conventions in this work associated with any composer or group of composers? (Review pages 389-390 in the text.)

Note here any sources you have used in studying the work - - e.g., program notes, album covers, books (beyond the text), articles, etc.

PART TWO: Critical analysis and evaluation of your experience in studying the opera, operetta or musical.

In Part One you have made informal notes on the work from various points of view. From your reflection on these, you are asked in this part to make a statement about your personal coherent perceptions of the work. Use any of the ideas from Part One you think are pertinent, plus additional ideas you have from reflection on the interrelations of these. Your statement should relate personal response to objective analysis and should be more than a mere repetition of the notes you have made. <u>It should be presented as a well-rounded, well-organized essay</u>.

PART ONE: Answers ranked: 0 - no credit 1 - fair 2 - good 3 - excellent Highest possible score- 21	PART TWO: Essay ranked: 0 - no credit 1 - fair (and multiplied 2 - good by 14) 3 - excellent Highest possible score- 42	PART ONE + PART TWO for Total Score Highest possible total- 63
Score	Score	Total

A GUIDE FOR CRITICAL ANALYSIS OF FILM

The art of seeing films is perhaps one of the most difficult to learn, for the study of film - - in the 20th century that most characteristic, popular, and seemingly ubiquitous of the arts - - creates special problems for the serious viewer. The appropriate subject of study, the film itself, consists of an intangible complex of images and sounds that appear and disappear in an instant. When they have vanished, there is little to consult but words, and as often as not the words are concerned with paraphrasable content, the story or narrative, and the ideas these inspire. And while these subjects hold undeniable importance, they offer only a fragment of the total film experience.

In the study of films, therefore, we place the emphasis on analysis of the visual and temporal structure which carry so much of the expressive content of films and at the same time offer delight in and of themselves. Analysis is not, of course, an end in itself, but a means of expanding awareness.

- - Lincoln F. Johnson

For this analysis you will be assigned or asked to choose on your own an example of film for critical analysis. Because film is a "time art" as well as "a combined art" the complex of appeals to our various senses moves by us so rapidly that it is difficult to reflect at the time on what has produced our responses to it. It is important, therefore, that you see the film being studied at least twice.

You should read the indicated sections in THE HUMANITIES before seeing the film the first time and then review them before seeing it a second time.

PART ONE

In Part One you will study the film from several points of view and make informal notes in the spaces provided.

PART TWO

In Part Two you will make a comprehensive statement about the film and your experiencing of it. This reflective evaluation should be carefully organized as a separate essay. Two thirds of the grade will be based on Part Two.

TITLE OF THE FILM________________________ DIRECTOR________________________

DATE OF FILM, IF KNOWN________________________ WHERE SEEN?________________________

WHEN?________________________

NAME________________________ CLASS MEETING TIME________________________

ADDRESS________________________ DATE________________________

FILM ANALYSIS NO.______________

4. Film is a "combined art" and therefore has available for use all of the elements of the arts which are integrated in it. We have become so accustomed to responding to the visual and auditory aspects of film as a unified experience that we are not usually conscious of their separate origins nor of the synchronizing and editing which has brought them together in the finished film. Are music and/or natural sounds used as background or to expand the meaning and emotional content of the film? What role do they play? Supportive of mood, place, time, action? Are colors used in any distinctive way? Was the film made "on location" or in a studio? What use is made of lighting? Are there sequences which seem included for their intrinsic merit as art rather than to develop mood, setting, period, or some facet of a character's personality? What is the style of dialogue? How much is conveyed visually? Through sound, speaking? (Review pages 190 and 203-205 in the text.)

5. Make notes here on the structure, the overall organization of the film. Is the organization important in itself, or does it simply provide an occasion for more important material? Is the subject, story, narrative presented sequentially? Is there an exposition, a crisis, a denouement? Is it all middle - - presentation of characters in action? Remember that film more often than literature, opera, ballet or theatre departs from traditional narrative conventions and expectations. (Review pages 420-422 in the text.)

6. Make notes here on two sequences which you thought especially effective uses of the film as art and analyze them in detail. How were elements and organization used to give them meaning beyond "paraphrasable content"? (Review the analysis of Kubrick's film, pages 206-208 in the text.)

7. What was the overall impact of this experience? Did the film leave you with questions? Did it change your mood? Did it challenge you to view your own life or the lives of others differently?

8. Of the many films with which you are familiar, which does this resemble most in style? Do you know other films made by the same director? Do these seem to confirm the "auteur theory" of film criticism? (Review page 204 in the text and "Auteur theory" in the Glossary.)

Note here any sources beyond the text which you have used in studying the film.

PART ONE: Informal notes on the film.

In this section you are asked to examine the film from several points of view and to make notes in the spaces provided. Formal sentences are not necessary, and you may work through the various points of view in any order you choose. There will probably be more things to note under some headings than under others, but you should make your coverage as complete as possible.

1. The opening sections of a film are important. They set the mood, tone, expectations of what is to follow. How does the film begin? How are the title and credits presented? What is the relationship of the title to the film? Is it descriptive, thematic, ambiguous, enigmatic, etc.? Are music or natural sounds used? (See "Establishing shot" in the Glossary.)

2. What is the film about? Remember that the ostensible subject matter, ideas, story may on analysis and reflection emerge as mere skeletons on which the deeper meaning of the film, its "content" is developed. Make notes on both explicit, nominal subject matter and on any less obvious meanings you sense in the film. (Review pages 35-38, 205, 420-422 in the text.)

3. Comment on the medium - - i.e., the camera and sound techniques used to put audio and visual images on film. For example, is there a tendency toward organizing scenes within a "frame"? What methods of transition are used (e.g., fade-in, fade-out, flashbacks, cutting from one speaker to another)? Does the camera act as the eyes of the director or the eyes of a character or characters? Does it record "objective" material, "subjective" interpretation, associations, symbols, etc.? Comment on "aesthetic distance" in the film. (Review pages 203-209 in the text and see "Transitional devices" in the Glossary.)

PART TWO: Critical analysis and evaluation of your experience in studying the film.

In Part One you have made informal notes on the film from various points of view. From your reflection on these, you are asked in this part to make a statement about your personal, coherent perception of the work. Use any of the ideas from Part One you think are pertinent, plus additional ideas you have from reflection on the interrelations of these. Your statement should relate personal response to objective analysis and should be more than a mere repetition of the notes you have made. It should be presented as a well-rounded, well-organized essay.

PART ONE: Answers ranked: 0 - no credit 1 - fair 2 - good 3 - excellent Highest possible score- 24	PART TWO: Essay ranked: 0 - no credit 1 - fair (and multiplied 2 - good by 16) 3 - excellent Highest possible score- 48	PART ONE + PART TWO for Total Score Highest possible total- 72
Score	Score	Total

9 ELEMENTS OF THE VISUAL ARTS

CONCEPTS

The physical means by which we come into contact with a work of art is its (1) ____________________. The qualities or properties of the work of art are the (2) ____________________ which the artist arranges in the physical material of the art. The nature of the medium determines the kinds of qualities which can be realized in it. In the medium of music, which is sound, the (3) ____________________ of the sound is an element. In wood, the medium which Moore used in his _Two Forms_, the curves of the surface and the color of the wood are (4) ____________________.

The elements of the visual arts are:

(5)____________________________ (9)____________________________

(6)____________________________ (10)____________________________

(7)____________________________ (11)____________________________

(8)____________________________

When we speak of _space_ as an element in the visual arts we mean the illusion of three-dimensional space on a two dimensional canvas, including the illusion of perspective. Four ways by which the artist can give us a sense of perspective in a painting are (12)________________, (13)________________, (14)________________, and (15)________________.

Match the following:

____ 1. hue (1) the quality of color determined by the amount of the complementary color in it.

____ 2. value (2) the quality by which we usually designate the colors of the spectrum.

____ 3. intensity (3) the quality of color determined by the amount of black in it.

Mark the following statements as <u>true</u> or <u>false</u>:

____ 1. White is the highest value in a color and black is the lowest.

____ 2. The complementary color of red is green.

____ 3. Light and shadow mean the same thing as value in painting.

____ 4. The artist can use light and shadow to model a figure or an object in depth.

____ 5. The three primary hues are red, blue and yellow.

____ 6. When we mix red with blue we get violet.

____ 7. Our perception of color is changed by the presence of other colors.

____ 8. Green and blue are warm colors.

____ 9. All shadows are black or grey.

____10. Red and yellow are associated with emotions of melancholy and serenity.

APPLICATION OF CONCEPTS

Each of the following is used in the text to illustrate the effect of a different kind of line: What kind of line is each used to illustrate?

1. Daumier's The Uprising: ______________________________

2. Van Gogh's Berceuse: ______________________________

3. El Greco's Purification of the Temple: ________________

4. The Charioteer: ______________________________________

5. Rembrandt's Three Trees: ______________________________

6. Miro's Painting: _____________________________________

Lines have direction. They are always doing something. Look at El Greco's Resurrection (Color Plate 6). Note how the splayed thighs in the form of a "V" at the bottom of the painting guide our eyes out and upward until they are pulled to arms that guide us upward to the center of interest.

Name the type(s) of line(s) which predominate in the following illustrations; and on the line below relate its/their use to the subject matter (the content) of the painting.

1. Lapith and Centaur (page 223) ________________________

____

2. Monet's Waterloo Bridge (page 233) ___________________

____

3. Riley's Shih-li (page 240) ____________________________

____

4. Kandinsky's Warlike Theme (Color Plate 9) _____________

____

5. Orozoco's Modern Migration of the Spirit (page 142) _______

____

6. Van Ruisdael's The Mill (Color Plate 41) _______________

____

7. Duchamp's Nude Descending a Staircase (page 122) ________

____

SELF-TEST IN PAINTING

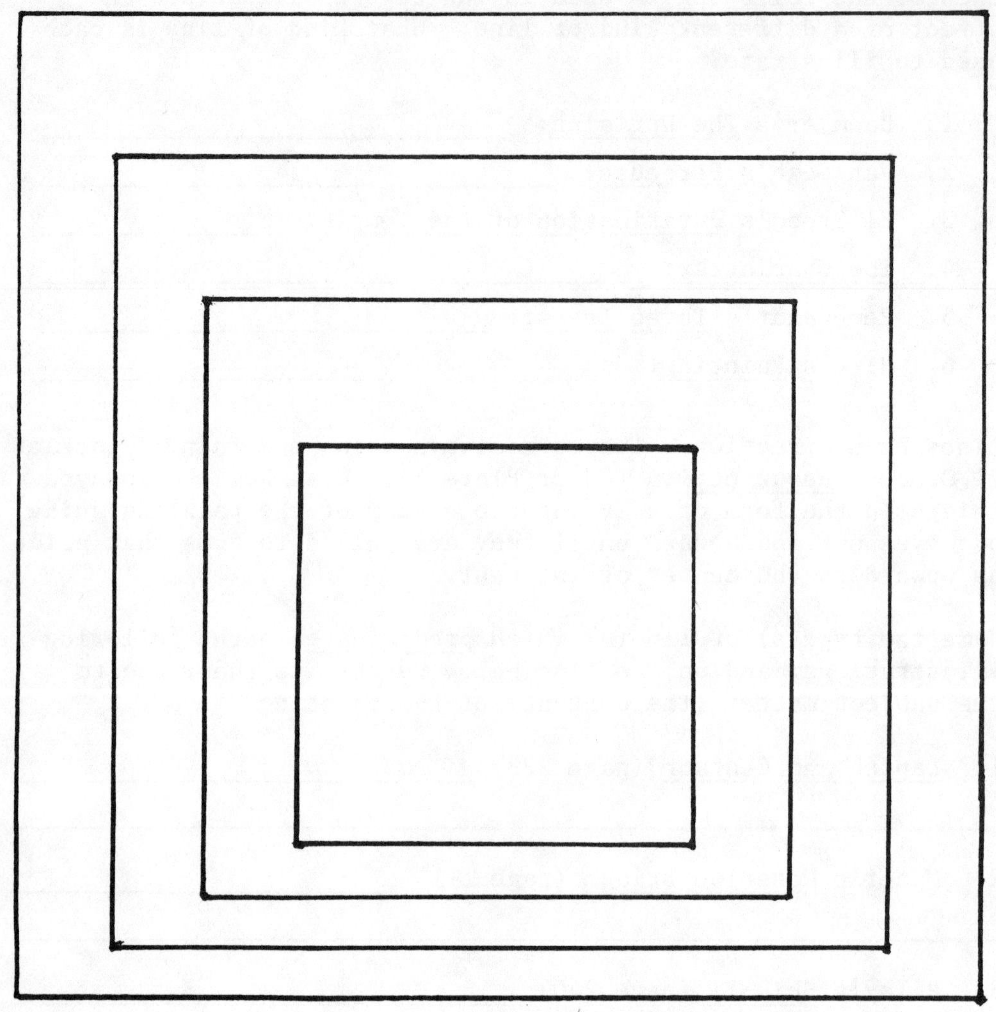

JOSEPH ALBERS, HOMAGE TO THE SQUARE: BROAD CALL

This painting is Color Plate 27 (following page 216). The exact proportions of the painting are reproduced in the sketch above. You will need both for this exercise.

Most interesting questions about art have subjective answers and we have tried to make this self-test interesting. So, when you think of a more suitable answer to a question than the possibilities given you, circle the alternative(s) you think are best and then write your answer in the space provided.

Problems of Subject

1. The real subject of the painting - - the problem Albers is concerned with - - probably is
   a. line
   b. shape
   c. color
   d. cubes
   e. your answer:

2. Which relationships are of most importance in the painting?
   a. color
   b. angle
   c. value
   d. your answer:

3. The overall feeling is one of
   a. anger
   b. harmony
   c. solidarity
   d. vibrations
   e. your answer:

4. The artist's attitude seens to be one of
   a. intense emotion
   b. care in representation
   c. formal analysis
   d. metaphysical speculation
   e. your answer:

5. Although the artist rejects many traditional aspects of painting, he does <u>not</u> reject
   a. emotional relationships of what is depicted
   b. perspective for spatial relationships
   c. chiaroscuro for modeling
   d. your answer:

Problems of Medium

6. From what you can see in the reproduction this work is most likely executed in
   a. oil paint
   b. silk screen
   c. pastel
   d. water color

Problems of Elements

In order to answer the following six questions, make yourself a "ruler" by marking on the edge of a separate piece of paper the widths of the spaces between the edges of the squares in the painting and compare them.

7. The width of the spaces between the side margins of the squares is exactly
   a. two times that of the spaces between the bottom margins
   b. three times that of the spaces between the bottom margins
   c. half that of the spaces between the top margins

8. The spaces between the top margins are
   a. two times as wide as the spaces between the bottom margins
   b. three times as wide as the spaces between the bottom margins
   c. two times as wide as the spaces between the side margins

9. The spaces between the side margins are
   a. equal
   b. the left is larger
   c. the right is larger

10. The distance between the bottom edge of the innermost square and the bottom edge of the outermost square is
   a. unique in the picture
   b. twice that of the inner left margin
   c. equal to the distance between the two outer top margins

11. The ratio of the distances between the outer margins - - i.e., bottom: side: top - - would be expressed
   a. 1:2:3
   b. 2:1:3
   c. 1:3:5

12. The distances between the outer margins are
   a. larger than inner margins
   b. smaller than inner margins
   c. equal to inner margins

13. The darkest hue is
   a. the central square
   b. the second square (next to the central)
   c. the third square
   d. the outer square

14. The red of the outermost square is
   a. duller by being mixed with green
   b. mixed with a little blue
   c. mixed with yellow
   d. your answer:

15. Looking intently at the picture you may observe apparent (not real) lightening and variation of the color. From your observation, which statement is not true?
    a. the color appears to vary and become lighter along the edges where color is juxtaposed
    b. when light color meets dark color the lighter color appears to be most susceptible to illusory changes
    c. the center of the middle square is the site of the most obvious perceptual distortions
    d. your comments:

Problems of Organization

16. Covering the top half of the picture with your hand, your first impression is that the squares
    a. recede at the center
    b. project at the center
    c. there is no sense of depth
    d. your answer:

17. Covering the bottom half of the picture with your hand, your first impression is that the squares
    a. recede at the center
    b. project at the center
    c. there is no sense of depth
    d. your answer:

18. The picture taken as a whole without a title might suggest
    a. a fire
    b. a flashing signal
    c. a shout
    d. your answer:

19. Aside from the visual, to which sense does this picture appeal most
    a. hearing
    b. touch
    c. smell
    d. physical balance
    e. your answer:

20. When you stare at the very center of the picture for 30 seconds and then look at a white wall or sheet of paper you see
    a. a light green after-image
    b. a dark blue after-image
    c. a pink after-image
    d. your answer:

Now that you have examined Alber's painting yourself, you should read again his own description of his Homage to the Square series on page 227.

Read also the little poem by Albers on page 226. Do you feel that he has succeeded in putting into the painting his experience with color as he describes it in the poem? Copy below three phrases from the poem which express _your_ experience with the painting.

1.____

2.____

3.____

You can experiment with how Albers gets his effects by coloring the sketch at the beginning of this exercise. Better still, you can collect many colors and shades of paper and cut them to the proportions in the sketch and superimpose possibilities on each other until you get the effect you wish. Then, as Albers did, you may wish to give the effect a suggestive title.

If you become interested in Albers' experiments with color you can look up his book on _Interaction of Color_ (New Haven: Yale University Press, 1963). You will be especially interested in the color plates in it.

SELF-TEST IN PAINTING

SANDRO BOTTICELLI: BIRTH OF VENUS, Color Plate 12 (following page 88)

Most interesting questions about art are subjective and we have tried to make this self-test interesting. So, when you think of a more suitable answer to a question, circle the alternative(s) you think are best and then write your answer in the space provided.

Problems of Subject

1. The picture has an atmosphere of
   a. formal ritual
   b. a candid snapshot
   c. gaity and celebration
   d. emotional emptiness
   e. your answer:

2. The expression on Venus' face is one
   a. of gentle melancholy
   b. you might see on Miss America
   c. of pride and power
   d. your answer:

3. The artist depicts Venus as a symbol of
   a. feminine sexuality
   b. innocence and purity
   c. dynamic personal magnetism
   d. ideal beauty

4. The Breezes (on the left) appear to be
   a. doing their job
   b. overcome with adoration of Venus
   c. solemn yet joyful
   d. stern and judgmental
   e. your answer:

5. The falling flowers, waves, leaves and hair are arranged
   a. in a naturalistic manner
   b. as decorative patterns
   c. according to the ancient canon of beauty

6. The medium is
   a. encaustic
   b. fresco
   c. tempera
   d. water color

Problems of Medium

7. This work appears to have been executed with
   a. brush
   b. pencil
   c. chalk
   d. palette knife

Problems of Elements

8. The lines are
   a. angular and harsh diagonals
   b. mostly right angles
   c. curves
   d. your answer:

9. On the whole the color effect is
   a. fresh and springlike
   b. brilliant
   c. simple earth tones
   d. your answer:

10. The colors are
   a. intense, vivid
   b. analagous
   c. delicate
   d. your answer:

11. Volume is achieved through
   a. high-contrast modeling
   b. rough, coarse brushstrokes
   c. strong color contrasts
   d. soft modeling
   e. your answer:

12. The artist appears to have been most interested in
   a. volume
   b. color
   c. line
   d. your answer:

13. The source of light is
   a. strong light from the upper right
   b. diffused light from the upper right
   c. strong light from the upper left
   d. diffused light from the upper left
   e. your answer:

14. The lines of the figure on the right give a sensation of
   a. weightlessness
   b. stability and serenity

c. directing our eyes toward the central figure
c. self-contained motion
e. your answer:

15. The type of balance is
    a. symmetry
    b. asymmetry
    c. a double pyramid
    d. your answer:

16. The hands are
    a. in natural ordinary positions
    b. a simplification
    c. posed
    d. your answer:

17. The treatment of space is
    a. based on the "laws" of perspective
    b. all on one plane
    c. that of "cut-out" figures superimposed on a receding landscape
    d. your answer:

18. The trees on the right
    a. are obviously drawn from nature
    b. contribute a feeling of stability
    c. are primarily used for color
    d. your answer:

<u>Problems of Organization</u>

19. Does the concept of the goddess Venus seem most meaningful to you in connection with
    a. the attendants
    b. the portrayal of a beautiful woman
    c. the springlike mood
    d. your answer:

20. The relationship of the figures is
    a. primarily psychological
    b. linear
    c. part of a pattern composed of patterns
    d. based on backward and forward movement in space
    e. your answer:

21. The bouyancy of the figures is due to
    a. a clear separation of figure and ground
    b. a lack of weight in modeling
    c. the large size of the figures
    d. your answer:

22. Covering the right attendant figure with your hand, you discover that
    a. the composition is still satisfying
    b. there seems to be incompleted motion toward the right
    c. there seems to be incompleted motion toward the left
    d. your answer:

23. In the artist's concept of myth, which predominates?
    a. serenity, harmony, calm
    b. the Renaissance ideal of man
    c. Godlike powers
    d. personalities
    e. your answer:

10 ELEMENTS OF MUSIC

CONCEPTS

The elements of music are:

1. ______________________ 4. ______________________

2. ______________________ 5. ______________________

3. ______________________ 6. ______________________

Match the following by writing the number of the correct definition at the right in the space provided.

________ 1. rhythm	(1)	A succession of musical sounds, each being heard in relation to the preceding and following sounds to produce a continuity.
________ 2. melody	(2)	The pace or speed of pulses in a musical composition.
	(3)	Music which does not tell a story.
________ 3. harmony	(4)	The simultaneous sounding of tones, to form a chord either for support of a melody or to be used in succession in creating a composition.
________ 4. tempo	(5)	Patterns of long and short duration within the more or less fixed meter of a composition.
________ 5. dynamics	(6)	The quality or "tone color" of a sound.
	(7)	The loudness or softness of a musical performance - - the force and volume of the sound.
________ 6. timbre	(8)	Music for voices alone and sung without instrumental accompaniment.

Associate a phrase in the right column with a phrase in the left, and place the correct number in the space provided:

_____ 1. descriptive music

_____ 2. number of vibrations

_____ 3. polyphonic harmony

_____ 4. pure music

_____ 5. time signature

_____ 6. tone color

_____ 7. homophony

(1) Two numbers at the beginning of a piece of music telling the number of beats to the measure and the value of each beat.
(2) Music which suggests or imitates objects of the world.
(3) Fortissimo.
(4) The sound of a combination of instruments of different timbre.
(5) A scale composed of all the tones in an octave.
(6) Pitch.
(7) Harmony in which a tune makes its own accompaniment as in a round.
(8) Music in which a single melody predominates accompanied by chords.
(9) Music which does not describe or imitate anything.

Because a succession of notes appears in musical notations from left to right, patterns of successive pitches are sometimes spoken of as the horizontal aspect of music. And because the simultaneous sounding of pitches is represented by putting one note above the other in musical notation, this aspect of music is sometimes called the vertical aspect. Which of the following might be described as (1) a horizontal aspect, (2) a vertical aspect, or (3) both.

________ 1. chord

________ 2. counterpoint

________ 3. harmony

________ 4. pitch

________ 5. homophonic

________ 6. rhythm

________ 7. melody

________ 8. dissonance

________ 9. texture

________ 10. meter

Match the following:

_____ 1. ma non troppo (1) with motion

_____ 2. con brio (2) gracefully

_____ 3. grazioso (3) but not too much

_____ 4. maestoso (4) majestically

_____ 5. con moto (5) with vivacity or spirit

Mark the following as belonging to one of the four categories below by placing the correct number in the space provided.

(1) Tempo indication (2) Dynamic marking (3) Time Signature (4) Clef Sign

_______ 1. 𝄞

_______ 2. presto

_______ 3. >

_______ 4. Allegretto

_______ 5. $\frac{4}{4}$

_______ 6. <

_______ 7. ¢

_______ 8. sf

_______ 9. Adagio

_______ 10. 𝄢

Complete the following sentences by writing in one item from each of the two scrambled groups below:

GROUP A	GROUP B
very loud	p.
growing louder	pp.
growing softer	sf.
suddenly loud	mf.
very soft	ff
soft	decres.
moderately soft	f.
moderately loud	mp.
loud	cres.

1. crescendo means _________ and is abbreviated _________.

2. decrescendo means _________ and is abbreviated _________.

3. forte means _________ and is abbreviated _________.

4. fortissimo means _________ and is abbreviated _________.

5. mezzo forte means _________ and is abbreviated _________.

6. mezzo piano means _________ and is abbreviated _________.

7. pianissimo means _________ and is abbreviated _________.

8. piano means _________ and is abbreviated _________.

9. sforzando means _________ and is abbreviated _________.

APPLICATION OF CONCEPTS

Correct the following by adding or subtracting from note values or by adding notes to make the measures conform to the time signature.

This exercise may look very difficult to you when you first encounter it, but it is probably easier than you think. In any case, it provides a good review of your understanding of the elements of music and you will learn some very important things from attempting it. DO NOT BE CONCERNED ABOUT HOW IT WILL SOUND. THAT IS NOT THE POINT OF THE EXERCISE. Below and on the following page there are six groups of five lines. They are actually copies of music manuscript writing paper of the sort composers use. Simply follow instructions step by step.

<u>Exercise 1</u>

On the first and second groups of lines write eight measures of music for the G clef in 4/4 time, four measures to each line. The first four measures should be an ascending phrase and the second four a descending phrase. Indicate that the eight measures are to be repeated. Indicate that the piece is to be played very fast.

<u>Exercise 2</u>

On the third and fourth groups of lines write eight measures of music for the F clef in 3/4 time, four measures to each line. In the piece use eighth, quarter, and half notes. Indicate that the notes in the fourth and eighth measures are to "flow" smoothly into each other, forming a unit. Indicate that the piece is to be repeated. Indicate that it is to be played slowly.

<u>Exercise 3</u>

On the fifth and sixth groups of lines write eight measures of music for the G clef in 3/8 time, four measures to each line. Use as much variety in duration of notes as you can. Indicate that all the notes are to be played staccato, with the exception of the last note which is to be sounded beyond the time strictly alloted it. Indicate that the tempo is to be bright and happy.

Exercise 1

Exercise 2

Exercise 3

LISTENING FOR THE ELEMENTS IN MUSIC

By providing you with alternatives, the following can be used to guide your listening for the elements of music and for what characterizes their use in any piece of music. You can use it for practice. Your teacher may ask you to complete it for some particular piece of music played in class.

RHYTHM

____ 1. The basic rhythm is
- (1) duple
- (2) triple

____ 2. The basic rhythm is
- (1) important in the piece
- (2) not obtrusive in the piece

MELODY

____ 3. The piece
- (1) uses only one melody at a time with accompaniment
- (2) is contrapuntal with one melody predominant at a time
- (3) is in counterpoint with two melodies of equal importance

____ 4. The phrases of the melody are
- (1) long
- (2) relatively short
- (3) very short

____ 5. The melody moves
- (1) mostly stepwise up and down the scale
- (2) mostly in relatively small intervals (larger than a step)
- (3) mostly in large intervals

____ 6. The motion of the melody is
- (1) predominantly ascending
- (2) predominantly descending
- (3) about equally divided between the two

____ 7. (1) The accents in the melody fall mostly on accents in the basic rhythm.
- (2) The melody is free-flowing without strict regard for the basic rhythm.

____ 8. The piece seems to be in
- (1) a major key
- (2) a minor key

____ 9. The piece is in character
(1) natural and relaxed
(2) tense and energetic

____10. The piece is in mood
(1) emotional, expressive
(2) reserved, dignified, static
(3) humorous, whimsical

TEMPO

____11. The tempo is
(1) very fast (presto)
(2) moderately fast (allegro)
(3) rather slow (adagio)
(4) very slow (largo)

____12. There is in the piece
(1) no marked change in tempo
(2) marked changes in tempo
(3) occasional retards followed by a return to first tempo

TIMBRE

____13. The impression of the piece is predominantly (choose as many as you need)
(1) Woodwinds
(2) Strings
(3) Brasses
(4) Percussion

____14. Tone color in the piece is
(1) of much importance
(2) of little importance

HARMONY

____15. There are in the piece
(1) very few dissonances
(2) some dissonances quickly resolved
(3) use of unresolved dissonance
(4) much use of dissonance which is resolved

DYNAMICS

____16. List by number the dynamics of the piece in proper order (choose as many as you need)
(1) very soft (pianissimo, pp.)
(2) soft (piano, p.)
(3) somewhat loud (mezzo forte, mf.)
(4) loud (forte, f.)
(5) as loud as possible (fortissimo, ff.)

VOCABULARY AID IN DISCUSSING MUSIC

This is a partial answer to the question, "What can you say about a piece of music?" It is simply suggestive and by no means exhaustive. You will want to consult it when you are discussing or writing about music. The index and Glossary in your text will help with words with which you are still not familar.

A. MELODY

1. Type: Prominent? Familiar? Singable? Simple? Classic? Dramatic? Vague? Unfamiliar? Instrumental? Complex? Romantic? Climactic?
2. Scale: Major? Minor? Chromatic? Modal? Pentatonic? Whole-tone? Quarter-tone? Atonal?
3. Shape: Scale motion? Chordal skips? Undulates? Narrow range? Wide range? Climactic high and low notes?
4. Phrases: Smooth? Jerky? Brief? Long? Regular? Irregular? Repetitive? Balanced? Cadenced? Legato? Pizzicato?
5. Timbre: Vocal? Coloratura? Lyric soprano? Mezzo? Alto? Tenor? Baritone? Bass? Instrumental? Strings? Woodwinds? Brasses?

B. RHYTHM

1. Meter: Duple? Triple? Compound? Variety?
2. Accent: Regular? Irregular? Syncopation? Strong? Weak? Sforzando?
3. Pulse: Steady? Hesitant? Playful? Hurried? Uncertain? Calm? Smooth? Cross rhythms? Polyrhythms?
4. Tempo: Lento? Adagio? Andante? Allegro? Presto? Ritardando?
5. Dynamics: Forte? Fortissimo? Piano? Pianissimo? Crescendos? Decrescendos? Sforzandos?

C. HARMONY

1. Tonality: Simple tonic-dominant? Monotonal? Modulatory? Chromatic? Frequent shifting? Atonal?
2. Texture: Consonance? Dissonance? Resolutions postponed?
3. Spacing: Antiphonal? Contrary motion? Horizontal? Wide ranged? Fugal or imitative?
4. Performing Group: Solo with accompaniment? Vocal group? Instrumental group? Chamber orchestra? Full orchestra? Combined vocal and instrumental?

D. FORM

1. Parts: Unitary? Binary? Ternary? Rondo? Sonata form? Through composed?
2. Fugue: Canon? Round? Imitative? Fugal? Number of Voices? Subjects? Countersubjects? Episodes? Stretto?
3. Theme and Variation: Number of variations? Character of variations? Passacaglia? Chaconne? Classic? Romantic?
4. Dance Forms: Folk Gigue? Minuet? Waltz? Foxtrot? Allemande? Courante? Sarabande? Polonaise? Mazurka? Polka? Rumba? Beguine? March? Tango?
5. Vocal Forms: Folk song? Ballad? Lyric? Art Song? Carol? Hymn? Chorale? Aria de capo? Madrigal? Motet? Opera? Orstoriio? Cantata? Mass? Requiem?
6. Sonata Forms: Sonata? Concerto? Symphony? Overture?
7. Free: Impromptu? Prelude? Intermezzo? Etude? Nocturne? Tone Poem? Rhapsody? Program?

A LISTENING TEST ON THE ELEMENTS OF MUSIC

The following questions will help you sharpen your perception of how the elements of music are used in any musical composition. Your teacher will play a piece in class and ask you to choose the answer which is appropriate to it. You can prepare for this by answering the questions as they apply to some pieces you choose on your own.

RHYTHM

_____ 1. The basic rhythm is (a) duple (b) triple

_____ 2. The basic rhythm is (2) important in the piece (b) not obtrusive in the piece

_____ 3. The rhythm (a) changes in the piece (b) remains the same throughout

MELODY

_____ 4. The piece (a) uses only one melody at a time with accompaniment (b) is contrapuntal with one melody predominant at a time (c) is in counterpoint with two melodies of equal importance

_____ 5. The phrases of the melody are (a) long (b) relatively short (c) very short

_____ 6. The melody moves (a) mostly stepwise up and down the scale (b) mostly in relatively small intervals (larger than a step) (c) mostly in large intervals

_____ 7. The motion of the melody is (a) predominantly ascending (b) predominantly descending (c) about equally divided between the two

_____ 8. (a) The accents in the melody fall mostly on accents in the basic rhythm (b) The melody is free-flowing without strict regard for the basic rhythm

_____ 9. The piece seems to be in (a) a major key (b) a minor key (c) changes from major to minor in parts (d) changes from minor to major in parts

_____10. The character of the piece is (a) natural and relaxed (b) tense and energetic

_____11. The mood of the piece is (a) emotional, expressive (b) reserved, dignified (c) humorous, whimsical (d) dramatic, exciting

TEMPO

_____12. The tempo is (a) very fast (presto) (b) moderately fast (allegro) (c) rather slow (adagio) (d) very slow (largo)

_____13. There is in the piece (a) no marked change in tempo (b) marked changes in tempo (c) occasional retards followed by a return to first tempo

TIMBRE

_____14. The tone color of the piece is supplied predominantly by (Choose as many as you need) (a) Woodwinds (b) Strings (c) Brasses (d) Percussion

_____15. Tone color in the piece is (a) of much importance (b) of little importance

HARMONY

_____16. There are in the piece (a) very few dissonances (b) some dissonances quickly resolved (c) use of unresolved dissonance (d) much use of dissonance which is resolved

DYNAMICS

_____17. List letters for dynamics of the piece in proper order (Choose as many as you need) (a) very soft (pianissimo, pp) (b) soft (piano,p.) (c) somewhat loud (mezzo forte, mf.) (d) loud (forte, f.) (e) as loud as possible (fortissimo, ff.)

A LISTENING TEST

The following questions are designed to be used with Bach's Air from Suite No. 3 in D, sometimes called "Air For the G String". The piece should be played at least twice for this test.

_____ 1. The rhythmic beats of the music are grouped: (1) in units of two; (2) in units of three; (3) in no particular units.

_____ 2. The music is: (1) strongly accented on the beat; (2) relatively unaccented; (3) accented on the off-beat.

_____ 3. The opening theme: (1) has many skips up and down; (2) moves predominately by steps up and down the scale; (3) has many sustained passages on a single note.

_____ 4. The harmony is: (1) uncomplicated, with few dissonances; (2) complex, with some dissonances; (3) complex, with many dissonances.

_____ 5. The music is in a: (1) major mode; (2) minor mode.

_____ 6. The music would serve as an accompaniment to: (1) a waltz; (2) a minuet; (3) a tango; (4) a pavane.

_____ 7. The music should be marked: (1) presto; (2) sforzando; (3) allegro; (4) adagio; (5) allegretto.

_____ 8. The music is performed: (1) by a string orchestra; (2) by a full orchestra; (3) by woodwinds; (4) by a brass ensemble.

_____ 9. The melody is carried by: (1) violins; (2) bass viols; (3) horns; (4) flutes; (5) clarinets.

_____ 10. The melody consists of: (1) short motifs; (2) short phrases; (3) long phrases; (4) choppy phrases; (5) no phrases.

_____ 11. After the opening theme: (1) variations of the first theme are played; (2) the first theme is played more slowly; (3) a new theme is introduced.

_____ 12. The piece ends: (1) on a restatement of the opening theme; (2) on a completely new theme.

_____13. Considering the piece as a whole: (1) the sections contrast very little; (2) the sections contrast very definitely.

_____14. Instrumental color: (1) varies considerably; (2) varies very little.

_____15. The music has: (1) one melodic line; (2) more than one melodic line; (3) one melody played in canon.

_____16. The music changes key: (1) often; (2) seldom; (3) never.

_____17. The form of the piece is most like a: (1) fugue; (2) aria; (3) canon; (4) rondo; (5) variation form.

_____18. The piece: (1) ends in a broad, finishing flourish of harmony; (2) does not seem to end, simply stops; (3) ends quietly on a restful chord.

_____19. The style of the piece seems closer to: (1) Bach; (2) Wagner; (3) Ravel; (4) Stravinsky; (5) Tschaikowsky.

_____20. The music is characteristic of the: (1) 15th century; (2) 16th century; (3) 18th century; (4) 19th century; (5) 20th century.

MUSIC LISTENING TEST

You are to answer the questions below about the short piece which will be played. The piece will be played twice. You may work through the questions in any order you wish. Place the number of the correct answer in the space provided.

_____ 1. The tempo of this piece should be marked (1) lento (2) adagio (3) presto (4) allegro (5) andante.

_____ 2. The meter is: (1) duple (2) triple (3) compound (4) nine-eight (5) other.

_____ 3. The meter: (1) changes often (2) never changes (3) changes once (4) changes twice (5) changes constantly.

_____ 4. The background instrument which gives harmonic support is a: (1) guitar (2) piano (3) harpsichord (4) clavichord (5) violin.

_____ 5. The dynamic level is predominately: (1) pp (2) p (3) fff (4) mf (5) sf.

_____ 6. The rhythm is: (1) always syncopated (2) never syncopated (3) sometimes syncopated (4) syncopated on one beat (5) none of these.

_____ 7. The most important solo instrument is the (1) Flute (2) Oboe (3) English Horn (4) French Horn (5) Clarinet.

_____ 8. Which of these instruments plays the highest pitches in the piece? (1) Cellos (2) Violins (3) Clarinet (4) Cembalo (5) Violas.

_____ 9. The tonality of the music is: (1) entirely major (2) entirely minor (3) minor with a major section (4) major with a minor section (5) changes from one to the other throughout.

_____ 10. The full cadence is used: (1) at the end of the piece only (2) at the beginning only (3) not at all (4) frequently throughout (5) at the beginning and end.

_____ 11. The tempo: (1) never changes (2) changes often (3) changes from slow to fast (4) changes from fast to slow (5) gets continuously faster.

_____12. The melody moves predominately by: (1) scale (2) small intervals (3) very wide leaps (4) half tones (5) whole tones.

_____13. Significant pauses or rests occur: (1) throughout the piece (2) only at beginning (3) not at all (4) at the end (5) in the middle.

_____14. The background instrument which gives harmonic support is a: (1) guitar (2) piano (3) harpsichord (4) clavichord (5) violin.

_____15. This composition would be classified as: (1) program music (2) pure music (3) narrative music (4) descriptive music (5) operatic music.

_____16. The harmony of the piece is: (1) entirely chordal (2) entirely melodic (3) both chordal and melodic (4) a continuous running figure (5) none of these.

_____17. This music would be normally performed: (1) in church (2) in a nightclub (3) on a concert stage (4) at a charity ball (5) by a marching band.

_____18. The melody consists of: (1) short motifs (2) long irregular phrases (3) no phrases (4) short regular phrases (5) one continuous phrase.

_____19. The instrument most distinctly heard in this music is the (1) oboe (2) clarinet (3) bassoon (4) cembalo (5) violin.

_____20. Considering the whole piece: (1) the sections contrast very little (2) there are no distinguishable sections (3) there are sections of definite contrast (4) there are only two sections (5) none of these.

SUGGESTIONS FOR LISTENING TO A MUSICAL COMPOSITION

You can ask youself the following questions when listening to music. They will guide your listening and sharpen your perceptions of what is taking place in the music. And they will help you identify what you hear with the technical terms in the text so that you can describe to others precisely and accurately what you are hearing.

1. SUBJECT

Is the composition a completely self-contained work of art? That is, does it aim at representing only that which is itself (pure or absolute music)? Is it part of a larger work?

Does the title of the piece suggest that it is about something- that is, that it is program music? Does either the title or the piece itself make its program clear to you or do you need to bring to your listening a knowledge of the program? What type of program music is it - - imitative, descriptive, or narrative?

II. FUNCTION

Was the piece composed with any particular purpose in mind? (March, lullaby, serenade, waltz.)

Was the piece composed for some particular occasion, festival, or celebration?

Does the piece introduce something or set the mood for some activity? (Prelude, Overture).

In what kind of setting would it normally be performed?

III. MEDIUM

The materials out of which music is made (medium) are the sounds of the instruments and voices which make it. The instruments or voices which the composer chooses to use for a composition force upon him certain limitations within which he must work. Some of the more obvious limitations have to do with how high and low the instruments or voices can play (pitch), the expressive qualities of tone they can make (timbre).

The group of instruments and/or voices you hear were chosen for this particular work because the composer thought them appropriate for it. Keeping this in mind will help you in appreciating the work. Is it an instrumental or vocal solo? Is there an accompaniment? Played on what instrument?

Is it a small orchestra (chamber orchestra), or a large orchestra (symphony), an orchestra accompanying several solo voices alternating or singing together (opera or oratorio)? Or some other combination?

The better you know the personalities and capabilities of the various instruments and voices the better you will be able to judge the composer's handling of the medium of his art. Listen for the way the composer takes advantage of their various qualities and ranges for purposes of variety, expression, emphasis, etc. Listen for solo passages, various combinations, etc.

IV. ELEMENTS

Melody

1. Do you hear the piece as predominantly unaccompanied tunes? Do you hear it as a melody with chords or accompaniment? Do you hear it as two or more melodies (counterpoint)? Does one melody predominate at times or is more than one heard simultaneously?

2. What can you say about the pattern of the melody or melodies? Does it progress mostly by single steps up and down the scale or are there larger intervals between the notes of the melody? Is the melody made up of short or long phrases? Does it have a predominately upward movement? a downward movement? or does it form combined patterns of both?

Harmony

1. Do the combinations of notes heard together (harmony) seem clear, simple, rich, complex, conventional, unusual?

2. Does the progression of the harmony (change from one combination of notes to the next) seem rapid, slow?

3. Is there little or much dissonance (unrestful combinations of notes) in the piece?

Rhythm

1. Is the pacing or speed (tempo) of the piece fast or slow? Are there notable changes in speed as the piece progresses or in parts of the piece? Are these changes gradual or sudden?

2. Do the basic beats of the rhythm fall into groups of two (duple meter) or into groups of three (triple meter)? Is there a change in this basic pattern during the course

of the piece? Is this basic rhythm of little or much importance in the total feeling you have for the piece?

3. What is the nature of the rhythm of the melody which is superimposed on the basic rhythm? Can they be distinguished one from the other?

Timbre

1. Listen for the different qualities of tone of instruments playing the piece. Is one instrument or group of instruments used more than others? Do you recognize the instrument or instruments being used?

2. Are there passages for solo voices or instruments?

3. Would you say the piece makes much or little use of tone color?

V. ORGANIZATION

Organization is the arrangement of similar and different things to make a pattern (give a feeling or order). In music, which is a time art, organization is concerned with arrangement of what follows what in a time sequence. After a theme or melody has been played, the composer may have the same melody played again (repetition) or introduce a new melody (variety). At the end of the second theme or melody, he may have the second melody repeated, have the first melody repeated, or introduce a third melody. The resulting pattern of repetition and variation is the form of the music.

One of the pleasures of listening to music is to be found in following the composer in his decisions as to whether to repeat a melody or introduce a new melody and in the methods he uses to get from one melody to another (transitions).

A simple system of representing this organization is to assign to each melody a letter of the alphabet, letting the sequence of letters represent the sequence of themes in the piece. You may come up with such organizations as these: AB or AABB (binary form, using two themes without a return to the first); ABA or AABBA (ternary form, in which there is a return to the first theme after the introduction of a new theme); ABACADA, etc. (rondo) or A1-A2-A3-A4 (in which the same theme is repeated over and over with some change in harmony, rhythm, etc. i.e., Theme and Variation.)

VI. STYLE

Style is a term applied to "manners" of handling the items

listed above. A style may be recognized as characteristic of a particular period of history, group of composers, individual composer, etc.

A feeling for subtle differences of style is likely to be developed only after long, careful listening to many styles of music. Perhaps in the early stages of listening to music analytically, it is best to try to listen for the broader distinctions of style. The following are two broad classifications of temperament or style, each of which includes smaller classifications; you can begin with these.

Classical

1. Does the composer's interest in his work seem to be its organization?

2. Do you find yourself responding to the music as tunes and melodies as such and listening for their development?

3. Does the composer show a tendency toward clear, balancing of part against part and definite contours of rhythm and harmony?

4. Is the piece made up predominantely of expected sequences of harmony, mostly consonant?

Romantic

1. Does the composer's interest in his work seem to be expression of feelings and emotions?

2. Do you find that your response is in the direction of emotional identification with the music?

3. Does the composer show a tendency toward fragmentary or unbalanced construction, and blurred contours of rhythm and harmony?

4. Are there many unexpected harmonic changes and much use of dissonance?

11 ELEMENTS OF LITERATURE—SENSE

CONCEPTS

Match the following:

____ 1. metaphor	(1) states explicitly the similarity between two things.
____ 2. simile	(2) a statement of the accepted and expected relationships of words in a sentence.
____ 3. grammar	(3) calls one thing something else which it resembles.
____ 4. reference	(4) a representation of a sensory experience in concrete words which engage the senses of the reader.
____ 5. allusion	(5) something suggested but not stated directly.
____ 6. implication	(6) an explicit naming of a person, thing, or event.
____ 7. image	(7) indirectly implying a person, place, thing, or the like.

Write in the term or phrase defined on the right:

____________________ 1. a privilege granted poets to depart from traditional grammar and sentence structure if they do so knowingly for a purpose.

____________________ 2. the literal meaning of a word--the thing, person, or event to which it points.

____________________ 3. the feelings, associations, and contexts a word evokes beyond its literal meaning.

____________________ 4. a style of discourse which states or describes ideas, events, or experiences in a logical, orderly manner in accordance with traditional expectations.

____________________ 5. a style of expression which presents feelings, information, ideas--the raw data of experience--in an arrangement governed only by the artist's sense of its rightness for his purpose.

Match the following:

____ 1. jargon	(1) words belonging to a particular profession, business, or trade.
____ 2. dialect	(2) words belonging to a particular geographic area.
____ 3. technical terms	(3) words that are made up or have recently been added to the language.
____ 4. neologism	(4) words used for other words they logically suggest.
____ 5. metonomy	(5) words which are obscure or belong to a specialized activity used pretentiously.

Three of these definitions you should have been certain of: They appear in the text. The other two you probably guessed at, helped by the fact that you had eliminated the other three definitions. But, quoting the text, "It is always a temptation to guess when one is uncertain, but it is never safe." You should check these in a dictionary. Were you correct?

APPLICATION OF CONCEPTS

An Example:

The poem below is printed in the text (page 305) as an example of Italian sonnet form. We are using it here to suggest how you can study any poem: First, you should look up all the words you do not know. Then, you should read it aloud for its sound patterns as they expand, amplify, or reinforce meanings. Then, you try to answer such questions as those posed here.

THE WORLD IS TOO MUCH WITH US
William Wordsworth
(1770-1850)

The world is too much with us; late and soon,
  Getting and spending, we lay waste our powers:
  Little we see in Nature that is ours;
We have given our hearts away, a sordid boon!
This sea that bares her bosom to the moon;
  The winds that will be howling at all hours,
  And are up-gather'd now like sleeping flowers;
For this, for everything, we are out of tune;
It moves us not.--Great God! I'd rather be
  A Pagan suckled in a creed outworn;
So might I, standing on this pleasant lea,
  Have glimpses that would make me less forlorn;
Have sight of Proteus rising from the sea;
  Or hear old Triton blow his wreathed horn.

References and allusions: Proteus was, according to Greek tradition, a god who inhabited the sea and who knew all things: past, present, and future. Proteus also possessed the ability to assume all sorts of shapes and was rarely beheld in his true god-like form and only in his true form could he prophesy. Because of his ability to assume myriad shapes Proteus came to be regarded as the origin of all living matter. Wordsworth intends all these ideas to be associated with his mention of Proteus. Triton is the son of Neptune, the sea god, and possessed the power to still storms or summon them up with a blast upon his sea-shell horn. The reference to Triton should be thought of in connection with earlier mention of the wind in the poem.

When you have read the poem several times, try to answer the following questions, preferably in writing. Then look at the suggested answers and see if you agree with the general idea expressed here.

Questions:

1. What is this poem about?

2. In what sequence does the poet present his subject to you? What effect does the poet get from this sequence?

3. Can you point out any words or phrases which seem to indicate clearly the poet's attitude toward his subject?

4. What level of vocabulary does the poet use? Are any words especially striking? What are the prevailing sounds of the words used?

5. What senses are appealed to by such words as "bares her bosom," "Howling," "wreathed," and "sleeping flowers"?

6. Point out any use of figurative language (words not intended literally).

7. Will "old Triton" blow his horn to raise or still a storm?

8. What qualities does this poem possess which make us think of it as poetry?

Suggested Answers to the Questions:

1. The poem expresses Wordsworth's concern at "the world" turning its back on nature, and concentrating on material values of "getting and spending." A hundred and fifty years after the poem was written we still feel the world is too much with us in ways that Wordsworth never dreamt of. The retreat of humankind from Nature, the source of its latent powers, into a materialistic world exasperates the poet. To make himself feel less forlorn he thinks nostalgically of an earlier day when persons were so close to Nature that they explained it in terms of a series of homely myths.

2. Down to the words "It moves us not" Wordsworth is experssing his disillusionment with the materialism of "the world." In the rest of the poem he expresses his nostalgia for the Pagan "creed outworn" in which humanity felt itself a participant of Nature and natural forces.

   It strengthens the intensity of the effect of his nostalgia, because we realize first how thoroughly he is disillusioned with "the world," and hence his nostalgia is motivated. The references to Nature in both parts of the poem reveal a development of thought, rather than merely a shift of thought.

The division of thought in a sonnet must follow either of two traditional forms. In his sonnet Wordsworth naturally makes a break after the eighth line for there were two distinct parts to his idea. This 8 plus 6 line organization is appropriate for question and answer, general statement and specific application of it. There is another kind of sonnet which breaks into groups of four, four, four and two lines. In this case the first three groups usually present various treatments of the same idea and the last two lines serve as punch lines or summary. (See the sonnet by Shakespeare in the text, page 305.)

3. Line 4, "a sordid boon"; "sordid" means cheap, unworthy, "boon" means a blessing or favor. Also line 2, where he speaks of laying "waste" our powers. These are strong words and indicate that Wordsworth feels strongly. Other passages bear this out. His exasperation is dignified, however, because he uses simple words and doesn't resort to grammatical obscurity to provoke feeling. His nostalgia is borne out by such words as "forlorn" and "<u>old</u> Triton."

4. The vocabulary is quite simple. He avoids "poetic" words. To us, today, "lea" (meaning meadow) might seem so, but it was not in Wordsworth's time.

   At first reading, "suckled" seems a rather conventional, perhaps "poetic" word. But the more you think of it, the more meaningful it becomes in light of the meaning of the poem. It refers to a primitive, natural, instinctive fact; it is just the recognition of such natural and instinctive acts that Wordsworth sees the world turning its back on. Wordsworth is urging a return to simple, primitive, natural times, and the word helps to evoke them and Wordsworth's attitude toward them. Note, too, the sea "bares her bosom" in line 5. This is a further emphasis on an elemental appeal to a <u>Mother</u> Nature.

   Look for the repetition of vowel and consonant sounds. "Too" and "soon" in the first line sound a desolate note. Notice, also, the repetition of "w" in the line: "The winds that will be howling at all hours." "Late" (line 1) "lay" (line 2) and "little" (line 3) produce an echoing effect.

5. The mere identification of imagery and the senses appealed to is less important than showing how these words quicken the imaginative communication of the poet's idea by sharpening and making specific his experience. "Wreathed," for example, appeals to the eye; but more important it appeals to the imagination, for we see not only the whorls of Triton's sea shell horn but we also think of it adorned with flowers, like the "sleeping flowers" or the "up-gather'd" wind.

6. "The world" (line 1)--meaning busy materialism rather than the planet. "This sea that bares her bosom to the moon"--telling us something of the expanse of the sea, that it is, so to say, unabashedly there, and referring to the sea as a nourishing source of natural power. "Sleeping flowers" means, of course, folded flowers, rather than flowers in open blossom. By comparing the wind to flowers Wordsworth is telling us of the gentle softness of the wind in certain moods.

7. To stir up a storm. Line 7 tells us the winds are up-gather'd now. A storm would not only reveal to the blind, materialistic worlds the latent force of nature which can dwarf man and his mundane preoccupations, but we also feel that Wordsworth himself would welcome the storm as an affirmation of Nature's power.

8. More than the fact that it is lined-up as poetry and that each line rhymes with several other lines, we feel that this is a poem, because Wordsworth is presenting his experience to us in langauge which appeals directly to our imaginations. It possesses the compact distillation of experience that we come to associate with poetry. The more we think about it, the more we are aware how a word or a phrase or a reference will open up for us and seem to convey a number of ideas on different levels, rather than being merely accurate, descriptive words.

SUGGESTIONS FOR

READING POETRY FOR ENJOYMENT AND UNDERSTANDING

1. Read it out loud, preferably with someone else. This is very important.

2. Reread it and let the sounds create a mood for you.

3. Reread it to become aware of the structural organization or divisions of thought.

4. Begin to make decisions. It helps to take notes at this point.

   (1) What is the main mood? Is it peaceful and harmonious or stimulating and energetic or dignified and thoughtful?

   (2) What is the main idea? Is the poet trying to explain a philosophy? Is the poet simply describing nature? Is the poet presenting an experience by describing it? Is he presenting an experience directly?

   (3) What devices are used to create sound effects? What kind of rhythms are used: harsh and jerky or smooth and flowing? What kind of vowels and what kind of consonants predominate? Are there frequent rhymes or none?

   (4) What made the idea or mood vivid and fresh? What sensations are alluded to--hot or cold, sweet smells or bad smells, harsh sounds or sweet music, etc.?
   What comparisons are used by simile, metaphor or other device?
   What is compared with what and what qualities do they share?

   (5) In presenting the mood or idea, why has the poet chosen the particular arrangement in stanzas, or the particular organization and development?
   (In a sonnet this is very important: Is the division 8 plus 4 or three quatrains plus 1; and what are the relationships of the thoughts in each group?)

   (6) Are there words or comparisons or rhythms or vowels which seem inappropriate to the rest of the poem and mar the main effect?

5. Reread it, and now bring out even more strongly the integration of rhythms, sounds, and ideas.

ON SPOTTING AN OLD FASHIONED FRANCISCAN AMONG DE KOONINGS WITHOUT BLINKING

"Puella est pulchra. Feminae
sunt sanctae." Nominative. First person
to translate correctly in one
breath
before all others
wins
her heart
for the day. Sister Perpetua, smelling
of lilac
dusting powder and noontime
kielbasa, used both hands
to teach firstyear Latin. Roomy
dark brown sleeves rarely
if ever
hid those four chalky fingers
'in toto.' Nobody dared
ask how.

The lone fat nude
with highheel spikes
slouched miraculously
in the open,
her sharpened teeth kept in
readiness
on duty for business
at all times
with no appointment necessary
or convenient. Can anyone
count her knuckles without
distracting the collegegirl guard
at the gallery
one way entrance? Slip her
two or three valium
in a coke — wait
for that unexpected siesta
snore
before doing some investigating.

The bifocaled nun
in passing
will admire your no-
nonsense plan of attack
with closemouthed smile
and half-bow.

J.D. BUTKIE

The poem entitled "On Spotting An Old Fashioned Franciscan Among De Koonings Without Blinking" is by J.D. Butkie, a young American poet. It would be classified by some critics as "confessional" poetry", a kind of stream-of-consciousness poetry in which the writer reveals a series of personal thoughts and images which on a first reading may seem random and haphazard, even irrational. The unity and coherence of such poems and of the experience they communicate must be found, if the poem is successful, in a careful reading of it, thoughtful reflection on the various "cues" in it, and the interrelationships of these. The title tells us the incident which provoked the content of this poem. The following questions are intended to guide you through the more difficult aspects of this poem. You should read the poem a couple of times so that you are familiar with all the words and ideas before undertaking them.

1. The first lines in Latin - - "A girl is beautiful. Women are sacred." - - relate at once to the title which it follows directly and to the lines which follow it.

   Who is the sacred woman?____________________What do these two lines tell you about the writer?____________________ Line two contains a kind of pun, a phrase which by its placement in the poem is made to "do double duty": What is it?_________________ Do you think he is teasing us momentarily into thinking he has made a mistake?____________________

2. In the middle stanza we are told directly that the writer is in a gallery and from the title we know that the exhibit includes De Kooning paintings. The best known works of De Kooning are his many, many sketches and paintings of women. Woman I (Color Plate 4) is one of the best known and is typical of many of them. Do you think it may have been this painting the author is describing?

   Explain:____________________

3. The quotation which begins the poem is probably from a Latin text the author studied. Seeing the "old fashioned Franciscan" seems to have caused him to remember it, for she is "sacred", but is the "lone fat nude" pulchra?
   Find three ways in which the two are specifically contrasted:

   1.____________________2.____________________3._________________

4. From the first stanza and the title we know that the "old fashioned Franciscan" in the gallery with the writer is a nun. We learn also that her presence has evoked a series of memories about Sister Perpetua who taught him first year Latin.

   What does he remember about Sister Perpetua? Why "four chalky fingers 'in toto'"? ______________ Why did the poet choose the word toto (from Latain totus) rather than all? __________ What was it that "Nobody dared ask how?" ______________ What did she eat for lunch? ______________ When did she teach her Latin class? ______________ Read through the poem again and find three additional facts about her.

   1. ______________ 2. ______________ 3. ______________

   Considering all of these, what appears to have been the attitude/relationship of the writer to his teacher? __________ How does your answer help explain the phrase "Without Blinking" in the title? ______________________________

"The first and last rule in knowing literature is that one should know what the words mean." So says your text. Here is help with two words in this poem. Kielbasa is a Polish sausage seasoned with garlic. Valium is a trade-mark for an anti-anxiety drug -- a combination of a tranquilizer and a muscle relaxant.

Now that you have considered these specific questions, here are some more general ones:

1. Is there a consistency in mood and tone throughout the poem or do you feel that the poet has in places lapsed from the mood established in the title?

2. Do the images used give you a sense that the poet was working from an actual incident -- that there is a wholeness and integrity of experience back of the bits and pieces he has given us?

3. Does the "associational flow" seem natural, genuine?

4. Consider the various personalities he invites us to recreate from "cues" -- teacher Sister Perpetua, the lone fat nude in the painting, the guard at the gallery entrance, the speaker himself. Consider the environments involved -- a classroom after lunch smelling of garlic and lilac with a blackboard and chalk where Latin is taught, a one-way entrance gallery, with a guard, de Kooning paintings, and a nun.

   How well has the poet compressed all these into a statement which has significance and economy? What do you wish he had added? What could he have left out?

WHAT IF I HAD, LIKE YOU SAID, MISSED THE BUS?--WELL, I WAS JUST OUT FOR A WALK ANYWAY

(For Jack Ward)

Speak poem--aroma of baked bread,
sweetly morseling--when asked:
What is it?
Not flaky Danish
nor fruity strudle but
wholesomness.

If the meant is not said,
only hinted at obliquely,
unspoken for, what thought
is nourished when nib-
ling sense rests content?

That were to invite a prosed contempt
with no divinity of discontent,
linearly descendant of any
bardic utterance or relevant
in what can be read: the sown
and harvested, published and perishèd.

Does not this which limpingly is read
reach you unleavened so unlike
what to spirit must be fed;
dough leavened rises yeasti-
ly by common hearth and gloats.

Sell my loaf? I'd as lief borrow crumbs
from the improvident, chirp bird-
wise with song whose fragrance
is mine;
redolent though I be
limnèd as a blind linnet.

Normand LaPorte Denis

WHAT IF I HAD, LIKE YOU SAID, MISSED THE BUS?--WELL, I WAS JUST OUT FOR A WALK ANYWAY

The Butkie poem aims at a kind of organic unity with the various images and suggestions falling together somewhat like a jigsaw puzzle to communicate the subjective experience the author had on a particular occasion.

The poem by Mr. Denis is typical of another kind of contemporary poetry--in this instance, more difficult than the poem we have been discussing. But it does yield meaning to a careful reading and what it has to say seems to be more serious, at least more philosophical than that in Mr. Butkie's poem. Before assisting you in any dialogue with it, we suggest that you read it a couple of times, (1) paying particular attention to the punctuation, noting especially those passages which are made parenthetical to normal, logical sentence structure by being set apart in hyphens; (2) testing the words orally for sound relationship and rhymes or near-rhymes as a reason for their having been chosen; and (3) being alert to any variations or "twists" to ordinary language and commonplace idiom as the poet attempts to give them freshness in the poem.

When you are familiar with the words of the poem, try answering these general questions:

1. The "You Said," in the title suggests that there are at least two people involved and the use of <u>like you said</u> instead of the more formal <u>as you said</u> suggests an informal relationship. From clues in the poem, what do you think are the setting and the occasion of the bit of conversational exchange in the title?

2. A metaphor, we know, is a figure of speech in which one thing is referred to as another thing. For example, we say, "Life is like a river," to enrich the meaning of "life" by having those qualities which we associate with a river expand our sense of it. Mr. Denis' complete poem is an extended metaphor in which one activity and its product are spoken of as another activity and its product. What are the two activities which are equated metaphorically and provide the basic materials of the poem?

3. When someone we have known for a long time does something we did not know that person could do and does it extremely well, we may say "You missed your calling," or "You missed the boat in not becoming a . . . ." Why do you think the author has chosen "bus" as a variant of this expression in the title? In terms of the basic metaphor of the poem, what is the equivalent of "only out for a walk"?

Before answering the remaining questions, read this short description of an hypothicated incident that could have led the author to write the poem.

> A young man who considers himself a poet, has written many poems but has never submitted them for publication because, he insists the reward for writing poetry is one's own delight in it, not the approval or disapproval of some reading public, nor money paid for it. He has invited a friend to dinner and for the occasion has done something he rarely does: baked fresh yeast bread. The friend is delighted and as a compliment says, "You really missed the boat, you know. You could have made a fortune as a baker." He replies, "Oh no, I only bake bread for the pleasure it gives me just as I write poetry because it pleases me. If I wrote *or* baked to sell, I'd be selling a part of myself which is really important only to me." Later reflecting on the bit of conversation, questioning himself as to the sincerity of this answer, a poem evolved.

1. How does the bit of conversation which is used as a title contrast in style with the poem which follows it?
   In Mr. Butkie's poem, "everyday" language is organized into poetic expression. Here the poet searches out words which are alliterative, which have assonance and which have pleasing rhythms, and which rhyme. Furthermore the words he chooses have in them an associational, ambiguous playfulness. Identify as many of these as you can. For example, in the last stanza he leaves us with "loaf" and Lief," and then the "leaf" and limned" in the last line become puns to create a tree for the linnet.

   Another example: college faculty members are frequently admonished that they must either "publish or perish"; note how this phrase is reversed in the last line of stanza 3 and--to tie it to the other part of the metaphor--is equated with "sow and harvested." Note also the double meaning of "unspoken for" in stanza 2. What is the personification implied in "dough leavened . . . gloats"?

2. Note the contrast between baking bread and writing a poem. Baked bread has an aroma. It is wholesome. It is the good harvest of that sown, leavened, and enjoyed by the common hearth. Poetry is flaky Danish and fruity; it does not say what is meant but only hints obliquely at things and does not nourish. It must be read limpingly.

You probably have noticed the deliberate ambiguities in the poem--a word used so that it can mean one thing or another thing, a phrase placed so that it may connect with what went before it or with what follows. These create a kind of shimmer of meanings, not unlike that created in some modern art, such as Albers' _Homage to the Square_: _Broadcall_, where a color seems to belong to one square and then another, or de Kooning's _Woman I_, where an area of color and lines seem to belong to one figure and then another.

The first two lines are an example: "Speak poem--aroma of baked bread, sweetly morseling--when asked": We cannot tell whether the poet is confirming the basic metaphor by asking the poem to speak _as_ (i.e. in the same way) bread morseling gives off an aroma, or whether the poem is being asked to speak _while_ the bread is morseling, or whether the poem is being asked to speak _about_ the bread morseling. If you were to question the poet as to which meaning he intended, he would probably say all three, or simply shrug.

We have mentioned before our innate human need to find an order in confusion, to bring the chaotic into some comprehensible focus. We have observed, also, the tension and involvement which accompanies our searching for an order. It is on these two human traits that poems such as Mr. Denis' depend for their effectiveness. We owe it to ourselves to try to understand what such poets are doing, how they are trying to reach us. Whether, in the final analysis, we judge them to be merely curious, interesting, good, or great is another matter.

The basic strategy in Mr. Butkie's poem is different. The sentences are straight forward. He compresses into simple, ordinary words carefully selected images which he gives us in an associational series. On first reading, the poem seems so simple on the purely linguistic level that applying traditional standards we could dismiss it as unpoetic. But such poems do create tension and, if well done, release: What does a Franciscan nun have to do with de Kooning's paintings and what significance does their being together have for the poet? Finding the answer to this kind of ambiguity is what pulls us into the poem and into the experience of the poet.

THREE POEMS

The three poems by E.S. Miller on the following page speak for themselves in simplicity, good humor, and brevity, but there are a few things we hope you will not miss.

THE FALL OF THE CONE

The atmosphere conjured by this poem is one of its charms. How is the once-upon-a-time, legendary tone achieved? You will remember from the text if not from elsewhere that in the nineteenth century there were many such poems about real and imagined legends. You may recall Coleridge's "The Rime of the Ancient Mariner," Keat's "The Eve of St. Agnes," and Wordsworth's "Lucy". For a particularly good example reread the stanza from Poe's "Annabel Lee" on page 301. Obviously the poet is depending on our half-remembered knowledge of such poems for his effect.

Here are a few specific questions: Why is there no period at the end of the first stanza? What is the rhyme scheme of this stanza? Is it repeated in the second stanza? Why does the poet change tense in the poem? What words not usually considered poetic are introduced to give the images concreteness? What passages are especially musical? What is the pun in the last line? Why "fall of the . . . <u>year</u> and <u>years</u>"?

ENCOMIUM VITAE and ENCOMIUM ARTIS

The use of Latin titles for this pair of poems is sure to remind you of the sentence usually attributed to Hippocrates: <u>Ars longa, vita brevis est</u>. ("Art is long, life is short.") Poet Miller is giving his own "twist" to this epigram in his poems "In Praise of Life" and "In Praise of Art."

ENCOMIUM VITAE: Who was Pericles? We know who Scheherazade was and because "We'd had a few" we are not surprised at her twenty-two violins becoming forty-four. But suppose you are told that Scheherazade was a nightclub in Paris with walls of mirrors, would this add or detract from the poem?

ENCOMIUM ARTIS: <u>particular</u> is a pun; what are the two meanings? Find another pun in the poem. What is it that <u>settles</u> in the second line? What is the name for the last foot in this poem?

These three poems and a fourth, GRASSHOPPERS, reprinted on page 198 without comment, are from E.S. Miller, <u>Selected Poems</u> in the Open Places Poets Series, Stephens College, Columbia, Missouri, 1972. The copyright is owned by the author and the poems are reproduced here with his permission.

THREE POEMS
E. S. Miller (1904)

THE FALL OF THE CONE

Many and many a year ago
the stars did their twinkling and sunshine shone
and turned to dew or turned to snow,
and a pine did its pointing and dropped a cone
on pigeon moss, trillium leaves,
pebbles, or slate shards under the eaves

over a bedroom window where
a lovely lady loved by dew,
stars, and sunshine is brushing her hair,
and those that love her she loves too,
and as she quickens she overhears
the fall of the cone and year and years.

ENCOMIUM VITAE

We've had a few.
Let's have some more
till Scheherazade's
twenty-two
advancing violins
are forty-four
and we go out
and never think about
the silly time when Pericles
built ruins.

ENCOMIUM ARTIS

When we outdie
particular death,
settle, and dirty
other dirt,
any black banana
or punk grapefruit,
if Picasso
were to paint it
would be still life
worth wiping us off of.

12 ELEMENTS OF LITERATURE—SOUND

CONCEPTS

Match the following:

____ 1. alliteration	(1) resemblance or similarity in sound of accented vowels.
____ 2. assonance	(2) words in which the final consonants agree but the vowels preceding them differ.
____ 3. consonance	(3) identical sounds in the same position in two or more lines.
____ 4. rhyme	(4) repetition of initial identical sounds in words which are close together.

Match the following:

____ 1. tone color	(1) the quality of a line's motion in tension with its basic beat--its shape as determined by accents, tone color, and inflection necessary to its meaning.
____ 2. rhythm	(2) a pattern of accents repeated throughout a line.
____ 3. meter	(3) words which have identical vowel and consonant end sounds, but different initial sounds.
____ 4. rhyme	(4) equivalent to timbre in music; a quality produced by repetition of sounds, phrases, or sentences.

APPLICATION OF CONCEPTS

Using the key given, identify by number(s) the word(s) which describe(s) the relationship between the pairs of words below it.

(1) alliteration

(2) assonance

(3) consonance

(4) rhyme

____ 1. kin - can

____ 2. lake - fate

____ 3. nettle - bottle

____ 4. pace - late

____ 5. kite - quite

____ 6. cinema - sinner

____ 7. luck - peak

____ 8. rope - coat

____ 9. bought - talk

____ 10. grass - alas

Write in the appropriate column three examples each of alliteration, consonance, assonance:

ALLITERATION

1. __________ - __________

2. __________ - __________

3. __________ - __________

ASSONANCE

1. __________ - __________

2. __________ - __________

3. __________ - __________

CONSONANCE

1. __________ - __________

2. __________ - __________

3. __________ - __________

APPLICATION OF CONCEPTS

- 1 -

The appeal of sound rhythms which reinforce meaning is universal. Mother Goose verses and nursery rhymes which go back hundreds of years illustrate this fact. The devices used are some of the same ones we find in more sophisticated, serious poetry. Probably you are familiar with this verse:

Jack Sprat could eat no fat,
His wife could eat no lean,
And so between the two of them
They licked the platter clean.

But probably you have not speculated about the source of its appeal, apart from the little, logical joke. Consider the first line. Why is it pleasant to say? Try changing a word or two:

Jack Smith could eat no grease

Clearly the assonance and consonance of Jack-Sprat-fat have something to do with the effect. Wife was probably originally Middle English wyf and pronounced wēf so that the assonance between his-wife-lean was more pronounced than in modern English.

Because this is a four-line stanza it is technically called a ____________________. The first, second, and fourth lines have ____________ poetic feet, but the third line has ____________ feet. There is in this verse no variation from the basic meter. Every foot is made up of a weak syllable followed by a strong syllable, called an ____________________ foot. Combining these facts about (1) meter and (2) length of line, we would say that the first, second, and fourth lines are (1) __________________ (2) ____________ and that the third line is (1) ______________ (2) ____________.

Another familiar nursery rhyme is one which is chanted by an adult as he or she jogs a child up and down on a knee or foot. The rhythm of the chanting and force of the jogging are adjusted to act out the characters portrayed in the sounds and rhythms.

Here goes my lord
   A trot, a trot, a trot, a trot!
Here goes my lady
   A canter, a canter, a canter, a canter!
Here goes my young master
   Jockey-hitch, jockey-hitch, jockey-hitch, jockey-hitch!
Here goes my young miss
   An amble, an amble, an amble, an amble!
The footman lags behind, to tipple ale and wine
   And goes gallop, a gallop, a gallop, to make up his time.

Consider the (1) meter and (2) line length:

The second line is (1) ________________ (2) ________________

The sixth line is (1) ________________ (2) ________________

The last line is (1) ________________ (2) ________________

As an exercise in how sounds and rhythms work, compose an updated version of this rhyme with characters which children today will recognize: for example, the mounted policeman in parks, cowboys, the rodeo rider, the racing jockey, etc. Or you may change the subject altogether and make it trains, cars, motorcycles, or anything which produces a variety of rhythms you can imitate in words.

- 3 -

The curfew tolls the knell of parting day,
The lowing herd wind slowly o'er the lea,
The plowman homeward plods his weary way.
And leaves the world to darkness and to me.

The stanza above is from "Elegy Written in a Country Churchyard," by Thomas Gray (1716-1771). The meter of the whole stanza is quite regular. Most of the feet are ______________, but there is one important variation, one foot that is different. It is found in line ______________ and is a ______________ foot which is quite effective in its placement. The type of foot which predominates in the lines and the length of the lines lead us to refer to them as ______________ ______________ lines. The rhyme scheme is ____ ____ ____ ____ ____ ____, and since there are four lines in the stanza we call it a ______________.

- 4 -

But at my back I always hear
Time's wingèd chariot hurrying near.

These two often quoted lines are from "To His Coy Mistress," by Andrew Marvell (1621-1678). Considering (1) the meter, (2) the line length and (3) the rhyme scheme, we would correctly refer to it as an (1) ______________ (2) ______________ (3) ______________.
The particular diacritical mark over the <u>èd</u> in <u>wingèd</u> is called a <u>grave</u> <u>accent</u> and directs the reader to ______________________________

____.

EPITAPH ON THE COUNTESS OF PEMBROKE

Ben Jonson
(1573-1637)

Underneath this sable hearse
Lies the subject of all verse:
Sidney's sister, Pembroke's mother.
Death, ere thou hast slain another
Fair and learn'd and good as she,
Time shall throw a dart at thee.

Marble piles let no man raise
To her name, for after-days
Some kind woman, born as she,
Reading this, like Niobe
Shall turn marble, and become
Both her mourner and her tomb.

Read the poem aloud a couple of times, savoring the rhythms and the sounds. Look up in any dictionary sable and Niobe. Consider the (1) meter, (2) the length of the lines and (3) the rhyme scheme. Now, complete the sentences below by writing the correct words in the spaces provided.

Most of the poem is in (1) __________ (2) __________ (3) __________ but there are two lines in the first stanza which are different. They are lines ____ and ____ and make a (1) ________ (2) __________ (3) __________. In tension against the basic meter a different kind of foot is introduced in some other lines for variety and to change the __________. Niobe was chosen for the allusion because she ______________________. One couplet does not rhyme, but it is a near-rhyme. The couplet is made up of lines ______________ and ______________________.

SCANSION OF VERSE

Your teacher may assign you a short poem or ask you to choose a poem to be used in this exercise in studying poetry.

I. METER

(1) Write out the poem on every other line. Read the poem aloud in order to place an accent mark (′) over each accented syllable in each line. Then place a (˘) over the remaining unaccented syllables. Separate each foot with a diagonal line (/). Give the names for the line lengths.

(2) Circle any unusual feet such as trochees, dactyls, anapests, or spondees and indicate the name of the exceptional foot.

II. TONE

(1) Mark the rhyme scheme of the poem, if any, with small letters to the right of each line. If the form is a traditional form, name it.

(2) Cite all the examples of alliteration, assonance, and consonance you can find.

(3) Indicate any evidence of onomatopoeia.

III. IMAGERY

(1) Indicate the specific senses to which the imagery of the poem appeals and indicate the passages that do so.

IV. FIGURES OF SPEECH

(1) Note all the metaphors and similes in the poem, if any.

(2) Cite any examples of personification.

(3) Explain any allusions.

BUFFALO BILL'S
E.E. Cummings (1894 - 1962)

Buffalo Bill's
defunct
          who used to
          ride a watersmooth-silver
                                        stallion
and break onetwothreefourfive pigeonsjustlikethat
                                                                      Jesus
he was a handsome man
                                    and what i want to know is
how do you like your blueeyed boy
Mister Death

BUFFALO BILL'S

We have made the point in the text about the difficulty of translating poetry from one language to another. It is just as difficult to translate poetry into prose. It is, therefore, unlikely that any of the answers to the questions posed below will completely satisfy you. However, put the number(s) of the one or two which come closest to your feelings in the space provided and then write your own answer on the line after the last alternative.

SUBJECT

____ 1. Which of the following sentences states best what the poem is about? (1) Boys should not admire great men who are old, for they will die; (2) Buffalo Bill should not be "whitewashed," but should always be represented with a gun shooting claypigeons; (3) Death claims all men, even the greatest and most glamorous; (4) We have difficulty in reconciling the dashing glamour of the living hero with his unbeing--death.

____

____ 2. Is the overall effect of the poem one of (1) burlesque? (2) understatement? (3) technical display? (4) journalistic reporting? (5) wit?

____

MEDIUM

____ 3. Expressions in the poem such as "Jesus" and "Mister Death" seem to be used to characterize the speaker. The language is that of (1) a wise and benevolent philosopher; (2) a sensitive but slightly cynical young person; (3) a sophisticated adolescent; (4) a calloused, seasoned frontiersman.

____

____ 4. Considering the liberties taken in arranging the lines on the page, do you think the poet is trying (1) to achieve an effectively balanced page; (2) to make the poem look interesting and different; (3) to suggest the accents, pauses, emphases to be observed in reading the poem; (4) to make the poem long enough to look important.

____

____ 5. Do you think the practice in some phrases of runningwords together justlikethis is followed by the poet (1) to provide a clue as to how it should be read; (2) to produce momentary confusion which will make the reader go back and read the passage again and more carefully; (3) to be different; (4) to communicate visually the idea of speed and accuracy.

____

____ 6. What is the tone established in beginning the poem with the phrase

Buffalo Bill's defunct	vs.	Buffalo Bill's dead	or	Buffalo Bill's passed away?

Does the word "defunct" in its context suggest to you that the speaker's attitude is one of (1) assumed irreverence? (2) distracting personal grief? (3) casual indifference? (4) scientific statement of fact?

____

ELEMENTS

____ 7. In lines four and five the phrase "a watersmooth-silver / stallion" appears. Do you think this is (1) partly a visual and partly an auditory image? (2) purely a visual image? (3) partly a visual and partly a feeling (tactile) image? (4) purely an auditory image?

____

____ 8. The particular musical quality of the phrase "a watersmooth-silver / stallion," is achieved through the use of (1) a regular iambic (u') rhythm; (2) effective rhyme; (3) liquid sounds (r's and l's) and nasal sounds (m's and n's); (4) using a noun for an adjective.

____

____ 9. Which of these lines do you think contains the best example of rhythm used to echo and emphasize meaning? (1) Line one; (2) Line six; (3) Line eight; (4) Line ten.

____

ORGANIZATION

____10. What seems to you to be the controlling factor in the organization of the poem? (1) A desire to achieve regularity in a traditional form: (2) an attempt to give the impression of spontaneous, unorganized speech which is accidentally suggestive; (3) an attempt to say something quite ordinary in an unusual way: (4) a desire to make the "poem" look "right" on the page.

THE ENORMOUS POET

Estlin Cummings'
defunct
    who used to
    write a watersmooth-silver
                                        lyric
and break onetwothreefourfive
imagesjustlikethat
                                              Jesus
he was a gladsome man
       and what i want to know is
where do we find another
     blueeyed boy
 Mister Death

It is no surprise that this famous poem, written as an ironic elegy to Buffalo Bill, should with so few changes serve as an epitaph for the man who wrote it. For Edward Estlin Cummings was certainly the showiest poet of his age, riding his prancing verses through dazzling jigsteps while beyond him a calliope played tunes of his own devising. He wrote carnival verse, brightly colored and splattered with a thousand sounds, and he pitched it all over the typographical lot in a frank attempt to grab the customer's eye and draw the customer in. If the carny's gift had been his only gift, though, far fewer city slickers would have stopped to listen. The fact was that he had pegged his gaudy tents to hard ground beneath a clearly visible sky, and when he died of a stroke last week, at 67, in a hospital near his New Hampshire summer home America lost not only its most attractive spieler but - with Frost - its finest lyric poet of this century.

INDIVIDUALIST: Cummings was both these things by design, if not quite by inevitability. His father was a fiercely nonconformist Unitarian minister, a scion of Cambridge intellectual society, and, by his son's account, a sort of witty John Bunyan out of doors; his mother was a joyous, beautiful woman of whom he later wrote, "if there are any heavens my mother will (all by herself) have one." Estlin grew up with a monumental sense of his own individuality - not always distinct from superiority - and a concomitant oneness with nature and estrangement from all who were not so individual.

Like most of the other young nonconformists, Cummings hied himself to Europe before 1917 to serve as an ambulance driver for the French, who became suspicious of some of his connections and gave him a small loyalty test. *"Est-ce que vous detestez les boches?"* they asked.

"Non, j'aime beaucoup les francais," he replied.

The French put the question to him again, he replied as before, and they threw him in jail for three months. Cummings' stand was largely a pose, for he did indeed detest the boche; it was in one way a fortunate pose, for out of it came a novel, "The Enormous

Room," that not only made him famous but may well have been the best of all the literature spawned by World War I.

Cummings stayed in Paris in the '20s, acquainted with but not a part of the inbred expatriate colony of Americans. For him as for everyone else, though, Ezra Pound was a new rising sun, and under Pound's influence Cummings tore apart the traditional frames of syntax, punctuation, and usage.

At first they laughed when he sat down at this strange-looking piano, and it was some time before most people could realize that the melody was as sweet and true as any that came out of normal-looking instruments. The typographical and verbal hi-jinks served a purpose - they helped the tired eye of man to see his ancient world as if for the first time, which all poetry must do - and they were fun for their own sake. The one thing wrong in laughing at Cummings has always been that it was so much more profitable to laugh with him:

While you and i have lips and voices
which
are for kissing and to sing with
who cares if some oneeyed son of a
bitch
invents an instrument to measure
Spring with?

Inevitably, the honors came in his late years, although they never measured him for a Pulitzer. And just as inevitably, most of the press clung to its image of him as a verbal stunt-man and went on spelling his name in lower-case. Meanwhile Cummings pointed out that he used capitals as the ancients did, to indicate important words. For some time now, E.E. Cummings has earned the right to be capitalized.

<u>Newsweek</u>, September 17, 1962.

GRASSHOPPERS

The blithe grasshopper
has no more trouble
in grass unscythed
than in the stubble.

The enthusiastic
grasshopper
hops over
the grass
with the thick
thews he has
to hop with.

E. S. Miller

13 ORGANIZATION IN THE VISUAL ARTS

CONCEPTS

The words form, type, plan, order, as used in the text, are all synonyms for (1)__________. The term we use for organization in music is (2)__________ and the term we use for organization in literature is (3)__________. Three examples of forms in music are (4)__________, (5)__________, and (6)__________. Three examples of types in literature are (7)__________, (8)__________, and (9)__________.

In the visual arts there are no names for types of plan, but there are four arrangements which are used frequently and are easily recognized: the (10)__________ plan; the (11)__________ plan; the (12)__________ plan; and the (13)__________ plan.

Plan in this sense is not very interesting as such. It is simply a frame or (14)__________ which holds the work together in some overall plan. The essentials in holding our attention and in giving the work expressive quality and content are arranged within the plan; this arrangement is sometimes called the (15)__________ structure. In this structure one principle holds for all the arts: (16)__________ and (17)__________, or (18)__________ and (19)__________.

The tympanum on a temple, the facade of a building, the proscenium arch of a stage, all function as (20)__________ for anything placed within them.

When the elements of the organization are well-contained within the (21)__________, it is sometimes called a closed form. If, on the other hand, parts of figures are cut off by the frame, as in a candid snapshot, it is sometimes called an open form. Using this terminology, Toulouse-Lautrec's In the Circus Fernando (page 318) would be an example of (22)__________, and Giotto's Death of S. Francis (page 314) would be an example of (23)__________. Another example of open form in the text is (24)__________ by __________ on page _____. Another example of closed form is (25)__________ by __________ on page _____.

The seemingly contradictory aspects of organization in great works of art which Rudolf Arnheim mentions in the quotation at the beginning of Part Three of the text (page 211) are (26)__________ and (27)__________. If we were to translate these two aspects into the terminology we are using in this chapter, we would call them (28)__________ structure and (29)__________ structure.

APPLICATION OF CONCEPTS

-1-

Examine Brueghel's _The Parable of the Blind_ (Color Plate 42, following page 440) and read the poem by Williams underneath it. In the left column below write four details in the painting which Williams comments upon. In the right column contrast these with four details in Brueghel's _The Journey of the Magi_ (page 317).

The Parable of the Blind	_The Journey of the Magi_
______________________________	______________________________
______________________________	______________________________
______________________________	______________________________
______________________________	______________________________

-2-

It is sometimes said that abstract art and especially abstract expressionism have taught us to see paintings in a way which was unknown (at least consciously) before the 20th century. In minimizing subject matter and its importance and in maximizing the expressiveness of purely formal aspects, they have sensitized us to an idiom of form and color and have given us a new way of "reading" traditional art. They have made us aware that the masters of the past were consciously and/or unconsciously using this innate language in their paintings to reinforce and communicate the content of subject matter. Some critics would go so far as to argue that traditional art, if it is good, can be enjoyed and appreciated when viewed as pure abstraction in color, line, perspective, etc., ignoring completely the subject matter or anecdotal content.

Do you find from your experience that this is correct? Select three paintings from the text and defend the point of view you believe to be true.

In abstract art, the plan is likely to be based on repetition and variety of the elements rather than on a traditional skeletal model. Find in the text (outside this chapter) three abstract paintings which illustrate this statement and state below (1) what elements are repeated, (2) what are varied, and (3) how tension (interest) is created in each.

______________ ______________________________ ________
Artist Painting Figure No. or Color Plate No.

1.____

2.____

3.____

______________ ______________________________ ________
Artist Painting Figure No. or Color Plate No.

1.____

2.____

3.____

______________ ______________________________ ________
Artist Painting Figure No. or Color Plate No.

1.____

2.____

3.____

TENSION AND RELEASE:

THE TWO ASPECTS OF ORDER IN THE ARTS

We sometimes become so absorbed in searching for the skeletal plan in a work of art that we forget that quickly perceived order would not interest us very long. If perfect order were the sole criterion of greatness in art, a circle would be the perfect art work. It is tension between order and disorder which holds our interest and centers our attention. This requirement of tension (some degree of disorder) and release (some degree of order) is a basic aspect of organization in all the arts.

Perhaps the principle is most readily understood in the literary arts. A novel, play or film in which there is no conflict, no involvement of our emotions as a resolution of problems presented is sought would be dull indeed. And a musical composition in which there is no dissonance, simply a flow of consonant harmony, a series of major chords, would not claim our involved attention for long. One has examples of this in some hymn tunes which are mainly for keeping a congregation together in singing words which are significant to a particular religious group. They have little musical interest in themselves.

Just so in painting. For example, Kandinsky's *War Themes* (Color Plate 9) is dramatic and arresting because of the diagonals of canon and ramparts pulling against restless curves, and because he has placed the high value yellows in very careful relation to the greens and blues, and set them against the oranges and reds in such a way that the eye moves over the canvas constantly searching for order in the chaos. Tension and release, the posing of a question and giving an answer, dissonance which resolves in consonance: These are aspects of organization which involve us. In the process of finding an order in the midst of chaos we find release from our tensions.

The mood or idea determines the choice of a plan for a work. Compare Kandinsky's *War Themes* with Vermeer's *Young Woman with a Water Jug* (Color Plate 43). In the Vermeer the plan itself is uncomplicated. The rectangles of the window and map create strong verticals and horizontals and with the horizontal table top give the work stability and also a sense of orderliness to the domestic drama being enacted. They guide the eye round the painting and into the light area where the activity takes place. The painting is saved from monotony by the diagonals of the arms, the opening in the white cape and the highlights on the face, the metal tray and the pitcher on the gleaming table. The Kandinsky on the other hand, at first glance leaves one with a sense of no overall plan, just confusion. Actually the blobs of smoke and light are set against the elongated rectangles in a space roughly rectangular, though broken. After all, he was trying to depict violence and conflict. He seems to be telling us in his painting that his is no world of repose and that tensions are everywhere. Vermeer, in contrast, is presenting us a quiet, ordered domestic setting in which some action, interesting but certainly not violent, is taking place.

The basic satisfaction of sensing and responding to repetition and variety, to confusion and clarity, to order and chaos, to tension and release is all too often an unclaimed reward in the arts.

DISCUSSION QUESTION:

After reading the above, consider the following illustrations and be prepared to explain for each (1) how tension has been created (2) what changes could have been made to lessen the tension and (3) what would have been gained or lost in doing so.

Kline, <u>Mahoning</u>, page 17.

Michelangelo, <u>Creation</u>, Color Plate 15, following page 88.

Picasso, <u>Les Demoiselles d'Avignon</u>, page 54.

Albers, <u>Homage to the Square: Broadcall</u>, Color Plate 27, following page 216.

THE IMAGE AS FOCUSED EXPERIENCE

Gyorgy Kepes whom we have quoted earlier on The Universal Language of Art has something important to say about our search for order in experience, our human trait of trying to find pattern in whatever confronts us.

It seems now to be generally agreed that whatever the origins of this need to organize our experience and of our perceptual equipment for doing so, it served as an important survival mechanism in the early stages of human history. When enemy tribes came together in battle, it was the tribe which could see a pattern in the individuals of the other tribe approaching them and deploy its members to meet them at the most critical and vulnerable points which was victorious. The ability to perceive the continuous flow of rain, snow, warm weather, cold weather, green vegetation, dying vegetation as a predictable cyclic pattern made agriculture possible.

This faculty to perceive what is experienced as pattern, an image, is of critical importance to both artist and scientist. There is a growing awareness that creativity in the arts, sciences, and social sciences is not as different as we once assumed. The materials on which professionals in these fields focus attention are different and the purposes in seeking patterns are different but the process seems similar in all. For example, a little book by Robert Nisbet, Sociology as an Art Form (New York: Oxford University Press, 1976) points out similarities in creativity in these two fields.

The artist appears to be interested in all phenomena, whether they have practical significance or not. The scientist is interested in the predictability aspects of order, in patterns which can be replicated confident that the results will always be identical, and patterns of relationships which can be used to do work, to manipulate nature. The artist is perhaps, as Kepes suggests, more interested in extending the concepts and images we have for the still silent, unarticulated experiences we have of our inner and outer world.

THE IMAGE AS FOCUSED EXPERIENCE

Each important contribution of image-making to the broadening of human understanding returns us to the same basic human urge: to reduce a multiplicity of sense impressions to a unified whole.

Common perception gathers a number of sense impressions into a gestalt, a patterned vision. The heightened perception of artistic vision collates sense impressions into vision of the high patterning of works of art: harmony, balance, sequence and rhythm.

The uncomplicated symmetry of prehistoric tools: the intricate axial inversions of neolithic ornaments; the rhythmic variations of Peruvian fabrics; the orderly pulsation of the mosaics of San Vitale; the unifying lines and planes of Piero della Francesca, Raphael, Sesshu, Bellini, Poussin, Juan Gris or Mondrian; - all these visual syntheses document convincingly our persistent need to focus and unify the diffuse variety of the changing seen world. Our sensibilities need to be sustained with the joy of felt orders.

Image symbols are the elemental structures of focused experience. The function of tool does not exhaust their role. As a basic aspect of the human organism, the image is a dynamic organizer of life, enabling us to deal with the environment and directing and controlling our development. Images shape and key our thoughts and feelings as the genetic material shapes and keys the composition, growth and reproduction of our bodies. The images we share encode our common culture; our private images encode our inner, unique lives, impressing on us both the richness of the sensed and the order of the understood.

-- Gyorgy Kepes

SELF-TEST IN PAINTING

LEONARDO DA VINCI: MADONNA AND S. ANNE

During the course of ten years Leonardo da Vinci made many cartoons (preparatory sketches) of a Holy Family group. One of them discarded by Leonardo was finished by his pupil, Bernardino Luini and is shown in Figure 17-1, page 428. Another of the cartoons from this period Leonardo himself developed into the painting Madonna and S. Anne (Color Plate 46, following page 440). There are significant differences between the paintings which pose interesting questions.

Most interpretations of works of art are of necessity more or less conjectural. Even artists themselves frequently do not know, or cannot or will not articulate the meaning a particular work has for them. The best guide to interpretation must be found in the work itself.

Study the composition of the Leonardo and Luini paintings carefully and of the alternatives given you, indicate the one you think most likely correct with a ✓ and the one you think least likely correct with O . This is not a test but an exercise to lead you into the study of the two paintings and problems of interpretation.

1. The principal subject in the Leonardo composition is
   _____ 1) St. Anne because she dominates
   _____ 2) The Virgin Mother because she is central
   _____ 3) The Infant because all lines center on Him
   _____ 4) The family group itself because of the tight organization

2. The artist's chief purpose seems to be
   _____ 1) to portray piety
   _____ 2) to communicate a sense of the humanity of Jesus
   _____ 3) to express reverence for motherhood
   _____ 4) an interest in composition rather than the subject

3. The picture taken as a whole suggests
   _____ 1) a matriarchal interpretation of the Diety
   _____ 2) emphasis on the humanity of Jesus
   _____ 3) a secular rather than a religious approach
   _____ 4) a design for a funeral monument

4. The child is not mentioned in the title
   _____ 1) because He is implicitly referred to in "Madonna"
   _____ 2) He is subsidiary in interest
   _____ 3) He is there only to identify the Blessed Mother
   _____ 4) the subject is not a conventional theme

5. The word "madonna" in the title
_____ 1) literally means "my lady"
_____ 2) in art usually identifies the Virgin and Child
_____ 3) in an old Italian style of address refers to a married woman
_____ 4) when capitalized means the Blessed Virgin

6. The landscape in the background
_____ 1) is that of a rural setting which explains the lamb
_____ 2) is typical of the artist's compositions in like subjects
_____ 3) gives depth to the composition and has no other significance
_____ 4) harmonizes with the blue drapery of the Virgin

7. There are obvious differences in the organization of the Luini painting and the Leonardo paintings and these make a difference in the content. Which of these differences do most to highlight the matriarchial lineage of Jesus?
_____ 1) the eliminating Joseph from the group
_____ 2) making St. Anne the apex of the organization
_____ 3) having St. Anne preside over the action of Mary and Jesus
_____ 4) having Jesus turn from the lamb to look at Mary

8. The main lines of composition
_____ 1) focus on the Child, making Him the central subject
_____ 2) approximate a spiral within a triangle
_____ 3) constitute a major and a minor triangle
_____ 4) unify two groups of subjects

9. When compared to the Luini painting it
_____ 1) is compositionally quite different
_____ 2) is less well organized because there are fewer subjects
_____ 3) makes the figure of St. Anne more dominant
_____ 4) identifies the lamb with St. John

10. Light in the painting
_____ 1) is diffused
_____ 2) is outdoors
_____ 3) seems to have its source above the spectator's left shoulder
_____ 4) is used for chiaroscuro effects in modeling the figures

11. Though not the <u>center</u> of interest in the composition, attention is drawn to the Child
_____ 1) by having lines of arms and legs converge on Him
_____ 2) by the direction of gaze of the main figures

_____ 3) by the light on His face
_____ 4) because of sentimental interest

12. Organizationally the child is not the center of interest
_____ 1) he is off-center
_____ 2) the triangle including his figure is not dominant
_____ 3) he is not mentioned in the title as part of the subject
_____ 4) his gaze is directed back to the central figure

13. The crooked elbow of St. Anne
_____ 1) breaks up the severity of the triangle
_____ 2) gives her more solidity
_____ 3) balances and contrasts with the outstretched arm of Mary

14. This is an unusual presentation of the Madonna
_____ 1) because she is not holding the infant (presenting Him)
_____ 2) because she shares interest with a figure dominating her in the composition
_____ 3) nothing indicates a dogmatic theme
_____ 4) no figures of patrons or angels are included

15. The expression on the face of St. Anne
_____ 1) suggests that of the *Mona Lisa* which Leonardo painted later
_____ 2) may suggest the secret of the mysterious smile of the *Mona Lisa*
_____ 3) is the strongest indication of the content of the painting as being that of the glory of motherhood
_____ 4) by her smile enforces the structure of the composition

16. Since one of Leonardo's discarded cartoons was the basis of Luini's painting, it appears that Leonardo was in it already striving for a composition to give prominance to St. Anne by
_____ 1) having her stand behind the Virgin
_____ 2) placing her between the Virgin and Joseph
_____ 3) highlighting her face
_____ 4) placing her face close to that of the Virgin in an enveloping expression

This print, Landscape with Bathers, is by Paul Cézanne. There are three additional works by Cézanne in your text: Well and Grinding Wheel (Figure 1-9, page 20), Madame Cézanne in the Conservatory (Figure 13-2, page 312), and Still Life with Apples (Color Plate 34, following page 216).

Of Cézanne, Jakob Rosenberg has written, "Nobody could equal him in placing figures into a landscape as inseparable parts of the whole, yet endowing them with plastic vigor. His figures fulfill both a rhythmical and a spatial function within the design, and thus become true partners of nature as essential carriers of the composition." 1

In this print there is a suggestion of a stream in the foreground, a landscape with bathers in the middle ground, and Cézanne's beloved Mont-Ste.-Victoire in the background. The eyes focus first on the male coming forward in the center. From this figure formal relationships play in all directions.

With these clues to studying the print consider the following questions:

1. First, look at the character of the lines, the free, spontaneous quality, the gradations in value. What kind of print do you think this is (i.e., etching, woodblock, etc.)?

2. Compare the photograph and painting of _Well and Grinding Wheel_ (page 20). How has the artist rearranged the landscape to establish a central area for the subject of the painting?

3. How has he arranged the landscape in the print to give depth to the scene?

4. How would the effect be changed if the reclining figure in the print were standing? What would be lost?

5. What compositional purpose is served by the dark area of trees on the left?

6. Why does the tree on the right lean to the left? Why is it in the print taller than the mountain?

7. Can you find the subtle verticles and horizontals which give the painting stability, which let us know which direction is up?

8. Compare the print with Still Life with Apples (Color Plate 34, following page 216). Are there similarities in the way Cézanne has created a central space, a middle ground, to focus interest on the subject of the painting. To what in the print might one compare the bare corner of the table in the left of the painting?

9. Compare Madame Cézanne in the Conservatory (Figure 13-2, page 312) with Van Gogh's La Berceuse (Figure 9-3, page 217). Portraits fall naturally into pyramidal organization and it is the mark of a good portrait that it escape the rigid triteness of the triangle. How has Cézanne created a sense of depth, counterbalanced the triangularity of the figure, and added visual interest to the whole canvas? Does the Van Gogh seem flat in comparison? Why? Are the rhymthical patterns Van Gogh uses to create unity more like those in the print or in the portrait by Cézanne?

10. Compare the point of view in the print of Landscape with Bathers and in the Still Life with Apples. In one the artist is at eye-level with the subject; in the other, he is above the subject. Perhaps there is a realism involved, but is there also a compositional reason?

11. Do you think the loose arrangement of the tablecloth in _Still Life with Apples_ tightens or loosens the organization? Does it appear that the loosely grouped apples in the lower left hand corner is about to roll off the table? Can you account for this in terms of perspective? Do you think that the distortion of the plane of the table is intended to produce this effect? Observe that this provides ambiguity in the eye level. Does this add tension (i.e., a sense of impending movement) to an otherwise static scene?

[1] The quotation is from Jakob Rosenberg's _On Quality in Art: Criteria of Excellence, Past and Present_ (Bollingen Series XXXV. 13: Princeton University Press, 1967), page 215.

SHEEP PIECE FOR KANSAS CITY

Henry Moore (1898-   ). British Sculptor. Sheep Piece for Kansas City (1972). (Bronze. Height: 14 feet and 6 inches. Grounds of the William Rockhill Nelson Gallery of Art, Kansas City, Missouri. Photographs by Roy E. Pell.)

Some sculpture is oriented frontally, that is, is designed to be seen from one vantage point. See, for example, Michelangelo's Tomb of Guiliano de Medici on page 312 of the text.

Moore's Sheep Piece was designed to stand in the open so one can walk around it and view it from all sides. The sculptor has tried to make it interesting, different, and representative of the subject matter from all points of view. If you were limited to one of the photographs on the following page for a textbook, which would you choose? Why?

How has Moore made the parts relate to each other as well as to the surrounding field? Is there a visual center of interest? From all views? How has he achieved this focus?

This sculpture "for Kansas City" is a bronze duplicate of one on the grounds of Moore's home, "Hoglands," in Much Hadham, England. A window in the studio where he works opens on a grazing pasture for sheep. He has made many sketches and etchings of the sheep, but this sculpture was done as "a gift to the sheep." As they wander about the pasture grazing, they walk under it where it protects them from the hot sun or cold rain and they rub against the inner surfaces which they like to do as a way of cleaning their wool. Moore himself has said that the sculpture takes its form from the animals and that from different points of view it suggests them huddling together for warmth, suckling and mating.

It is important to note that the piece is over 14 feet high for us to estimate the size of the openings on all sides.

Look once again at Moore's Two Forms (page 34 of the text) and Reclining Figure (page 40 of the text). What similarities in style to this sculpture can you identify? Simplified forms from nature? Forms tied visually to the earth? Surfaces catching play and movement of light on them as we move about them?

A large beautiful color photograph of the original showing sheep walking through the holes, rubbing against protrusions in the concave areas, and snuggling together in the shadow is used as the back cover of Moore's book Sculpture and Environment (New York: Harry N. Abrams, Inc., 1977).

HENRY MOORE'S
SHEEP PIECE FOR KANSAS CITY
(1972)

TENSION AND RELEASE IN SCULPTURE

Sculpture (untitled) by Dorothy Berge, Colony Square, Atlanta, Ga. Photograph courtesy Paul Liberman, Atlanta, Ga.

Study this impressive sculpture in terms of its organization. How is tension between order and disorder and consequently interest generated by the artist? Note the proportions and relationships of the parts to each other; the organization of verticals, horizontals and diagonals; the shape of the topmost part in relation to the part below it; how the bottom line of the right section of the top part connects with the top line of the left section of the part below it, etc., etc. This is a start toward analyzing the piece. Be prepared to discuss your evaluation of its effectiveness.

14 ORGANIZATION IN ARCHITECTURE

CONCEPTS

Mark the following True or False:

_____ 1. The use of disintegrating materials accounts for our knowing so little about the buildings of the early inhabitants of the Mesopotamian Valley.

_____ 2. The temple was the characteristic building during the Roman Empire.

_____ 3. Civic buildings, aquaducts, bridges are the most characteristic constructions of the Greeks.

_____ 4. The three stages of architecture between A.D. 400-1500 are known as Early Christian, Romanesque, and Gothic.

_____ 5. Thick heavy walls, small window openings and a stone roof are three characteristics of early Christian basilicas.

_____ 6. Romanesque means "Romanish", i.e., similiar to Roman.

_____ 7. The term Renaissance meaning rebirth takes its meaning from the Christian concept of reincarnation.

_____ 8. During the Renaissance a type and style of building developed which in England is called Georgian and in America Colonial.

_____ 9. Byzantium, Constantinople, and Istanbul are successive names for the same city.

_____10. Baroque style was developed and used by the church to dramatize the liturgy of Christianity through environments of bold contrasts of light and shadow, striking ornate forms, sculpture and painting.

_____11. There are Gothic motifs on Brooklyn Bridge.

_____12. The Gothic cathedral often took centuries to build.

_____13. The frieze in the Doric order comes between the cornice and the architrave.

_____14. Egyptian architecture was modest in size compared to Greek architecture.

_____15. Stone lintels cannot bear as much weight as wood lintels.

_____16. The Parthenon is one of the best known of Greek temples.

_____17. The tympanum is an arch-shaped recessed space over a doorway in Gothic architecture.

_____18. Organic architecture in the twentieth century is identified with the work of Buckminster Fuller.

_____19. Severe vertical and horizontal lines are characteristic of international style architecture of the twentieth century.

_____20. The modules of a geodesic dome and of an international style building are the same shape but a different size.

_____21. Reinforced concrete is the medium used in the Sydney Opera House (page 3 in the text).

_____22. Adobe is made from clay dried in the sun.

_____23. Glass brick are transparent.

_____24. Buildings can be made taller with a round arch than with a pointed arch.

_____25. Two short barrel vaults are crossed at right angles to make a groin vault.

CONCEPTS

Match the following:

_____ 1. ka

_____ 2. hypostyle

_____ 3. pylon

_____ 4. drum

_____ 5. triforum

_____ 6. flower columns

_____ 7. pendentive

_____ 8. bud columns

_____ 9. ziggurat

_____10. clerestory

_____11. apse

_____12. transept

_____13. nave

_____14. narthex

_____15. ambulatory

(a) A massive gateway covering the front of a building.

(b) A place built to walk in.

(c) Smaller at the top than at the bottom.

(d) A semicircular space covered with a half-dome at the east (or altar) end of a church.

(e) Dependent upon the human body, even mummified, for its life.

(f) The cross arms of a church, at right angles to the nave.

(g) A tube-shaped extension under a dome to lift it so that visually it clears the body of the building below.

(h) An outside porch or inside vestibule of a church, a transition from the world outside to the holy place inside.

(i) Mud-brick stepped pyramids with ramps leading from tier to tier.

(j) The long central area flanked by aisles with the altar at one end and the entrance at the other in a basilican plan church.

(k) A kind of hall in which rows of columns support the roof.

(l) A triangular part of a sphere that fills the space between a round dome and a square supporting structure.

(m) Has capitals like an inverted ball.

(n) The wall space in the nave in a Gothic church between the sloping roof and the vaulting of the aisle.

(o) A story above a larger story below with side windows to permit light to enter into the central space(s) of the building.

APPLICATION OF CONCEPTS

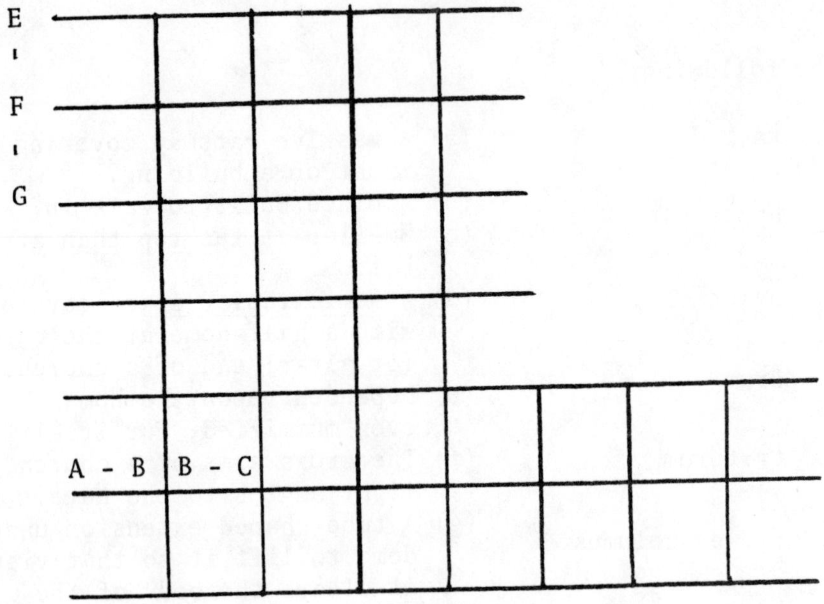

E
F
G
A - B B - C

The abstract diagram above represents a building using "skeleton" construction seen in profile. The horizontal lines represent floors, the vertical lines the steel columns supporting the floors.

______ 1. What architectural principle is illustrated at section A-B of the second floor?
   1. the round arch
   2. the corbel arch
   3. the cantilever
   4. the post and lintel
   5. none of the above

______ 2. What architectural principle is illustrated at section B-C of the second floor?
   1. the round arch
   2. the corbel arch
   3. the cantilever
   4. the post and lintel
   5. none of the above

______ 3. The use of a structural steel frame
   1. forces the builder to use his walls to support weight
   2. permits the builder to use a wall merely as a screen if he wishes

3. allows the builder to depend upon the arch principle for support of weight
4. requires the architect to use a cantilever system of construction
5. eliminates the need for post and lintel construction in architecture

______ 4. Which of the following seems to you the least practical possibility for the spaces E-F, F-G, etc, between the ends of the floors. They could be
1. filled in with a brick wall
2. left open for balconies with bannisters
3. covered with a tinted glass curtain wall
4. covered with environmental, reflective glass
5. covered with attractive grill work

______ 5. If the tower on this building (the tallest part) were extended upward, the building would resemble most
1. The Everson Museum (Figure 1-1, page 2)
2. The John Hancock Building (Figure 4-17, page 106)
3. Lever House (Figure 4-15, page 102)
4. The United Nations General Assembly Building (Figure 13-14, page 325)
5. The Inland Steel Building (Figure 13-23, page 325)

______ 6. In general, Greek architects were most concerned with
1. the problem of good exterior design
2. interior appointments and comfort
3. the creation of impressively-large buildings
4. getting a roof line that matched the feeling of the surrounding area
5. the quality of stone that would lend itself best to large-scale construction

______ 7. Which of the following statements is NOT true of a Greek temple ?
1. It contains a central room called the cella
2. It has porticos on both front and rear
3. It is built on a foundation called the pediment
4. It has rows of columns around all four sides called colonnades
5. It has corrections for optical illusions made possible by short bulges or entases in the columns and entablatures

______ 8. The "Porch of the Maidens" is a part of
1. the temple of Zeus at Olumpia
2. the Athena Nike on the Acropolis
3. the Erechtheum on the Acropolis
4. the Parthenon on the Acropolis
5. the Temple of Poseidon

______ 9. The Parthenon is noted for
1. a quality of vast monumentality
2. a quality of repose, proportion, rhythm, and restraint
3. the extreme complexity of the composition when seen as a geometrical solid
4. its pediment, but not for its columns which are heavy and clumsy
5. the fact that it is so old and yet so perfectly preserved

______10. The early Christian basilicas
1. had no transepts
2. were strongly vertical in their emphasis
3. could easily be extended in length, but could only be extended in width the distance the wooden beams would carry
4. are described by all of the above
5. are described by 1 and 3, but not by 2

______11. The use of barrel vaulting
1. became general among the Greeks of the Golden Age
2. had been known by the Romans in their larger building
3. demanded walls of extreme thickness to resist the stress of the roof
4. is characterized by all of the above
5. is characterized by 2 and 3, but not by 1

______12. Post-and-lintel construction
1. did not become popular before the High Renaissance
2. was exclusively a development of the Ionic order in Greece
3. was used in building the Parthenon, the Erectheum, and the Propylaea
4. was used in building the Cathedral of Chartres
5. is seen only in Oriental buildings

______13. The only completely original element of Gothic architecture was
1. groin vaults
2. flying buttresses
3. architectural sculpture
4. bell towers
5. the clerestory

______14. The Medici palace represents a stage of architecture at which
1. the old cathedrals were being converted into palaces
2. the fortress was on its way to becoming a town house

3. after the Crusades, the mosques were turned into castles
4. palaces were converted into apartment houses

_____15. In its present form St. Peter's in Rome differs from Michelangelo's plan in
1. possessing a dome
2. adhering to the pattern of the Roman basilica
3. being in the shape of a Greek cross
4. in having an elaborate ornamental facade
5. using round arches to admit more light on the sides

_____16. According to Frank Lloyd Wright, architecture
1. cannot be both enjoyable and functional
2. should be Gothic or Romanesque for colleges
3. should be the same for all altitudes
4. should harmonize with its site and surroundings so that it seems to grow naturally in them
5. should sacrifice beauty and harmony with surroundings in order that greater utility may be gained

_____17. Which of the following would Frank Lloyd Wright consider LEAST in planning a home?
1. the site of the proposed building
2. advanced technologies available for construction of the home
3. the materials available for construction of the building
4. the homes which had been built previously in the neighborhood
5. the personal needs of the individuals who were to occupy the home

_____18. Which one of the following statements is accurate?
1. Frank Lloyd Wright influenced the Internationalists in the development of their style
2. Wright's style developed out of the International Style
3. The Internationalists and Wright developed their styles independently
4. The International Style and Wright's style have nothing in common

_____19. Eclecticism in architecture is
1. the use of the Greek style for modern buildings
2. the use of external details from two or more historical styles
3. the abolition of applied ornament
4. the theory that the outside of a building should express its interior function

5. the theory that buildings should be constructed from native materials

______20. The most distinctive feature of Wright's interiors is
1. the open flow of space
2. the use of wood rather than plaster
3. the careful planning of furniture location
4. the insurance of privacy by the separation of each room from its neighbor
5. the provision of large wall surfaces for mural decoration

What historical architectural styles are represented by the three sketches below? Name the style of each and give three reasons for your choices:

1. ______________________

____

____

____

2. ______________________

____

____

____

3. ______________________

____

____

____

TWO CHURCH STYLES

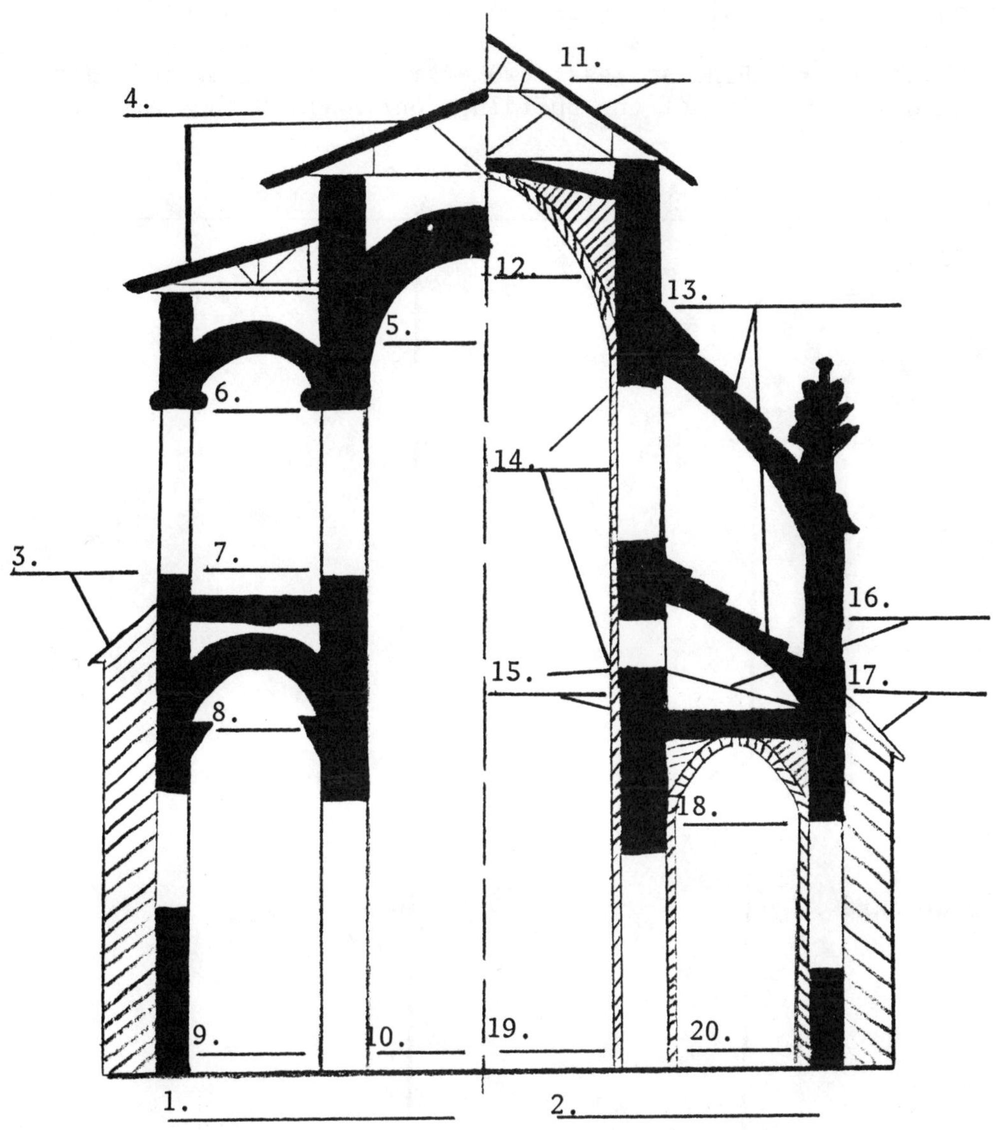

This sketch juxtaposes a half-section of two styles of churches. Label each half-section, and identify the parts by writing on each line provided one of the following terms: roof, buttress, flying buttress, loft, clerestory, triforium, round arch vault, cross arched vault, aisle, nave.

TERMS FOR ARCHITECTURAL DETAILS

Define and when possible sketch (below the term) the following architectural details. Use your text, class handouts, dictionaries, whatever. Find at least two examples of each. Indicate the name and location of the buildings on/in which they are to be found.

TERM - SKETCH	DEFINITION	EXAMPLES
1. stringcourse		
2. battlement		
3. narthex		
4. quoin		
5. mansard roof		
6. clapboard		
7. facade		
8. keystone		
9. curtain wall		

TERM - SKETCH	DEFINITION	EXAMPLES
10. cantilever		
11. fanlight		
12. ornamental balustrade		
13. cartouche		
14. coffered ceiling		
15. broken pediment		
16. engaged columns		
17. clerestory		
18. pedimented windows		
19. ornamental urns		

TERM - SKETCH	DEFINITION	EXAMPLES
20. cornerstone		
21. arcade		
22. dentil		
23. finial		
24. bay		
25. dome on drum		
26. truss		
27. crocket		
28. cupola		
29. gambrel roof		
30. gingerbread		

DISCUSSION QUESTIONS:

-1-

During the Gothic Revival in England and the United States, John Ruskin, the English author and critic, in several books urged the building of Gothic structures. His argument in The Stones of Venice (1851-1853) was that Gothic Churches had been conceived and built by good people and that therefore, they could conversely create good people from among the wicked. While this may sound either mystical or simplistic, more and more attention is now being given to the ways in which buildings affect us. Some writers go so far as to suggest that the buildings in which we live can destroy us psychologically without our being aware of what is happening.

Are you sensitive to how different buildings affect you? Would you like a room with wall paper in a design like that of Riley's Shih-li (Figure 10-2, page 240) or Vasarely's Vega (Figure 10-1, page 239)? How do you respond to long, narrow, barren corridors? Are you comfortable in rooms which have clinically clean hard plastic or metal walls and floors, as though they had been built to be sprayed out with a hose as soon as you leave. Examine your feelings about the interiors you know and be prepared to contribute to a discussion of the effects buildings have on persons working or living in them.

-2-

Buildings constructed in International Style have similar, easily recognized characteristics throughout the world - - rectangularity, skeletal frames, many stories, and extensive use of glass for exterior walls. The height makes necessary elaborate machinery such as elevators and escalators to move furniture, materials and people about inside the building. The extensive use of glass makes the interiors quite responsive to changes in the temperature and necessitates complicated climate conditioning mechanisms. In view of our dwindling energy sources and the economic and social crisis accompaning their depletion, it becomes questionable whether such buildings and the complex technology upon which they depend will continue to be practical. Discuss this issue. What practical alternatives would you suggest should the energy crisis continue to worsen?

-3-

A familiar technique of promoting a product is to associate it in advertising with a particular type of person, a particular life style, or a particular social class. Many advertisements associate a product with a particular style of interior design or with the exterior of a particular architectural style. Find and bring to class several examples. Be prepared to explain what the style is and the image of the product the producer is trying to create.

-4-

It has been said that when a chef makes a mistake on a stew he throws in a few onions; that when a surgeon makes a mistake he buries it; and that when an architect makes a mistake he plants ivy.

DOMESTIC ARCHITECTURE IN THE UNITED STATES

The text covers in some detail the major historical styles of architecture, but the discussion there is limited to buildings constructed for public purposes - - religious, governmental, and educational. We find these styles today in our public buildings, sometimes carefully followed, sometimes used eclectically (mixed with other styles) and sometimes used simply as a vague reference. During the Victorian period churches and schools were usually Gothic; banks and office buildings, classical or Renaissance, and state houses were classical or Georgian. Even factories, garages and department stores borrowed details and facades from earlier styles until modern architecture began to stress clean functional forms above decoration. This short supplement is included here to familiarize you with the way in which the historical styles discussed in the text are reflected in residential buildings.

The very earliest American domestic architecture was indigenous - - the sod hut, tepee, igloo, log cabin, and adobe shelter. These were practical, functional buildings using the materials at hand creatively, but they were relatively impermanent.

The styles of domestic architecture which were current in the colonial period were brought with them by the colonists. They are styles developed in an earlier period and a different place. That is why they are called eclectic (or borrowed). That is also why to call a building simply American Colonial is somewhat redundant and not very precise until you add "Tudor," "Georgian," "Gothic," "Dutch," or "Spanish." When Colonial is used alone, as in the Field Guide to Old-House Styles which follows, it usually refers to a very early Georgian style. The term Victorian architecture, too, simply tells us the period in which a style flourished, not what the style is.

Geography and climate have led to modifications in some traditional styles to produce new styles. For example, Georgian has been modified in the southern United States by adding wide verandas, sometimes surrounding the whole house, and two story columns to support an extended roof to provide shade for the windows below.

The study of American Domestic Architecture is thus a study of eclectic remnants from the past, some of which were once functional but are now merely decorative. It is also a study of how changing needs, changing tastes and technological developments have affected inherited styles. You are not likely to find many exact copies of early styles.

Four of the styles which the colonizers brought with them to the new country are Tudor Colonial, Georgian Colonial, Dutch Colonial, and Spanish Colonial.

The English brought with them what is now called Tudor Colonial style. Half-timbered construction was used widely in the villages of England, France, Germany and elsewhere, but it was not a formalized style; it was an elastic method of construction influenced by local tastes and materials. The method used heavy timbers and filled spaces between with plaster or rubble and clay. The exposed timbers were sometimes horizontal, sometimes diagonal trusses to support verticals. Designs varied greatly. The design which was common on houses in the Tudor Colonial style the colonists brought with them is but one. But Tudor houses had other distinctive features as the description below indicates.

England was also the source of Georgian style houses which became popular in the 18th century. These were based on the symmetry and detail of Renaissance buildings. They were sometimes relatively simple and compact as in the sketch which follows entitled "Colonial 1690-1760", or large and elaborate as in the sketch below.

The Dutch influence on domestic architecture is seen in very compact two story houses with dormers to let light into the second story. In the Eighteenth century a gambrel roof was frequently added to provide more space on the second floor.

Spanish Colonial houses were made of stucco, adobe, plaster. In form, they were large, simple, grouped masses. The walls were thick, the openings small and the roofs tile. Frequently the house enclosed an inner court. Balconies, grills, ornamental tile, and projecting timbers are often present. With modifications, this style still flourishes, especially in western and southwest portions of the United States where the thick walls, narrow windows and shaded courtyards are functional in hot climates.

On the following page we have summarized important characteristics of these four generic styles. And in the Field Guide to Old-House Styles which we have reproduced in the pages which follow, you will find a more detailed description of adaptations made of these as well as additional styles developed in later periods when there was a revival of interest in Gothic, Greek, and Italian styles of buildings.

FOUR COLONIAL STYLES OF ARCHITECTURE

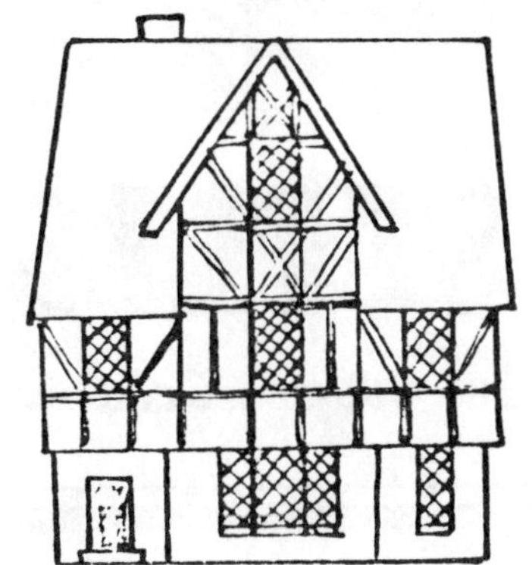

Tudor Colonial

1. Exposed beams on upper stories.
2. Low-eaved but high-gabled thatched roof design.
3. Diamond latticing of windows sometimes filled with bottle glass.
4. Second story projecting over first.
5. Stucco and dark stained beams.
6. Low beamed ceilings.

Georgian Colonial (late example)

1. Red brick with white shutters or white wood with green shutters.
2. Chimneys in pairs soaring over steep roof with dormer windows especially in the south.
3. Balustrading at gable or eaves.
4. Balanced fenestration and wings.
5. Columns often reaching two stories.
6. Renaissance ornamentation.

Dutch Colonial

1. Small modest two storied clapboard or stone. Plans may be rectangular or irregular.
2. Dormer windows in steep roof.
3. Balanced fenestration with shutters.
4. Upturned roof over veranda or porch.
5. Minimum ornamentation.
6. Some are similar to Cape Cod, but can be quite elaborate.

Spanish Colonial (late example)

1. Thick walls of stucco or local adobe material.
2. Small rectangular or arched windows without enframement. Shutters on interior sometimes.
3. Usually a low gabled red tile roof with overhanging eaves.
4. Occasional projecting timbers.
5. Iron balustraded windows.
6. Arcaded court and spiraled ornaments.

Field Guide To

OLD-HOUSE STYLES

Published by The Old-House Journal

THIS GUIDE IS DESIGNED to familiarize the reader with the architectural details of the most common old-house styles. Old houses derive their charm from the richness and variety of details that the old-time builders crafted with their hands.

EACH DETAIL BY ITSELF is subtle...it's the combining of different, related details that makes "style." Because of the subtlety of individual details, all too often they are destroyed during a remodelling. These character-destroying alterations could be better called "remuddling."

THE OUTLINE PRESENTED HERE enables you to identify the architectural heritage of most American old houses. Very few houses represent a "pure" style. Designers were continually trying out different combinations of traditional details. Also, many houses have been altered during the years in keeping with the latest fad. Today you're likely to find Colonial houses with Victorian additions...and Victorian houses with Colonial Revival additions. Once having mastered a few basic principles, however, your eye will begin to discern what is original to a house, and what has been added—or removed—in keeping with the latest fashion.

IT IS HOPED that a greater appreciation of architectural detail will inspire more old-house owners to preserve and restore their houses in harmony with the original intent of the builder. It is relatively easy for the home craftsman to preserve detail that is already in place. But it is difficult and/or expensive to replace architectural detail once it has been thoughtlessly removed.

THE CAREFUL ATTENTION TO DETAIL that went into the construction of old houses is a cultural treasure that cannot be replaced. Keeping up an old house is keeping faith with past—and future—generations.

Colonial 1690-1760

CHARACTERISTIC DETAILS: Large central chimney; narrow clapboards; simple frames around doors and windows; few—if any—small windows (lights) around doors. Windows had numerous small panes—frequently 12 over 12. In South, similar designs were executed in brick. Few have survived without addition of wings, ells and lean-tos, and other changes in details.

Saltbox 1700-1770

CHARACTERISTIC DETAILS: The roof line defines the saltbox. It evolved from the practice of adding a lean-to on the back of a house in order to gain extra space. Sometimes a change in the angle of the back roof shows where the lean-to was added. The design became so popular that some houses were built with the long back roof as part of the original structure.

Cape Cod 1710-1830

CHARACTERISTIC DETAILS: Frame structure, one and one-half storeys high; low pitched roof; large central chimney; no dormers. Light for attic comes from windows in gable ends. To increase attic headroom, builders sometimes used a bowed ("ship's bottom") roof. Originally covered on all sides and roof with wood shingles that weathered gray. Later houses used clapboards. Three basic designs: Half House—two windows to side of front door; Three-Quarters House—two windows to one side of door and one to the other; Full Cape—two windows to each side of door.

Early Georgian 1720-1760

CHARACTERISTIC DETAILS: Symmetrical design based on Roman classicism. Set on high foundation, with emphasis on entrance bay in middle of house. Wide panelled door had row of rectangular lights in door, or transom light above. Columns or pilasters frequently framed door, with pediment above. Plain colonial eaves were replaced with cornice, often with classicial features such as dentils. When dormers were used, they had triangular pediments and were spaced symmetrically. Usually had pitched roof, sometimes hipped. Executed in brick or wood.

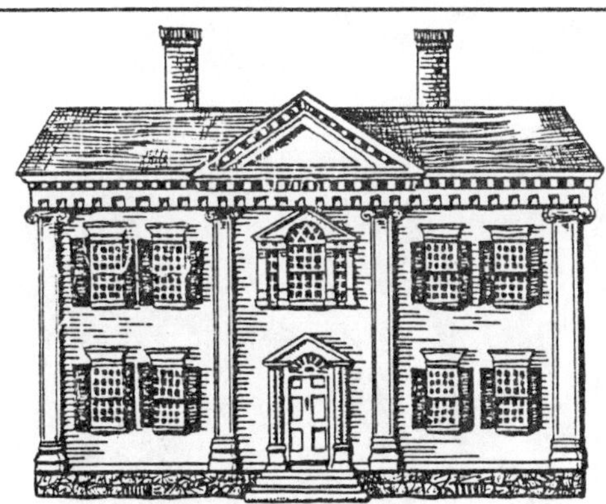

Late Georgian 1760-1780

CHARACTERISTIC DETAILS: Heavy use of classiical details...doorways surrounded with pilasters or columns, surmounted by cornice and/or pediment; semi-circular fanlight over door. Palladian (triple) window on second floor in center. Cornice on window caps. More elaborate houses would have projecting entrance pavillion topped by a pedimented gable. Use of columns and pilasters became more lavish, as did use of classical details in the cornice. Corners on masonry houses usually had stone quoins; on wood houses the quoins were often simulated in wood.

Federal 1780-1820

CHARACTERISTIC DETAILS: After the Revolution, house designers rejected much of the classical decoration of Late Georgian, but retained basic Roman symmetry. The result is often hard to distinguish from Early Georgian. Doorways retained pilasters and columns, usually topped with flat entablature. Elliptical fanlights over doors were popular. Simple frames around windows; corners unmarked by quoins or pilasters. Hipped roofs became more common, sometimes rimmed by a balustrade. Flat boarding sometimes used on exterior for a more classical effect.

Greek Revival 1815-1840

CHARACTERISTIC DETAILS: Emphasis on columns (or pilasters), capitals and low triangular gabled pediment—all to create the effect of a Greek temple. Focus shifted from the long side of the house to the gabled end. Pedimented gable appears to rest on classical entablature, which is in turn supported by columns. More elaborate homes had a columned entrance portico—especially popular in the south. Windows are strongly vertical, with six-over-six panes. Lines are simpler and cleaner than Roman-influenced Georgian.

Gothic Revival 1835-1880

CHARACTERISTIC DETAILS: Objective was to recapture the romance of medieval buildings. Emphasis was on vertical effect, achieved through multiple sharply pointed gables with slender finials at the peaks. Windows were tall and slender, sometimes topped with a lancet arch. Casement windows with leaded diamond-shaped panes were also popular. Wooden verge boards under eaves—and other decorative woodwork—was cut with medieval motifs such as trefoils, quatrefoils, gothic crosses and other pointed symbols.

Italianate 1845-1885

CHARACTERISTIC DETAILS: Designed to resemble Italian country villas. Asymmetrical arrangement of squared shapes and lines. Flat or low-pitched roofs; extended eaves that emphasize deep and heavy cornices set with ornate brackets. Plain horizontal decorative bands. Tall, slender windows, some with rounded heads. Square-pillared porches; semi-circular arches; tall square tower or cupola; balconies set on stout, ornate brackets.

Mansard 1855-1885

CHARACTERISTIC DETAILS: Easily recognized by highly distinctive roof line. Extra living space on top floor is gained by bending out the slope of the roof. The Mansard roof is pierced by a dazzling variety of dormer windows: Rectangular, pointed, gabled, round—even double rows of dormers. Dormers often ornamented with pediments and console buttresses. Slate often used on steep slope of roof. Also called Second Empire style.

Queen Anne 1875-1900

CHARACTERISTIC DETAILS: A picturesque massing of variety of shapes and textures in a non-symmetrical composition. Gables, dormers, chimneys, round turrets and oriel windows used freely. Porches feature delicately turned spindlework; horizontal decorative bands. Brick chimneys usually fluted, with large caps. In brick, terra cotta used for decoration. In wood, smooth boards are mixed with clapboards and shingles for variety.

Carpenter Gothic 1870-1910

CHARACTERISTIC DETAILS: Sawn wood ornament at peaks of gables, in verge boards under gables, and on porches. Even porch railings and aprons sometimes have sawn patterns. Designs may be holes and slots cut out of wood—or pieces applied to other boards. Sawn brackets appear on porch posts and on cornice. Ornament depends more on whim of the carpenter-builder than on any architectural style. This type of ornament also called "gingerbread."

Federal Italianate Mansard Greek Revival Queen Anne

CITY ROW HOUSES: Although they had only the front surface to work with, designers captured the essence of various styles in row houses... Doorways with fanlights and sidelights in Federal; Arched windows and heavy brackets on Italianate; Using the Mansard roof with countless dormer variations; Dentilled cornice with classical columns and architrave on Greek Revival doorway; Dazzling variety of gables, bays, textures and horizontal banding on Queen Anne.

This *Field Guide to Old-House Styles* was published by *The Old House Journal Company* (199 Berkeley Place, Brooklyn, N.Y. 11217) in 1974, and is copyrighted. It is reproduced here by special permission of the publishers.

AMERICAN DOMESTIC ARCHITECTURE

A Book:

Daniel M. Mendelowitz, A History of American Art. New York: Holt, Rinehart and Winston, Inc., paperback edition, 1973.

This volume is a well-illustrated introduction to the visual arts in the United States. The portions dealing with architecture are excellent. An important feature is that while the arts other than architecture are less exhaustively dealt with than in some specialized books, they are here integrated with the architecture in an unusually interesting and stimulating manner.

A Magazine:

The Old-House Journal is a magazine published by Old-House Journal, 199 Berekley Pl., Brooklyn, N.Y. 11217.

It contains articles on old houses, on ways of preserving them and on a multitude of other topics of interest to persons who wish to learn more about our architectural heritage. Perhaps your library subscribes. We think you will enjoy it.

The Field Guide to Old-House Styles is one of The Journal's publications. It is reproduced here by special permission. It publishes other inexpensive materials which you may wish to inquire about.

A Trust:

A National Trust for Historic Preservation was chartered by Congress in 1949 when private citizens and government leaders became increasingly alarmed at the rapidity with which monuments to our nation's past were being destroyed. Its activities at present extend to preserving old houses and other architecture. It publishes materials of interest in the study of American architecture, and a quarterly magazine. Descriptive materials and a list of publications may be obtained by writing: National Trust for Historic Preservation, 740-748 Jackson Place, N.WW., Washington, D.C.

A GUIDE FOR CRITICAL ANALYSIS OF ARCHITECTURE

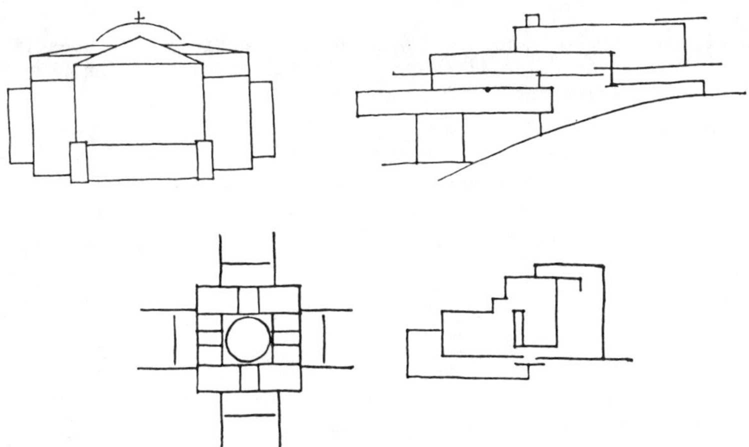

For this analysis you should choose a building you will be able to visit and study. It should be a building of some distinction and one which you will enjoy learning more about. It is suggested that you read this Guide through and review the passages in the text to which you are referred before undertaking the study.

PART ONE

In Part One you will study the building from several points of view and make informal notes in the spaces provided.

PART TWO

In Part Two you will make an over-all critique of the building. This reflective evaluation of the building and of your experiencing of it should be carefully organized as a separate essay. <u>Two thirds of the grade given will be based on Part Two</u>.

NAME OF THE BUILDING______________________________

LOCATION______________________________

ARCHITECT, IF KNOWN________________ DATE CONSTRUCTED, IF KNOWN______

NAME____________________ CLASS MEETING TIME________

ADDRESS____________________ DATE____________

ARCHITECTURE ANALYSIS NO.________

PART ONE: Informal notes on the building.

In Part One you are asked to study the building from several points of view and to make notes in the spaces provided. Formal sentences are not necessary. You may work through the various points of view in any order you choose. There will probably be more things to note under some headings than others, but you should make your coverage as complete as possible.

1. Make notes of what the building is, its purpose, function. How does it reflect values in the culture in which it emerged? (Review pages 32-33 on "Purpose" and pages 97-105 on "Function and Form" in the text.)

2. What seem to have been the "controlling" considerations of the architect? To make it serve a particular function? To make it a public expression of some kind? To make it a different, highly individual architectural creation? Some combination of these? Are the shape, function, decorative, expressive details and relation of parts well integrated? Are there climatic, geographical, period, or social-cultural influences reflected in the building? (Review pages 97-105 and 353-356 in the text.)

3. What are the mediums used? Why do you suppose they were chosen? Have they been used effectively? Explain. (Review pages 133-134 and 353-360 in the text.)

4. Describe the principles of construction used? Were they dictated by the medium? By the function? By the expressive intent? (Review pages 338-360 in the text.)

5. Indicate the characteristics of the building that relate to some particular period, geographic region, social-cultural context, or style of architecture. If you know of other buildings by the same architect or of similar buildings, you may wish to compare this building to them. (Review pages 338-363 - - especially the summary of styles on pages 361-363 - - and pages 431-432 in the text.)

6. Draw here sketches of the building in significant profiles. Include only important visual lines, and decorative, stylistic features. (See sketches of Palladio's Villa Capra and Frank Lloyd Wright's John C. Pew House on the cover of this Guide.) Make a rough sketch of the floor plan if you have access to the interior. In addition, attach a photograph or other picture of the building.

Note here any sources beyond your own observations and the text which you have used in writing your analysis of the building.

PART TWO: Critical analysis and personal perception.

In Part One you have made informal analytical notes on the building from various points of view. From your review of these and reflections on them, you are asked to in Part Two to demonstrate your personal, coherent perception of the building. Use any ideas from Part One that you think pertinent, plus additional ideas you have from reflecting on the interrelations of these. Your statement should relate personal response to objective analysis and should be more than a mere repetition of the notes you have made. It should be presented as a well-rounded, well-organized essay.

PART ONE: Answers ranked: 0 - no credit 1 - fair 2 - good 3 - excellent Highest possible score-18	PART TWO: Essay ranked: 0 - no credit 1 - fair (and multiplied 2 - good by 12) 3 - excellent Highest possible score-36	PART ONE + PART TWO for Total Score Highest possible total-54
Score	Score	Total

15 FORM IN MUSIC

CONCEPTS

Match the following:

In Binary Form

________ 1.

________ 2.

________ 3.

________ 4.

In Ternary Form

________ 5.

________ 6.

________ 7.

________ 8.

A. there are three separate sections, each of which is complete in itself.
B. there are two halves which form a unified whole, the second being the logical and necessary completion of the first.
C. the first section is not harmonically "closed," but ends on some other tone than the tonic, usually the dominant.
D. the first section is harmonically "closed" and ends on the tonic, giving a sense of completeness.
E. the same or similar thematic material is used throughout.
F. different, frequently contrasting, thematic material is used for the second section.
G. the organization is a continuous one.
H. the organization is a sectional one.

The musical forms on the left would be best represented by which of the schemes on the right?

_____ 9. Rondo

_____10. Theme & Variations

_____11. Minuet-Trio

_____12. Binary Form

A. A - B - A

B. A - B - C - D - E
   1 2 3 4

C. A - A - A - A - A

D. A - B - A - C - A

E. A - A - B - B

How would you put the forms on the right together to make a typical classical symphony?

_____13. First Movement

_____14. Second Movement

_____15. Third Movement

_____16. Fourth Movement

A. Rondo

B. Minuet-Trio

C. Theme and Variations

D. Sonata Form (sometimes called sonata-allegro form or first movement form)

Match the following:

_____17. Oratorio

_____18. Passion

_____19. Cantata

A. A shorter and usually less dramatic form than the other items named in this section.

B. An unstaged opera, usually on a sacred subject, making much use of recitative.

C. Has as its subject the events of the last week in the life of Christ.

Match the following:

_____20. Opera

_____21. Suite

_____22. Symphony

_____23. Passacalia

_____24. Requiem

A. A sonata for orchestra

B. A collection of dances in the same key

C. A drama set entirely to music

D. A name given to a mass for the dead which omits the Credo and Gloria

E. A type of variation in triple rhythm in which a bass melody is repeated over and over below varying harmonies, timbres and dynamics.

The Common or Ordinary of the Mass:

_____25. Kyrie	A. A statement of belief: "I believe in..."
_____26. Gloria	B. A prayer for mercy: "Lord have mercy upon us; Christ have mercy upon us; Lord have mercy upon us."
_____27. Credo	C. A prayer beginning, "O Lamb of God, that takest away the sins of the world, have mercy..."
_____28. Sanctus	D. A song of praise, beginning "Glory be to God on high, and in earth peace, good will to men..."
_____29. Agnus Dei	E. A song of praise beginning "Holy holy, holy, Lord God of hosts."
_____30. Benedictus	F. Really the last part of the Sanctus, but usually treated musically as a separate number, beginning "Blessed is he, who cometh in the name of the Lord."

APPLICATION OF CONCEPTS

STROPHIC AND CONTINUOUS COMPOSITIONS

The through composed art song is illustrated by Schubert's "Erlkonig" (The Erl King), in German and English, on pages 388-389 in the text. But you must hear this song performed to appreciate how effectively Schubert has dramatized the story with his musical setting of it.

We have included here a strophic popular song which has evolved from an art song by Jean Paul Martini (known as Martini el Tedesco). The music for the first section of the art song, <u>Plairsir d' Amor</u>, is quoted on page 367 of the text. You will be able to sing the popular song and you should compare the music with the music for the art song.

FROM ART SONG TO FOLK SONG
Plaisir d'Amour

The song "Plaisir d'Amour" quoted on page 367 of the text as an example of ternary song form is almost the only remembered composition of Jean Paul Martini Il Tedesco. Martini was a German opera composer who adopted France as his home. It was there that he achieved his fame as a composer and thus became known as Martini Il Tedesco (Martini the German).

This pleasant, singable melody has passed in the folksong repertoire, and the words have been added to and changed as it has passed from singer to singer in oral tradition. The melody has undergone less change. (You may be familiar with a version recorded by Joan Baez). The popular version omits the middle section of the part quoted in the text and thereby changes the piece from a through-composed art song into a strophic folk song. The first section of the music in the text is repeated over and over for each stanza.

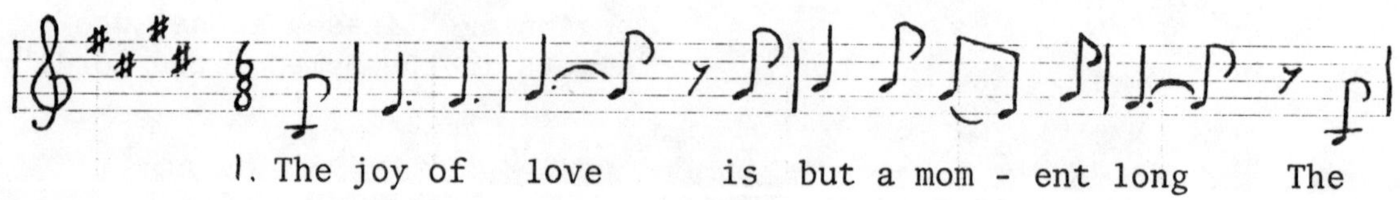
6/8
1. The joy of love is but a mom - ent long The

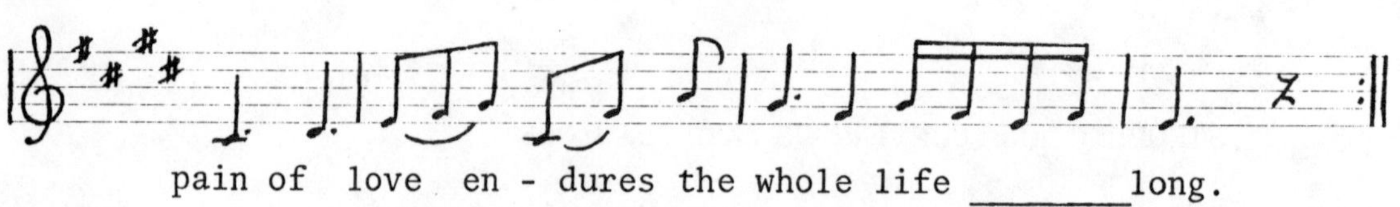
pain of love en - dures the whole life ________long.

2. Your eyes kissed mine, I saw love in them shine
You brought me heaven right then when your eyes kissed mine.

3. My love loves me, and many a wonder I see
A rainbow shines in my window, my love loves me.

4. But now he's gone, as dream fades into dawn;
Still the words stay locked in my heart,
"My love loves me."

The passage quoted in the text is only the first section of the song and the passage quoted here is only the first section of that. The complete art song can be found in the <u>Fireside Book of Love Songs</u> edited by Bradford Boni and Norman Lloyd (New York: Simon and Schuster, 1954), pages 165-171.

THEME AND VARIATIONS

This is one of the easiest forms to follow in listening. In Chapter 7 on the Mediums of Music we included three pieces in this form to help you learn to identify instruments with the sounds they make:

> Britten's _Variations and Fugue on a Theme from Purcell_
> Ravel's _Bolero_
> Schubert's _Fourth Movement from the Trout Quintet_

You will want to go back and review these and listen to them again as examples of this form.

The example of Theme and Variations in Chapter 15 of the text, pages 370-372, is the First Movement from Mozart's Sonata K331. After you have listened to it, you will want to hear the three additional examples which follow.

Haydn's _Surprise Symphony_, Second Movement

The "slow movement," of this symphony, as second movements are sometimes called, is pleasant to listen to and easy to follow. The theme which is played twice before the first variation is a simple folk tune, one to which we sometimes sing the alphabet. The "surprise" which gives the symphony its title, occurs in a very sudden loud chord which ends the second playing of the theme.

To appreciate the effect of this chord we must imagine an eighteenth century audience of sedate, bewigged ladies and gentlemen sitting quietly, listening attentively to the graceful, delicate, melody; and we must remember that in classical symphonies the dynamics of a movement were normally constant throughout. We quote here the theme and provide a description of the four variations.

1. The first variation repeats the main theme with counterpoint by the violins.

2. In the second variation, the eighth notes are changed to sixteenths, with a "bouncing" effect. This variation starts very loud and becomes softer. It is repeated in a minor key. The two halves are treated differently. The opening measures of this variation are quoted on page 244 of your text.

3. The strings and woodwinds play together while the flute sings a new melody.

4. This variation uses large chords and a broad swinging rhythm with many scale-like passages.

Handel's, "The Harmonious Blacksmith"

In Handel's <u>Harpsichord Suite in E Major</u>, which is usually known under the name "The Harmonious Blacksmith", there is a theme and five variations. The binary theme quoted above is serene and tranquil, even if it does sound a bit like a blacksmith beating on his anvil. In all five variations the pace remains the same, but the number of tones to a measure is increased each time the melody is repeated. Because each variation is increasingly complex and makes greater demands on the virtuosity of the harpsichordist, one has a sense of climax as the final variation is reached.

Brahms' *Variations on a Theme by Haydn*

This is a very frequently played piece and you are perhaps familar with the theme, but the chances are that you have not listened to it for its formal structure and have not, therefore, appreciated the skill with which Brahms turns it an impressive orchestral composition.

Johannes Brahms, VARIATIONS ON A THEME BY HAYDN

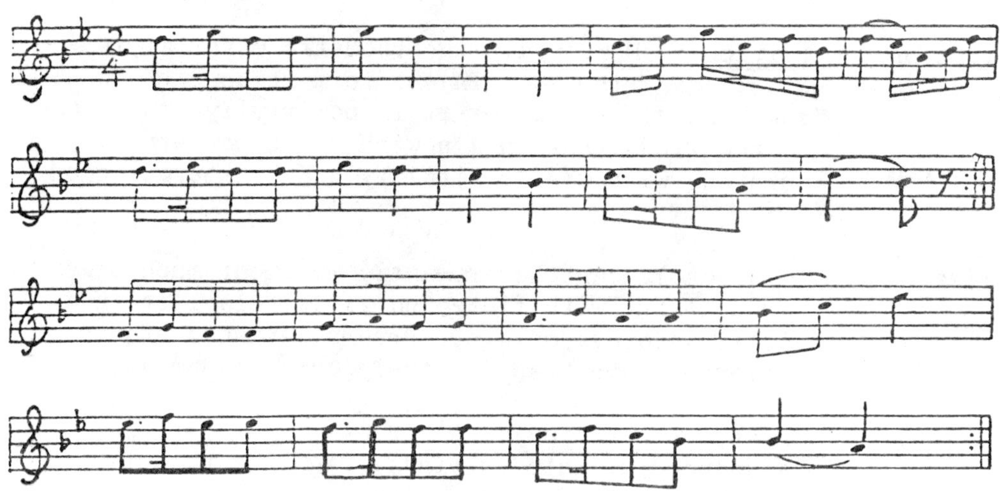

The Haydn theme quoted above is called the Saint Anthony Chorale, very likely because of some religious association antedating even Haydn's use of it. The tune in quatrain form (AABA) is delivered at once with delightful simplicity by oboes and clarinets with bassoons, horns, and double-basses defining the duple rhythm.

Variation 1: (*Poco piu animato*): Two contrasting melodic lines run in the counterpoint against the basic theme which you hear in woodwinds and in brasses. The strings enter with an inversion of the A theme.

Variation 2: (*Piu vivace*): The orchestra is divided roughly into antithetical statements with bold sharp contrasts in rhythm and dynamics.

Variation 3: (*Con moto*): Like a little romantic song in the night, gentle-voiced, a little timid perhaps, and full of sentiment.

Variation 4: (Andante con moto): Oboe and horn, in octaves, begin the melody over pizzicato bass, accomplishing a bizarre tone color curiously at contrast with the string accompaniment. Later the melody is assigned to the strings, mostly in their lower register.

Variation 5: (Vivace): This is a flippant distortion of Haydn's quasi religious tune. It is most irreverently tossed about, with shining fragments scattered throughout the orchestra.

Variation 6: (Vivace): Here again the thematic material is widely distributed. In one form it appears in low basses, in another it is powerfully projected by the winds, but in a new rhythmic pattern bursting with virile vitality and boisterous good humor.

Variation 7: (Grasioso): Another romantic movement much like his Lullaby, with flute and viola, clarinet and violin as protagonists. Brahms lavishes exquisite tenderness upon many a lovely curving phrase.

Variation 8: (Presto non troppo): An inversion of the theme is sounded by muted strings. Against them is brought a colorful combination of piccolo, clarinet and bassoon.

Finale (Andante): This movement begins with a passacaglia which is a form of theme and variations in which the theme always remains in the bass. The first five measure figure of the Haydn theme is used as a ground bass in the double-basses, serene and dominating in spite of the exciting variations piled above it in other sections of the orchestra. There is a powerful dialogue between strings and woodwinds, yet the majestic basses continue their solemn and insistent repetition. Finally the ground-bass becomes contagious among the strings. A superb climax is developed with a final outpouring of the basic theme by the entire orchestra.

MINUET AND TRIO

After you have listened to the Minuet and Trio from, Mozart's Eine Kleine Nacht music on pages 375 and 376 of the text, you should be able to follow most pieces in this form. Unlike other movements of a symphony in which the form is not designated, Minuet and Trio is almost always named as the form of the piece. In classical symphonies, those of Mozart and Haydn for example, the third movement is almost always in Minuet and Trio form. You will have no difficulty in finding examples to listen to.

Beethoven used a Scherzo (literally "joke") rather than the traditional Minuet for symphonic third movements and many nineteenth century composers followed him in doing so. The form remained unchanged - - i.e., that is scherzo-trio-scherzo. Again you will find the name of the form on recordings and scores. Compare the two labels of recordings in this book - one of a symphony by Mozart, the other of one by Beethoven.

FUGUE

The exposition of Bach's Little Fugue in G Minor is quoted on pages 374-375 of the text. You will certainly want to hear this piece and we strongly suggest that you hear it in the Stokowski transcription for orchestra. Purists are sometimes critical of transcriptions of a composition from the music medium the composer chose to another music medium. However, in this instance and in other instances where Bach's organ works have been transcribed for orchestra, it should be remembered that the organ was, in the beginning, and continues to be, a kind of "toy orchestra" with pipes cleverly designed to imitate flutes, trumpets, strings and other instruments. If you examine the stops on the keyboards of an organ you will see that they are so labeled.

To help you follow your listening we have included a chart indicating the instruments which play the variations of the fugue. Doing this will give you additional exercise in learning to recognize the timbre of the various instruments of the orchestra.

Bach's **Little Fugue**

Stokowski Orchestration

S—Subject
C—Counter Subject
P—Pedal Point
E—Episode
T—Stretto

Measures	1-5	6-11	12-16	17-21	22-24	25-32	33-40	41-45	46-49	50-55	56-62	63-68
	First Entrance	Second Entrance	Third Entrance	Fourth Entrance	Episode	Fifth Entrance	Sixth Entrance	Seventh Entrance	Episode	Eighth Entrance	Stretto	Ninth Entrance
	Exposition				Development							
Flutes								P				P
Oboes	S	C	C	P								P
English Horn		S	C	C								P
Clarinets						S						P
Bassoons			S	C		P						
Bass Clarinet				S								
Trumpets												S
French Horns							P					S
Trombones												S
Tuba						P						S
Harp											T	
First Violins					E	C	C	C	E	S	T	C
Second Violins					E	C	C	C	E	S	T	C
Violas					E				E	C	T	C
Cellos							S	C	E	P	T	C
Bass Viols								S		C		

THE INSTRUMENTAL SONATA, THE SYMPHONY, AND THE CONCERTO

In spite of the explanation in the text, the term sonata is likely to cause some confusion because it has different meanings in different contexts. A history of the term may clarify the different meanings.

Originally, sonata meant simply a piece which was "sounded" on an instrument, in contrast to cantata, a piece which was sung. Today, used alone, it has come to mean a multimovement piece for one or more instruments following a general set order of movements. Thus we have sonatas for piano, for violin and piano, for flute and piano, etc. A symphony is a sonata for full orchestra. A concerto is a sonata for one or more solo instruments and orchestra. Instrumental quartets and quintets are sonatas for the number of instruments indicated. These are all multimovement pieces of three or four sections or movements.

This is simple enough. The confusion comes about because the first movement of all these multimovement compositions is almost aways in one form and that form is technically called sonata allegro form. And sonata allegro frequently gets shortened in writing to sonata, the identical name for the long multimovement form of which it is only the first movement. Which of the two is meant can only be determined from the context. To avoid this confusion, because the first movement of the multimovement sonata is almost always a sonata allegro, the form has sometimes been called simply First Movement form. (This shortening of long technical terminology is similar to that which led to our referring to the pianoforte, the instrument which was the successor of the harpsichord and can play both loud and soft, in a shortened form, simply as the piano.)

In listening to the sections of the multimovement sonata, the summary below may help you determine their musical form. A movement may be in any of the forms outlined at the left. The questions at the right should help you determine which of the forms you are listening to.

GUIDE FOR LISTENING TO COMPOSITIONS IN SONATA FORM

Is there an introduction of some kind before the first important theme is heard (opening chords, an introductory passage, a prelude, overture)? What is the purpose of this material? What is its relation to what follows it?

Does the title indicate that the composer is following a traditional organization? (First movement form, fugue, rondo, etc.) How much of the indicated organization are you able to follow as you hear the music? If you get lost, where?

THEME AND VARIATIONS A, A^1, A^2, A^3, etc.	Is the piece made up of a theme repeated over and over in various rhythms, keys, with different harmonies, textures, etc.? After the theme is stated, how many variations are there? Try to determine in your listening what is done to the original theme in the various variations. Which seem most effective? Why?
RONDO A B A C A D A, etc.	
Main Theme	How many times is the principal or first theme repeated in the piece?
Alternating Themes	What is the nature of the alternating themes? Do they contrast in any way (mood, rhythm, etc.) with the principal theme? As you listen to the piece, can you indicate the order of theme by assigning a letter of the alphabet to each theme in order of appearance?
FUGUE	
Exposition	Characterize the subject as it is heard in single voice in the exposition. How many entries of the subject are there in the exposition? Can you list the order of entry (soprano, alto, etc.)?
Development	Can you count the entries of the complete subject in the development (middle entries Can you identify the nature of any of the other developmental devices uses - - augmentation, figure development, inversio etc.?

MINUET-TRIO FORM

A	Minuet A A B a B a	What is the nature of the theme in the opening and closing sections? Is it lyric and graceful like the classical minuets? Or is there an abruptness, involving surprise, whim, or bustling humor, like the scherzo?
B	Trio C C D c D c or C C D C D C	Does the trio section standing between the opening and closing sections contrast with or simply continue the mood of these sections?
A	Minuet A B a	

FIRST MOVEMENT FORM (Sonata allegro)

Exposition Theme A Theme B	Can you distinguish in your listening between the thematic material and transitional material? Try to characterize the first theme, the second theme. The exposition is sometimes repeated.
Development	What are some of the more important methods which the composer has used in developing the materials set forth in the Exposition? (Changes in dynamics, harmony, accompaniment, rhythm? Contrapuntal treatment? Combinations of themes? Figure development?)
Recapitulation	How exact is the restatement of the first and second themes of the Exposition? Is there a coda? What is its nature?

It should, of course, be understood that as with all art traditions and forms that have evolved with various composers and artists using, adapting, changing them, there are no once-and-for-all-time rules as to what a sonata should contain, no unchanging, specified order of forms for the various movements. Nonetheless there are some generalizations which will hold in <u>most</u> cases.

The SYMPHONY and INSTRUMENTAL SONATA use the forms above in this order:

First Movement: First Movement Form (i.e. Sonata Allegro Form).
Second Movement: Usually slow but in any form.
Third Movement: Minuet-Trio Form or Scherzo-Trio Form.
Fourth Movement: Usually Rondo Form but may be any form and usually fast.

The CONCERTO is like the symphony but with these differences:

1. The exposition of the first Movement instead of being repeated is written through twice: first in abbreviated form for Orchestra with the first and second themes in the tonic key and then in full form for solo instrument and orchestra with the second theme in the dominant key. Or if the first theme is in a minor key, the second theme is usually in the relative major key. For example, if theme A is in E minor, theme B will often be in G major.

2. Near the end of the recapitulation of the First Movement there is usually a cadenze - - a passage in which the orchestra does not play and the solo instrument plays technically difficult material to display to advantage the virtuosity of the solo performer and the capabilities and beauty of the instrument. Cadenzas were originally improvised spontaneously by the performer on themes of the movement. Now they are usually composed, but a free, uninhibited improvisational style is still used.

3. In the concerto the minuet-trio or scherzo, which is usually the third movement of symphonies and instrumental sonatas, is omitted. Thus, the Concerto usually has only three movements.

4. The last movement, whether third or fourth, is usually, as in the symphony, in Rondo Form and is designed to show the brillance and virtuosity of the solo instrument.

FIRST MOVEMENT FORM

Sonata allegro form is called First Movement Form because it is almost invariably the form of the first movement of a symphony, concerto, and instrumental sonata. This form is illustrated in the text with the first movement of Mozart's _Eine Kleine Nacht Music_ on pages 378-383. The exposition of this movement is quite typical of classical symphonies, but the development section is much shorter than usual. To extend your experience with the form we suggest that you listen to the first movements of Mozart's Symphony in G Minor and Beethoven's Symphony No. 5 in C Minor. These are not only considered among the greatest symphonies of these composers, but the two themes in the exposition of each contrasts sufficiently to enable you to identify them and to follow what happens to them in the development sections. The themes of the exposition of both are quoted below.

EXPOSITION

Theme A

Transitional Passage

Theme B

EXPOSITION

Theme A

Symphony No. 5 in C minor
First movement

Ludwig van Beethoven
German (1770-1827)

Theme B

THE MASS

Several masses are mentioned in your text and there are literally hundreds of others. They vary greatly as they express the emotions and feelings aroused in the individual composer by the text of this ritual of the Church. Because the text is known to the intended audience, great liberties can be taken in setting it in order to generate music which is beautiful, appropriate, and expressive of the composer's feelings. A single syllable may be repeated many, many times to fit the demands of the music, or a single significant word, embroidered and embellished, may become the basis for a complete section of the music. An analogy may be drawn with the colorful illumination of holy texts by medieval artists. The illuminations were not simply to delight the eye of man but to delight God whose "word" was being honored and glorified.

Because it is beautiful and short we are recommending for your listening The Mass in G of the 20th Century French composer Francis Poulenc (1899-1963), and have included the Latin text and an English translation. You will notice that the Credo which is a part of most masses is not set in this one. The text is, of course the same for all masses and you can use the translation given here to listen to other masses as well.

TEXT FOR THE POULENC, MASS IN G

I. KYRIE

Kyrie eleison.	Lord, have mercy upon us.
Christe eleison.	Christ, have mercy upon us.
Kyrie eleison.	Lord, have mercy upon us.

II. GLORIA

Gloria in excelsis Deo.	Glory in God in the highest.
Et in terra pax hominibus bonae voluntatis.	And on earth peace to men of good will.
Laudamus te.	We praise Thee.
Benedicimus te.	We bless Thee.
Adoramus te.	We adore Thee.
Glorificamus te.	We glorify Thee.
Gratias agimus tibi propter magnam gloriam tuam.	We give Thee thanks for Thy great glory.
Domine Deus, Rex caelestis. Deus Pater omnipotens.	O Lord God, Heavenly King, God the Father almighty.
Domine Fili unigenite Jesu Christe.	O Lord Jesus Christ, the only-begotten Son.
Domini Deus, Agnus Dei, Filius Patris.	O Lord God, Lamb of God, Son of the Father.
Qui tollis peccata mundi, miserere nobis.	Who takest away the sins of the world, have mercy upon us,
Qui tollis peccata mundi, suscipe deprecationem nostram.	Who takest away the sins of the world, receive our prayer.
Qui sedes ad dexteram Patris, miserere nobis.	Who sittest at the right of the Father, have mercy on us.
Quoniam tu solus sanctus	For Thou only art holy.
Tu solus Dominus.	Thou only art Lord.
Tu solus Altissimus, Jesu Christe	Thou only, O Jesus Christ, art most high,
Cum Sancto Spiritu, in gloria Dei Patris.	Together with the Holy Ghost, in the glory of God the Father.
Amen.	Amen.

(Credo comes here in most Masses)

III. SANCTUS

Sanctus, Sanctus, Sanctus Dominus Deus Sabaoth.	Holy, Holy, Holy, Lord God of hosts.
Pleni sunt caeli et terra gloria tua.	Heaven and earth are full of Thy glory.
Hosanna in excelsis.	Hosanna in the highest.

IV. BENEDICTUS

Benedictus qui venit in nomine Domini.	Blessed is He that cometh in the name of the Lord.
Hosanna in excelsis.	Hosanna in the highest.

V. AGNUS DEI

Agnus Dei, qui tollis peccata mundi: miserere nobis.	O Lamb of God, Who takest away the sins of the world, have mercy upon us.
Agnus Dei, qui tollis peccata mundi: dona nobis pacem.	O Lamb of God, Who takest away the sins of the world, grant us peace.

DISCUSSION QUESTIONS:

-1-

The opening section of sonata allegro form, the opening section of a fugue, and the opening scenes of a narrative plot are all called the exposition. Explain in sufficient detail to make the analogy clear what these have in common.

-2-

Some people insist that absolute music is a pure art and that all extra-musical associations generated by it are extraneous and hindrances to enjoying it for itself.

Notwithstanding, other people have often observed that sonata-allegro structure is similar throughout to that of a literary plot. The exposition is like the exposition of a play or novel: the introduction of the two contrasting themes is like the initial exposition of the conflicting forces in the literary forms. In the development the materials are treated so as to create contrast, conflict, tension, suspense, a climax as in an actual plot. Finally in the recapitulation, the themes return in their original form, suggesting the happy or at least logical ending of the play or novel.

What are the values and dangers of this analogy? Does it provide a framework within which one has realistic expectancies of what will follow what? Does it encourage irresponsible projection of a story into pure music? State your position on this issue from personal experience.

REVIEW EXERCISE

Now that you have become familiar with some basic music terminology, you can learn much about the music you are going to hear from information on concert programs or on record labels. The two labels shown here are typical ones. (1) What is the form of the piece on the Columbia label ______________? (2) Is it a typical example of this form or does it depart from it? ______________ (3) The first movement is marked Allegro con brio which means that it will be played ______________. (4) The second movement, sometimes called "the slow movement" is marked Andante con moto which means that it will be played ______________ . (5) The third movement is a ______________ and will be played ______________. (6) The 4th Movement, the ______________ will be played in the same tempo and mood. (7) Even if you do not know the dates of Beethoven and of Mozart, what on the label would lead you to think that Beethoven's Symphony No. 5 is a later work than that of Mozart? (8) ______________ Describe the tempo you expect to hear in each of the movements of the Mozart on the Angel label: (9) 1st Movement: ______________ (10) 2nd Movement: ______________ (11) 3rd Movement: ______________ (12) 4th Movement: ______________ Since these seem to be typical examples of the large multimovement form represented, what would you expect to be the form of both 1st Movements? (13) ______________ of both 3rd Movements? (14) ______________ How do these two Movements differ? (15) ______________

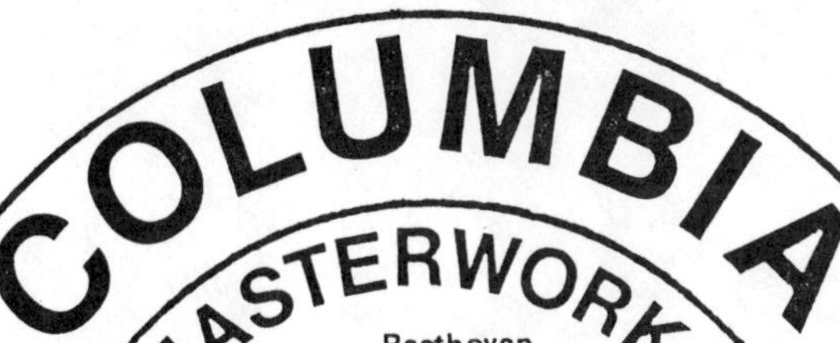

Beethoven
SYMPHONY NO. 5
IN C MINOR, Op. 67
BRUNO WALTER conducting the
PHILHARMONIC SYMPHONY ORCHESTRA
OF NEW YORK

ML 4790 (x"Lp" 15237)

First Movement: Allegro con brio
Second Movement: Andante con moto
Third Movement: Scherzo (Allegro)
Fourth Movement: Finale (Allegro)

SIDE 1

STEREO
S. 38183

MOZART
SYMPHONY NO. 40 IN G MINOR, K. 550
(1) - First Movement: Molto Allegro
(2) - Second Movement: Andante
(3) - Third Movement: Minuet (Allegretto) & Trio
(4) - Fourth Movement: Finale (Allegro assai)
THE PHILHARMONIA ORCHESTRA
conducted by
OTTO KLEMPERER

16 ORGANIZATION IN LITERATURE AND THE COMBINED ARTS

CONCEPTS

Complete the following by writing in the correct words.

1. The necessary parts of plot are (1) an exposition, (2)__________ __________, (3)__________, (4) a climax, (5)__________ and (6)__________.

2. Two ballets with music by Tchaikovsky are (7)__________ and (8)__________.

3. Drama and opera in addition to being auditory arts are (9)__________ arts. Dance is a (10)__________ art and since it usually is accompanied by musical or percussion instruments is an (11)__________ art.

4. Three ballets with music by Stravinsky are (12)__________, (13)__________ and (14)__________.

5. The two reasons that Nijinsky gave for insisting that all dancers in The Afternoon of a Faun face front with head and feet in profile were (15)__________ and (16)__________.

6. Recalling material from Chapter 15, the difference between The Nutcracker and The Nutcracker Suite is (17)__________ __________.

Dance

In the left hand spaces write five characteristics of classical ballet and in the spaces to the right, write five contrasting characteristics of modern dance.

CLASSICAL BALLET	MODERN DANCE
____________________	____________________
____________________	____________________
____________________	____________________
____________________	____________________
____________________	____________________

Opera

Match the following words with the phrases which explain their association with opera:

____ 1. aria	(1)	A drama that is sung
____ 2. ballet	(2)	A type of musical declamation that follows the natural inflections of speech
____ 3. opera	(3)	A solo song--a lyric moment in the action
____ 4. libretto	(4)	A small vocal group consisting of three or more voices
____ 5. recitative	(5)	A large vocal group
____ 6. ensemble	(6)	An opera with spoken dialogue
____ 7. orchestra	(7)	A musical phrase assigned to a character in an opera
____ 8. chorus	(8)	The instrumental accompanying body which also functions independently in the overture, interludes, etc.
____ 9. comic opera	(9)	A component that provides the diversion of the dance
____ 10. leit motive	(10)	The text

Film

Choose the correct answer and place the number in the space provided.

____ 1. Among the following, which is primarily responsible for a film's excellence, once a promising story has been chosen?
(1) script writer (2) film editor (3) director
(4) actors (5) cameraman

____ 2. Of the following, which is not considered among the great directors?
(1) John Ford (2) Ingmar Bergman (3) Jean Renoir
(4) Jonathan Edwards (5) Federico Fellini

____ 3. A novel, a movie, and a painting are alike in that they all
(1) depend upon their creator's judgment in selection
(2) tell a story
(3) must convey a moral message
(4) are primarily meant for large circulation
(5) have received their greatest achievements in the United States.

____ 4. The distinguishing thing about the movies as an art form is
(1) photography in color (2) flow of visual images
(3) beautiful actresses (4) background music
(5) realistic settings

____ 5. The finest films of the past have shown that social criticism and film
(1) can be combined successfully.
(2) are invariably associated.
(3) are never associated.
(4) must be handled comically to be successful.

____ 6. Which one of the following is not true? The cinema is the most flexible of art forms because, among other advantages,
(1) the scenes can change with great rapidity
(2) the flashback technique enables almost unlimited compressibility and expandability of time
(3) montage, the superimposition of various scenes on each other, permits action to continue and the passage of time to be shown
(4) the multiple exposure is so successful a device in narration
(5) it gives delight and meaning to life through beauty

____ 7. Which of the following is not true? Exposition is
(1) a kind of prose writing
(2) the opening section of sonata-allegro form
(3) the announcement of the subject of a fugue in different voices
(4) the pas de deux for the ballerina and danseur noble
(5) the part of a narrative plot introducing us to the characters and situation.

APPLICATION OF CONCEPTS

Below there are series of words. In each series all the words but one belong to one category (have to do with one subject). Write the word which does not belong in the first space below the series and identify the category of the remaining words in the second space.

Example: a) Howard Hughes, b) Pauline Kael, c) Andrew Sarris, d) Rex Reed e) John Simon
Howard Hughes (a) does not belong.
The category is film critics.

1. a) aria, b) ensemble, c) overture, d) recitative, e) arabasque

________________________ does not belong.

The category is ______________________________________.

2. a) Verdi, b) Nijinski, c) Wagner, d) Mozart, e) Monteverdi

________________________ does not belong.

The category is ______________________________________.

3. a) ballerina, b) pointilism, c) danseur noble, d) pas de deux, e) en pointe

________________________ does not belong.

The category is ______________________________________.

4. a) Martha Graham, b) Isadore Duncan, c) Mary Wigman d) Igor Stravinsky, e) Ted Shawn

________________________ does not belong.

The category is ______________________________________.

5. a) exposition, b) denouement, c) climax, d) conflict
e) decrescendo

________________________ does not belong.

The category is ____.

6. a) assonance, b) alliteration, c) rhyme, d) consanance,
e) dissonance

________________________ does not belong.

The category is ____.

7. a) Keats, b) Milton, c) Byron, d) Swinbourne,
e) Tennyson

________________________ does not belong.

The category is ____.

8. a) ballet, b) waltz, c) polka, d) minuet, e) rhumba

________________________ does not belong.

The category is ____.

9. a) simile, b) rhythm, c) metaphor, d) metonymy,
e) synecdoche

________________________ does not belong.

The category is ____.

10. a) epic, b) lyric, c) ballad, d) short story, e) drama

________________________ does not belong.

The category is ____.

11. a) <u>entrechat</u>, b) <u>sforzando</u>, c) <u>pas de chat</u>,
d) <u>cabriole</u>, e) <u>attitude</u>

________________________ does not belong.

The category is ____.

12. a) Iliad, b) Song of the Nibelungs, c) Beowulf, d) Odyssey, e) The Faerie Queene

_______________ does not belong.

The category is _______________________.

PLANNING AN OPERA

How might you develop an opera from this nursery rhyme?

Jack and Jill went up the hill
  To fetch a pail of water.
Jack fell down and broke his crown
  And Jill came tumbling after.

Remember that you have virtuoso singers, an orchestra, a chorus, a ballet troupe, a stage set, and costumes to work with. You'll need to invent an exposition: who are these people, what is the situation? Why did Jack and Jill undertake this feat? Were they chosen or did they heroically volunteer or did they do it as "a lark"? Were they lovers? Does it end in a double death? Did Jill follow Jack in his fall deliberately? Is it a romantic tragedy, a mock tragedy, a high tragedy, etc.? Review the components of opera. Where would you use an aria, duet, trio, quartet? How would you use the chorus? What kind of music would you want? Would there be an ensemble number in it? Would there be an opportunity for ballet in it?

PLANNING A PLAY

Clip a report of an incident which you think has dramatic possibilities from a newspaper. Outline it as it might be turned into a play. For example, at what point in the incident would you have the play begin. How would the exposition of characters and situation be presented? Below in the left hand column are the specific materials every plot must contain. Opposite them indicate the parts of the incident which would fulfill each requirement:

____

Title

1. <u>exposition</u>

2. <u>inciting incident</u>

3. <u>conflict, rising action</u>

4. <u>turning point, climax</u>

5. <u>falling action</u>

6. <u>conclusion, denouement</u>

OPERA

Opera is sung drama or, to put it another way, it is drama which has been set to music. The words of the drama are referred to as the libretto. This is sometimes available in the program itself or for sale at performances because it is difficult even for persons who speak a language to understand it when it is sung. One way of looking at opera is to consider it as made up of various components. These are:

1. Passages of recitative, that is, sung or chanted dialogue. Because the dialogue follows the phrasing and inflection of natural speech, recitative passages are not usually very melodic or musical in themselves, but they do move the action forward more rapidly than do arias, duets, trios and choruses.
2. Arias. These are set pieces for a single voice. They are quite melodic, often dramatic, and usually reveal in the music and the words much about the characters singing them. They are used at highly emotional or critical points in the opera. Frequently they are very demanding and provide an opportunity for the soloist to display vocal quality and technical ability. They are likely to be the pieces in the opera you know and remember, for they are musically separable from the opera and are frequently performed without any reference to the story itself.
3. Duets, trios, etc. These, like arias, are set pieces which are self contained musically. Duets, for example, are frequently love scenes to be sung by the hero and heroine of the opera. But they may be sung by two other characters brought together in other situations.
4. Ensembles. Ensemble is used in discussing opera to refer to a particular kind of song for usually four to six singers. It resembles an instrumental ensemble in that each singer sings a different melody expressing his or her particular emotions. Since they all sing at the same time, naturally one cannot understand what each of the singers is singing, but ensembles usually occur at points after the character and points of view of the singers have already been established and the different melodic lines blend as dramatically as in a lively string quartet.
5. Dances. Most opera companies have a ballet troupe, for many operas make use of dance for variety, enjoyment, and as a part of the spectacle. Many composers have contrived their libretti so as to involve ballroom scenes, dream sequences, festivals or other celebrations so as to include dancing.
6. Spectacle. Of course spectacle is a part of all opera. Opulent settings of exotic, distant lands and places, elaborate costumes and the like. Sometimes they seem quite fitting as in Aida and Madama Butterfly. At other times they seem somewhat contrived as in Act III of La Boehme

when the curtain swings open to reveal a scene on a sidewalk cafe in Paris in winter when chairs and tables are normally taken inside. But the snow drifting down on the colorful, muffled, costumed characters is so exciting that we hardly notice the discrepancy. And what a spectacular opening it makes for this act!

7. Choruses. Set pieces for a large number of voices. The "Soldier's Chorus" from *Faust* is well known apart from the opera. Choruses are frequently used in group scenes.

Of all the long forms of music, opera is perhaps the best known. To be fully appreciated it should, of course, be seen and heard in a stage performance. Many people, however, find the conventions of acting and drama frustrating in operatic performances, because the realism of gesture and the motions of the singer are necessarily restricted to such an extent that they often seem artificial. The composer necessarily is chiefly concerned with the music. It is also true that the story of the opera is hard to follow because the words are often in a foreign language. There is, at present, in the United States, an increasing tendency to sing opera in English, especially comic opera, if the translation adequately follows the vocal line and at the same time keeps to the meaning of the original. In any case, it is a great help to have a libretto to the opera which gives the words in both the original and in the English translation. Summaries of the plot are almost always given on the program. Also, it is possible to prepare for the enjoyment of an opera by reading the story and the main themes of music in such a source as Newman, *Stories of the Great Operas*.

More people enjoy opera now than they have at anytime in the past in spite of the extraordinary expense in assembling singers, an orchestra, a ballet corps and spectacular sets. A recent survey by the Metropolitan Opera Guild reported in *Opera News*, Nov. 1977, reveals some interesting statistics. In the United States in 1976-77 there were 492 opera companies and an additional 422 groups in colleges and universities. Of the works performed 226 were from the standard repetoire, and 201 were contemporary works. In all, there was a total of 7389 performances. The ten works from the standard repetoire which were performed most were the following in order of number of performances:

1. *The Barber of Seville* (Rossini)
2. *Madama Butterfly* (Puccini)
3. *The Marriage of Figaro* (Mozart)
4. *La Boehme* (Puccini)
5. *Die Fledermaus* (Strauss)
6. *Carmen* (Bizet)
7. *Cosi Fan Dutte* (Mozart)
8. *Gianni Schicchi* (Puccini)
9. *Tosca* (Puccini)
10. *The Magic Flute* (Mozart)

Even though many people do not live in centers which can make opera available on the stage, there are increasing opportunities for hearing it over the radio and on records. The concentration on music apart from stage effects has certain advantages. The same principles which make for good organization in any art apply here. The type of melody given a singer or group of singers should correspond with the mood and action. In fact, music can create the mood without the words. When we know, however, that Radames in Verdi's Aida has betrayed his country and has been condemned to die by the priests, and when we learn that Aida has come to his tomb prepared to die with him, we can better appreciate the intermingling of voices and themes. We hear Aida's mystical ecstacy; and then we listen to the duet of the lovers against a background of chanting of priests. As the rhythms and melodies pull against each other, the tensions increase until Aida's farewell to the world floats over the drone-like prayer of her rival, Amneris, and the music has left us with a sense of victory over the tragic death of the lovers. The appropriateness of the treatment of each element of melody, rhythm, and harmony is clear in the final tomb scene; and our satisfaction increases as we realize the complete coherence of the combinations of elements, and of the drama and music.

To introduce you to opera and how it works we suggest that you listen to the Tomb Scene from the last act of Aida. A libretto with comments are included to guide your listening. Of the components named above you will find here a spectacular stage set divided into two floors, recitative passages as Radames exexplains where he is and in the exchanges with Aida when he recognizes her, short arias of melody over metric accompaniment, as when Radames agonizes that one so beautiful should die so young for love of him, the final love duet of Radames and Aida, and, at the very end, something resembling an ensemble with Radames and Aida continuing their duet as Amneris joins them singing a prayer for peace and the priests in chorus add their invocation to the total effect.

Libretto for AIDA

The Tomb Scene (Act IV, Scene ii)

The Stage is divided into two floors. The upper floor represents the interior of the Temple of Vulcan, resplendent with light and gold; the lower is a subterranean crypt. The temple consists of many columns, a colossal statue of Osiris.

Radames is in the subterranean crypt. Above, two priests are engaged in putting the stone in place which seals the tomb.

Program Notes	Italian Text	English Translation
	Radames	*Radames*
Ominous chords, minor harmony	La fatal pietra sovra me si chiuse	The fatal stone is closed above me.
Chords punctuate	Ecco la tomba mia.	Behold my tomb.
monotone vocal phrases	Del di la luce piu non vedro.	I'll never see the light of day again.
On name "Aida" pitch	Non rivedro piu Aida . . .	Never see Aida again.
rises for first	Aida, ove sei tu?	Aida, where art thou?
time	Possa tu almeno viver felice	May you at least live happily
	E la mia sorte orrenda sempre ignorar	And never know my dreadful fate.
Mounting tension	Qual gemito! Una larva!	A groan! A ghost!
	Una vision.	A vision.
	No; forma umana e questa . . .	No, it's a human shape . . .
	Cielo!—Aida!	Heavens! Aida!
	Aida	*Aida*
	Son io.	It is I.
	Radames	*Radames*
Emphatic declamation	Tu . . . in questa tomba?	Thou . . . in this tomb?
	Aida	*Aida*
Thudding minor harmony	Presago il core della tua condanna	My heart foretold your sentence
	In questa tomba che per te si apriva	Into this tomb which opened for thee
	Io penetrai furtiva	I furtively made my way.
	E qui lontana da ogni umano sguardo	And here far from every mortal glance
Modulation to major	Nelle tue braccia desiar morire	In thy arms I wished to die.
	Radames	*Radames*
Change to duple rhythm	Morir! si pura e bella!	To die! So pure and beautiful
More regular melody	Morir per me d'amore	To die for love of me;
Accompaniment imitates part of melody	Degli anni tuoi nel fiore	In the flower of thy youth
	Fuggir la vita!	To fly from life!
	T'aveva il cielo per l'amor creata	Heaven created thee for love,
	Ed io t'uccido per averti amata!	And I kill thee having loved thee!
Melodic climax	No, non morrai!	No, thou shalt not die!
	Troppo io t'amai . . !	Too much I loved thee!
	Troppo sei bella!	Too beautiful art thou!

Program Notes	Italian Text	English Translation
Change to triple rhythm, pulsation less stressed Detached notes of melody More skips in melody	*Aida* (ecstatic) Vedi? di morte l'angelo Radiante a noi sí apressa? Ne adduce a eterni gaudii Sovra i suoi vanni d'or. Su noi già il ciel dischiudersi; Ivi ogni affanno cessa; Ivi comincia l'estasi D'un immortale amor.	*Aida* Seest thou the angel of death Radiant approaches us? He takes us to eternal joys Under his golden wings. Above us heaven opens; There every grief ceases; There begins the ecstasy Of an immortal love.
Sacred song and dance of priests in temple	*Priests* Immenso, immenso Fta!	*Priests* Mighty, mighty, Phtah!
Oriental-sounding melody	*Aida* Triste canto!	*Aida* Sad song!
Accompaniment; chords on harp	*Radames* Il tripudio dei Sacerdoti!	*Radames* The celebration of the priests
The priestly song continues	*Aida* Il nostro inno di morte . . .	*Aida* Our hymn of death!
	Radames Ne le mie forti braccia Smuovere ti potranno, o fatal pietra!	*Radames* Not even my strong arms Can move thee, O fatal stone!
	Aida Invan! . . . tutto e finito Sulla terra per noi	*Aida* In vain! All is finished On earth for us.
	Radames (resigned) E vero! E vero!	*Radames* It is true! It is true!
Beginning of final duet Duple rhythm. Tension produced by skips, by harmony, and by high notes.	*Aida* O terra addio; addio valle di pianti Sogno di gaudio che in dolor svani A noi si schiude il cielo E l'alme erranti	*Aida* O earth, farewell! Farewell, vale of tears Dream of joy that vanished in grief. Heaven opens to us And our wandering souls
Melodic climax	Volano al raggio dell' eterno di	Fly into the rays of eternal day.

Radames
(repeats words of "O terra addio" with Aida occasionally echoing a phrase.)

(*Amneris*, the princess who loved Radames jealously and had him condemned to death, appears in the temple, dressing in mourning, and prostrates herself upon the stone sealing the tomb.)

Program Notes	Italian Text	English Translation
	Priests Immenso Fta, noi t'invochiam!	*Priests* O Mighty Phtah! Thee we invoke!
Broad phrase Soprano and Tenor sing duet in unison. Tension increased by reinforcement of melodic line	*Aida & Radames* A noi si schiude il cielo O terra addio; addio valle di pianti	*Aida & Radames* Heaven opens to us! O earth, farewell; farewell, vale of tears.
	Amneris (praying) Pace t'imploro	*Amneris* Peace, I implore thee!
	Aida & Radames Sogno di gaudio che in dolor svani	*Aida & Radames* Dream of joy that vanished in grief
	Amneris Salma adorata	*Amneris* Beloved soul!
The repetitions are required by the musical form rather than by mere dramatic emphasis	*Aida & Radames* A noi si schiude il cielo	*Aida & Radames* Heaven opens to us!
	Amneris Isi placata	*Amneris* Isis, be appeased!
	Aida & Radames E l'alme erranti Volano al raggio dell' eterno di.	*Aida & Radames* And our wandering souls Fly into the rays of eternal day.
	Priests Noi t'invochiam. *Aida & Radames* Il cielo, il cielo.	*Priests* We invoke thee. *Aida & Radames* Heaven, heaven.
	Priests Immenso Fta!	*Priests* O mighty Phtah!
	Aida & Radames Si schiude il cielo.	*Aida & Radames* Heaven opens.

(Aida sinks lifeless into the arms of Radames.)

Program Notes	Italian Text	English Translation
The violins repeat, very high, the melody of the duet The melody almost seems to evaporate.	*Amneris* Pace t'imploro; Pace t'imploro; Pace!	*Amneris* Peace I implore for thee; Peace I implore for thee; Peace!

End of the Opera

17 STYLE

CONCEPTS

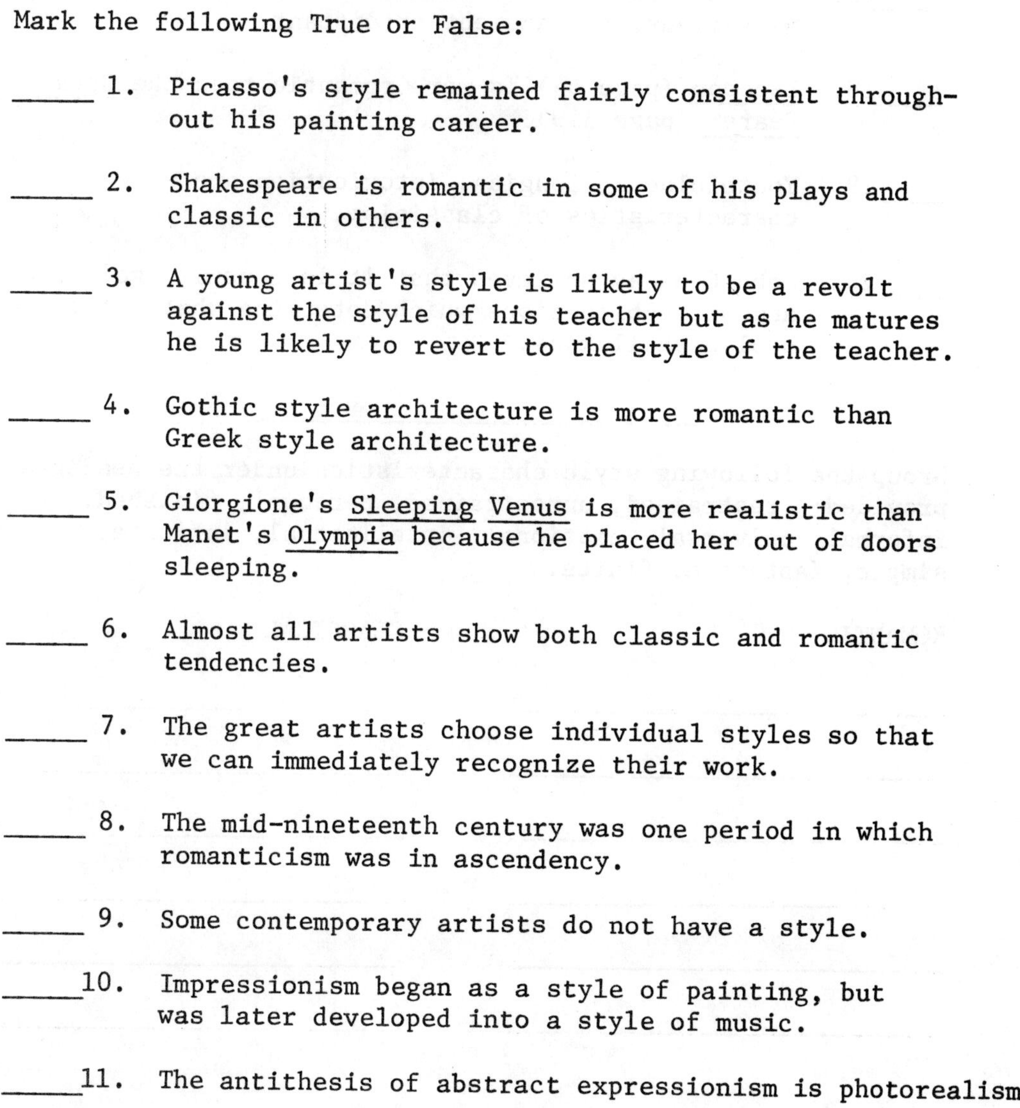

Mark the following True or False:

_____ 1. Picasso's style remained fairly consistent throughout his painting career.

_____ 2. Shakespeare is romantic in some of his plays and classic in others.

_____ 3. A young artist's style is likely to be a revolt against the style of his teacher but as he matures he is likely to revert to the style of the teacher.

_____ 4. Gothic style architecture is more romantic than Greek style architecture.

_____ 5. Giorgione's *Sleeping Venus* is more realistic than Manet's *Olympia* because he placed her out of doors sleeping.

_____ 6. Almost all artists show both classic and romantic tendencies.

_____ 7. The great artists choose individual styles so that we can immediately recognize their work.

_____ 8. The mid-nineteenth century was one period in which romanticism was in ascendency.

_____ 9. Some contemporary artists do not have a style.

_____ 10. Impressionism began as a style of painting, but was later developed into a style of music.

_____ 11. The antithesis of abstract expressionism is photorealism.

_____12. Style refers to the subject matter rather than to the form given it.

_____13. The symphonies of Mozart and Haydn are classical in style.

_____14. Op art means optimal art - - i.e., in contrast to minimal art.

_____15. A style developed in one art is sometimes copied in another.

_____16. The romantic artist is likely to forsake tradition in order to make a personal statement.

_____17. Favorite subjects of romanticism are nature, the mysterious, the ancient or distant.

_____18. Laocoon (page 64) is more romantic than the Spear Bearer (page 319).

_____19. Youthfulness, longing, intoxication are characteristics of classicism.

_____20. John Canaday believes that it is museums, galleries and art publications which determine what art the public shall know.

Group the following style characteristics under the headings provided: restrained, unrestrained, personal, finished, informal, universal, emotional, intellectual, infinite, simple, fantastic, finite.

ROMANTIC	CLASSICAL
______________	______________
______________	______________
______________	______________
______________	______________
______________	______________
______________	______________

APPLICATION OF CONCEPTS

-1-

There are illustrations of four works by El Greco in the text. They are:

Purification of the Temple, page 216
RESURRECTION, Color Plate 6, following page 56
St. Jerome, page 316
View of Toledo, Color Plate 47, following page 440

From these four paintings list four qualities which appear to be characteristic of El Greco's work, his style.

1.____

2.____

3.____

4.____

-2-

We have in the text illustrations of four works of Van Gogh. They are:

La Berceuse, page 217
Landscape with Cypresses, Color Plate 2, following page 56
Self-Portrait in a Straw Hat, page 140
Starry Night, page 84
Woman Cleaning a Cauldron, page 150

Study the paintings and list what seem to be four characteristics of Van Gogh's style:

1.____

2.____

3.____

4.____

In his book, Classic and Romantic Music,[1] Friedrich Blume, the well-known musicologist, uses various suggestive words and phrases to distinguish between the romantic temperament and the classical temperament as exemplified in music. Several of these are listed below:
"extragavant" "immoderate" "exuberance" "wholeness"
"universality" "simplest possible means of expression"
"beyond the level of human feeling" "individually human"
"orderly" "freedom" "according to law" "mysticism"
"enthusiasm" "ecstatic poetizing" "rapturous intensity"
"with much feeling" "multiple changes of key may occur"
"follows the norm" "refined development" "the personality of the creative artist speaks of its own inner self"
"simplicity" "natural" "to voice the inexpressible"

Copy each of the phrases under the heading to which you think it was applied.

CLASSICAL ROMANTIC

1 Friedrich Blume, Classic and Romantic Music: A Comprehensive Survey. Translated from the German by M.D. Herter Norton (New York: W.W. Norton & Company, Inc., 1970.)

DISCUSSION QUESTIONS:

-1-

The third edition of Webster's New International Dictionary (1960) was based on the principle that a dictionary should be descriptive and not prescriptive. The spellings, usages, and definitions given are those commonly in use, not necessarily the traditionally correct ones; they are descriptive of our language as it is now used. Webster's Third, as it came to be called, did not presume to judge, only to describe. It immediately gave rise to a controversary. Dwight Macdonald observed that it "impoverishes the language by not objecting to errors if they are common enough." It added many new words, many of them technical terms, not in the first edition (1934) but it dropped many more. William L. O'Neill points out that "This meant that half the words in the English language were lost between 1934 and 1961."

There are many issues to discuss about Webster's Third:

1. Was the position taken by the editors part of a larger cultural upheaval in the 60's - - the emergence of a counter culture which challenged the idea that anything is good or correct or wholesome or desirable simply because it is traditional?

2. Who should determine what is good form, correct usage? Who does determine these things? Who in the past did?

3. Chairman and chairwoman are probably in your dictionary. Is chairperson there? Is it likely to be? What does this tell us about words and culture?

(The information and quotations in this paragraph are from William L. O'Neill's Coming Apart: An Informal History of America in the 1960's. (New York: Quadrangle/ The New York Times Book Co., 1975), p. 200 n.

-2-

Saarinen in Chapter 4 of the text sets forth theprinciples which are important to him in architecture, but these are not style; they are the bases from which his individual treatment of them produces a style. Reviewing the three examples of his architecture in the text, what would you say is characteristic of the style which emerges from the principles?

DISCUSSION QUESTIONS:

-1-

-2-

18 THE TRAGIC AND THE COMIC

CONCEPTS

Match the following:

_____	1. Comedy of character	(1) low comedy
_____	2. Tragedy of character	(2) high comedy
_____	3. Comedy of situation	(3) low tragedy
_____	4. Tragedy of situation	(4) high tragedy

Match the following:

_____	1. Satire	(1) good natured and kindly.
_____	2. Humor	(2) an imitation which turns the serious into the ridiculous.
_____	3. Wit	(3) word play which is amusing.
_____	4. Pun	(4) words with the same or similar sounds but different meanings.
_____	5. Malapropism	(5) transposition of initial letters of two or more words.
_____	6. Spoonerism	(6) misuse of a word for one resembling it.
_____	7. Parody	(7) is or pretends to be aimed at righting a wrong.

Mark the following as characteristic of

(1) Greek tragedy

(2) Shakespearean tragedy

(3) Nineteenth century and Modern tragedy

_____ 1. The heros are of high birth and noble character.

_____ 2. The heros are noblemen but with a flaw in character which leads to conflict and their eventual fall.

_____ 3. The incidents take place within a frame in which the gods are supreme: defying or breaking the law of the gods brings tragedy.

_____ 4. The action takes place within a frame of strong religious belief.

_____ 5. The conflict is with the gods and their degrees.

_____ 6. The conflict is with society and social circumstances.

_____ 7. The conflict is within the individual - - character strengths in conflict with weaknesses.

_____ 8. The protagonist is an ordinary person from the middle classes.

_____ 9. Written to be performed in an amphitheater.

_____10. Written to be performed on a stage with a procenium frame.

_____11. Written to be performed in an enclosed courtyard with second and third story porches serving as balconies.

_____12. The action takes place in an atmosphere of varied, unclear, and confused values.

Mark the following as (a) characteristic of tragedy, (b) characteristic of comedy, or (c) characteristic of both.

_____ 1. tends to make us laugh.

_____ 2. is more intellectual than emotional.

_____ 3. depicts human beings who command our respect and concern in their problems.

_____ 4. presents us human beings in rebellion against the universe or a part of themselves.

_____ 5. treats the frailities, frivolities, and limitations of human beings as amusing, entertaining.

_____ 6. treats the protagonists with aesthetic distance so that we do not become emotionally involved in their struggles.

_____ 7. involves us emotionally in the struggles of the protagonists.

_____ 8. treats potentially serious subject matter with a detachment.

_____ 9. the characters have a three dimensional quality.

_____10. the individual characteristics do not seem very important.

_____11. is not common today as a pure type.

_____12. is a combined art.

_____13. has an exposition, conflict, and denouement.

_____14. when used as a noun to refer to a type of literature, usually refers to a dramatic work.

_____15. the necessity of the outcome is made clear early in the work.

19 JUDGMENT

CONCEPTS

This chapter suggests three qualities of art which should be examined and considered in making a final estimate of its greatness. These are listed immediately below. Place the number of one of these three in the blank preceding each of the words below with which it is associated in the text.

(1) Sincerity

(2) Breadth and depth of meaning

(3) Magnitude or effectiveness

____ 1. awesome	____ 9. individual
____ 2. authentic	____10. provocativeness
____ 3. genuine	____11. evocative of reflection
____ 4. scope	____12. honest
____ 5. universal	____13. integrity
____ 6. powerful	____14. sentiment
____ 7. sublime	____15. difficulty
____ 8. levels of meaning	____16. complexity

We have often heard the expression, "I do not know what is good but I know what I like." Art collector Vincent Price professes a different position: "I like what I know." (Presumably the "know" in the statement means the same thing as "understand." Be prepared to discuss the implications of both statements as they relate to judgment of art as discussed in this chapter.

APPLICATION OF CONCEPTS

A DESCRIPTION of a work of art states the immediately observable facts about it.

FORMAL CRITICISM is based on analysis of the formal aspects of the work. It explores ____.

HISTORICAL CRITICISM is criticism which ____.

INTERPRETATIVE CRITICISM draws upon all three of these in making JUDGMENTS about a work.

Look again at the sculpture of *Christ and S. John*, reproduced in Figure 3-10, on page 68, and discussed on pages 68 and 78-9. Compose below three statements about it which might appear in a historical critique of the piece and three statements which might appear in a formal critique.

HISTORICAL CRITICISM:

1. ____
____

2. ____
____

3. ____
____

FORMAL CRITICISM:

1. ____
____

2. ____
____

3. ____

____

POETRY
Marianne Moore

Read Marianne Moore's poem which begins this chapter through a couple of times, then mark the following statements as accurate or inaccurate representations of ideas in the poem. It is, of course, the very nature of poetry that the full meaning of it cannot be translated into prose. This is an exercise to demonstrate this fact and to involve you in arriving at your own interpretation of the poem. You will want to discuss your answers with other students and your teacher to see the extent to which your interpretation is shared by them.

____ 1. We do not admire what we do not understand.

____ 2. The importance of the subject does not necessarily result in good poetry.

____ 3. The genuine includes physical, involuntary level responses.

____ 4. It is useful to have one's emotions stimulated by the genuine.

____ 5. Poets should be literalists of the imagination.

____ 6. That which is trivial is not consequential.

____ 7. The "fiddle" of poetry is "the raw material of poetry."

____ 8. Fiddle in the poem probably means aimless playing with words with little feeling involved.

____ 9. Poetry should be clear, understandable, not unintelligible.

____10. Poets should be above insolence and triviality.

Mark the following True or False:

_____ 1. The meaning of art can be put into carefully chosen words.

_____ 2. Abstract expressionism was at the height of its popularity in the 1930's.

_____ 3. Any final evaluation of art is impossible.

_____ 4. The beginning student should not try to formulate opinions about what is great art.

_____ 5. One test of the greatest art is that it is understood by everyone.

_____ 6. The auteur theory of criticism argues that the director's integrity should find expression in all of his or her films.

_____ 7. The best guide to the sincerity of a work is the artist's commentary on it.

_____ 8. The style of Beethoven's early symphonies is similar to the style of Mozart's symphonies.

_____ 9. One guide to greatness in art is its popularity among the artist's contemporaries.

_____10. Sentiment is a genuine feeling and does not violate the principle of integrity.

_____11. The usefulness of criticism is that it may help us see and hear what we have not heard ourselves.

_____12. Susan Sontag does not consider it the critic's business to tell us what art means.

_____13. It is doubtful that it is appropriate to apply traditional canons of greatness to modern art.

_____14. Sublimnity in contemporary art is to be found only in drama.

_____15. Formal criticism can tell us more about contemporary art than it can about traditional art.

Rank the following as the text applies them to art:

_____	1. pretty	(1) the highest
_____	2. grand	(2) second highest
_____	3. graceful	(3) third highest
_____	4. sublime	(4) fourth highest
_____	5. beautiful	(5) fifth highest

DISCUSSION QUESTIONS:

-1-

Rudolf Arnheim, in a quotation on page 211 of the text, states that the great works of art are complex but that we also praise them for "having simplicity". Reread the whole quotation. To which of the three qualities of great art discussed in this chapter does the quotation most clearly relate? How?

-2-

Albert E. Elson in Purposes of Art, cited earlier, has said of histories of art: "In a real sense, art history is the record of how individual historians react to their subject." If this is true, what is the value in reading histories of art? How does one know which history of art to trust?

Art historians like journalists attempt to answer the questions of what, where, when, how and why. Applied to an art object these become: What is it, when and where was it created, how was it done and why. Some of these questions can be answered with certainty, others with less certainty, others must at best be answered with an informed guess. Rank the questions in terms of the probably realiability of the answers. Discuss the reasons for your ranking. Which do you consider most important in assessing the value of a work of art: those questions which can be answered objectively, or those which must be answered with some degree of subjectivity?

-3-

The point has been made in the text and in many other places that quality in art means more than technical virtuosity. Discuss this proposition, explaining the importance you think the artist's technical skill should be given in evaluating the worth and significance of art. If you consider technique of secondary importance, what is of greatest importance? Try to articulate carefully those qualities which make for great art - - beyond or in addition to technique.

-4-

It is often said that both natural sensitivity and training enter into the judgment of art. Discuss this statement. Sensitivity to what? Visual, aural, and tactile elements? To their interrelationships? To their expressive content?

What kind of training would you think important in becoming a critic? A familiarity with the great critics of the past and/or a wide familiarity with art itself? Which would you consider more important? Should a critic of painting be a practicing painter, or a film critic have had experience in writing scenarios and in acting and in directing films? Or is this not necessary?

-5-

On page 16 of this book there are listed 6 legitimate reasons for pursuing an interest in art. Reread the whole list. You will notice that it begins with liking the _subject_ of the work and ends with liking the philosophical _content_ - - that is, the values revealed in the way it is executed (completing the circle of _subject_ to _content_). All too often our academic training in art perception reverses the order so that our interest is soon exhausted by being told the "message" or given a verbal summary of _content_ so that we miss entirely the _experiencing_ of it which must come at the primary, sensory levels of 1 - 3. It is at these levels that the _content_ is _experienced_ in ways we cannot articulate well (as we demonstrated in the analysis of DeKooning's _Woman I_ and of Kubrick's _Space Odyssey: 2001_). Recall a painting that you have seen and known _about_ for many years, something like _Whistler's Mother_ (a name given by others to the painting but rejected by the artist), or da Vinci's _Mona Lisa_. How much have you really _seen_ in the painting you chose? At what levels have you _experienced_ it? Be prepared to discuss the painting and your acquaintance with it over the years.

20 A FINAL WORD

CONCEPTS

Mark the following True or False and for all (whether you mark them true or false) make a statement or give an example which justifies your answer on the line below it.

_____ 1. In the past, "Schools of painters" sometimes developed around great painters, but we have had no such "schools" in the twentieth century.

____

_____ 2. Art, by breaking up our learned orientations, can enable us to experience more of reality.

____

_____ 3. Whatever changes occur in styles of expression, knowledge is one thing which does not change from age to age.

____

_____ 4. The crumbling of boundary lines between the arts both reflects and creates the emergence of a new social structure.

____

_____ 5. Theater is the last of the arts to reflect change in the general culture.

____

_____ 6. Blind conformity to the systems on which our social order rests can impoverish our full functioning as human beings.

____

_____ 7. There is an analogy between the democracy of musical themes in canonic style and the democracy of tones in Schoenberg's music written in his tone-row style.

____

_____ 8. One lesson from history is that art which on initial encounter seems strange, shocking, chaotic, may after longer acquaintance with it, seem pleasant, enjoyable, and ordered.

____

_____ 9. "To imitate nature in her method of operation" is not the same thing as "To imitate nature in her appearances."

____

_____10. Every work of art reflects layers of artistic decisions through which accidents become finally a part of an integrated unity.

____

_____11. Myth is as true as history.

____

_____12. Because art does not depend upon discursive rhetoric, established rules and grammar for its ability to communicate, it can sometimes tell us more about a person or a culture than language.

____

Match the definitions in the left column with the words and phrases in the right column.

_____ 1. atonal	(1)	discovering by accident or alertness what was not directly sought
_____ 2. aleatory art	(2)	an event or series of events designed to evoke spontaneous emotional and/or physical reactions in spectators, turning them into participants
_____ 3. serendipity	(3)	the process used is allowed to determine the phases and final outcome of the undertaking
_____ 4. action painting	(4)	having no central tone or key
_____ 5. happening	(5)	exploits our optical faculties for its effects
_____ 6. op art	(6)	determined by chance

Look up the following words in a dictionary which gives etymologies. Write after each word its origin and explain how the origin relates to its present meaning:

1. tragedy

2. serendipity

3. aleatory

DISCUSSION QUESTIONS:

Review the following quotations in their contexts:

1. "Art seeks some reconciliation of opposites". (The text, page 473.)

2. "The origin of art: The discrepancy between physical fact and psychic effect". - - Josef Albers. (The text, page 29.)

3. "Tension and Release: The Two Aspects of Order in the Arts: (This book, pages 203 and 204.)

4. "There are two basic morphological archetypes . . . expression of order . . . expression of chaos . . ." - - Gyorgy Kepes. (This book, page 6.)

After reflecting on the passages referred to as they relate to each other, either making the same or a similar point or contradicting each other, write below at least five specific points you will contribute to a discussion of them.

1. ____________________

____

2. ____________________

____

3. ____________________

____

4. ____________________

____

5. ____________________

____

THE WATERSHED OF MODERNITY

and

HAPPY NEW EARS!

These two short pieces which follow provide a chance for you to look back upon the art of the past, to speculate about art of the present, and art of the future.

1. A break-up is perhaps the shortest summary possible of Bell's concept of modernity. Katharine Kuh in Break-up: the Core of Modern Art (Greenwich, Connecticut: New York Graphic Society Ltd., 1965) explicates a similar thesis concerning arts. But Bell goes beyond this. In what other arts does he see a break-up? Can you explain why he calls it a break-up? Can you give examples of a break-up of genres? Of traditional distinctions between the arts? Of traditional subject matter in the arts?

2. "All this conditions our appreciation of the past". Can you explain what Bell means by this? See discussion question 2 on page 201 of this book for a clud.

3. It is of some interest that Kandinsky, usually credited with the first completely abstract paintings, and Schoenberg, usually credited with establishing atonal music as a genre, were friends. Schoenberg greatly admired Kandinsky's On the Spiritual in Art in which he makes a theoretical defense of abstract art as expressive. The appearance of abstract paintings by Kandinsky and of atonal music by Schoenberg coincided in the first decade of our century.

4. Cage observes that much modern art deliberately avoids a center of interest so that our eyes wander through a painting experiencing each configuration as we encounter it. The atonal serialism and twelve-tone row of Schoenberg had a similar effect in music. In abandoning a traditional key center and insisting that every tone be made as important as every other he dispersed interest evenly throughout a piece. There is no tonal center from which we depart and return but a flux of auditory configurations experienced as they are presented to us with no sense that we are going anywhere; we are simply going, enjoying what appears next. Aleatory music in which chance, not premeditated design, determines the sequence and has the same effect.

5. Test Cage's thesis about the lack of a center of interest in modern painting by re-examining the paintings of Pollock, Kandinsky, Miro, Albers, Vasarely in the test.

6. In the text and in this book we have made the point that skeletal organization is of little interest as such and does not hold our attention for long. Where in his essay does Cage make a similar point?

7. Note that both Cage and Bell speak of a change in our conception of time as an orderly sequence of events and of space as foreground and background. What is meant by Cage's term "space-time" for this change? There is a clue in his statement that the distinction between space arts and time arts is an oversimplification.

8. Cage says that significant changes occur first in the space arts (architecture, painting, and sculpture) and that they appear afterward in the time arts (music and the performance arts). Can you document this statement with examples from your knowledge of the arts? Bell, for example, cites impressionism in the visual art of the 1870's as a forerunner of modernity, but the impressionistic music of Debussy and Ravel did not appear until more than a decade later. But this is a single example. We have already noted that Kandinsky and Schoenberg arrived at expressionism in music and painting at the same time. Think of other examples.

9. Cage seems to rejoice that significant changes in the arts now occur "every twenty minutes," and that is the point of the pun in the title of his essay, which asks <u>us</u> to rejoice. Other writers have argued that new experimental movements in the arts cannot today stay "underground" long enough to mature, to become disciplined in the new thing they are doing. These critics feel that the mass media now exploits anything different in the arts so quickly for news value that an experimental trend becomes exhausted and we become bored with it before its mature possibilities have been explored. Have you seen something new and interesting in the arts appear and then disappear before you could make up your mind whether or not it had "lasting appeal"? In this connection you may wish to reread John Canaday's statement on pages 429-430 of the text. How do you feel about the rapidly changing styles in the arts?

10. What in Bell's statement corresponds to Cage's statement that in our time "distinctions are disappearing"? What distinctions does Cage cite to support his statement?

11. If, as Cage argues, the distinction between the space and time arts is disappearing, all the arts it appears from the essay are moving toward becoming time arts, especially the conditions of music. Walter Pater (1839-1894), the English critic, said long ago (in his essay on Leonardo da Vinci in <u>The Renaissance</u>) the same thing: "All art constantly aspires towards the condition of music." Many critics have made the same observation. Ingmar Bergman, for example (page 421 in the text), says that he experiences film as music. Consider the characteristics of music which this analogy suggests. There are no assigned symbols in music; the meaning is general, not specific. We experience music as it presents itself to us in time; there is no center of interest to which we can go immediately. <u>Experiencing</u> it is the only way we can encounter it; meaningful verbalization about the arts is always difficult; in music it is almost impossible. Can you extend the list?

THE WATERSHED OF MODERNITY

The period from 1890 to 1930, the watershed of modernity, includes as an integral part of the revolution in sensibility (as well as the revolution in mind) analytical cubism and abstraction in art, and "color impressionism" and the break-up of chordal tonality in music as well. To put forth a particular thesis of my own, the nature of modernity, as a social and esthetic movement, is that it represents an "eclipse of distance" - of psychic distance and esthetic distance - - between the spectator and the work of art in all the spheres of culture. It involves the destruction (in the ideal-type sense) of rational conceptions of time as an orderly sequence of events; of space as an ordered composition of figure and background - which had been the dominant mode since the Renaissance, and which had achieved genre in Lessing's Laokoon. Post-modernity, beyond this, breaks up existing genres and traditional distinctions between the arts, and where, in Dewey's phrase, "Art is experience," it seeks to establish all experience, or happenings, without any shaping, as art. And all this, too, conditions our appreciation of the past.

- - Daniel Bell, The Reforming of General Education (New York: Columbia University Press, 1966), page 233.

HAPPY NEW EARS!

by John Cage

Max Ernst, around 1950, speaking at the Arts Club on Eighth Street in New York City, said that significant changes in the arts formerly occurred every three hundred years, whereas now they take place every twenty minutes.

Such changes happen first in the arts which, like plants, are fixed to particular points in space: architecture, painting, and sculpture. They happen afterward in the performance arts, music and theatre, which require, as animals do, the passing of time for their realization.

In literature, as with the myxomycetes and similar organisms which are classified sometimes as plants and sometimes as animals, changes take place both early and late. This art, if it is understood as printed material, has the characteristics of objects in space; but, understood as a performance, it takes on the aspects of processes in time.

I have for many years accepted, and I still do, the doctrine about Art, occidental and oriental, set forth by Ananda K. Coomaraswamy in his book *The Transformation of Nature in Art,* that the function of Art is to imitate Nature in her manner of operation. Our understanding of "her manner of operation" changes according to advances in the sciences. These advances in this century have brought the term "space-time" into our vocabulary. Thus, the distinctions made above between the space and the time arts are at present an oversimplification.

Observe that the enjoyment of a modern painting carries one's attention not to a center of interest but all over the canvas and not following any particular path. Each point on the canvas may be used as a beginning, continuing, or ending of one's observation of it. This is the case also with those works which are symmetrical, for then the observer's attention is made mobile by the rapidity with which he drops the problem of understanding structure. Whether or not a painting or sculpture lacks a center of interest may be determined by observing whether or not it is destroyed by the effects of shadows. (Intrusions of the environment are effects of time. But they are welcomed by a painting which makes no attempt to focus the observer's attention.) Observe also those works of painting, sculpture, and architecture which, employing transparent materials, become inseparable from their changing environments.

The tardiness of music with respect to the arts just mentioned is its good fortune. It is able to make deductions from their experiences and to combine these with necessarily different experiences which arise from its special nature. First of all, then, a composer at this moment frees his music of a single overwhelming climax. Seeking an interpenetration and non-obstruction of sounds, he renounces harmony and its effect of fusing sounds in a fixed relationship. Giving up the notion of *hauptstimme,* his "counterpoints" are superimpositions, events that are related to one another only because they take place at the same time. If he maintains in his work aspects of structure, they are symmetrical in character, canonic or enjoying an equal importance of parts, either those that are present at one instant, or those that succeed one another in time. His music is not interrupted by the sounds of the environment, and to make this a fact he either includes silences in his work or gives to his continuity the very nature of silence (absence of intention).

In addition, musicians, since they are several people rather than one person as a painter or sculptor is, are now able to be independent each from another. A composer writes at this moment indeterminately. The performers are no longer his servants but are freemen. A composer writes parts but, leaving their relationship unfixed, he writes no score. Sound sources are at a multiplicity of points in space with respect to the audience so that each listener's experience is his own. The mobiles of modern sculpture come to mind, but the parts they have are not as free as those of a musical composition since they share a common suspension means and follow the law of gravity. In architecture, where labor is divided as it is in music, music's freedom is not yet to be observed. Pinned to the earth, a building well made does not fall apart. Perhaps, though, when the dreams of Buckminster Fuller become actualities, houses, for example, that are dropped from the air instead of bombs, architecture, through flexible means unfamiliar to us now, will initiate a wholly new series of changes in the arts.

Changes in music precede equivalent ones in theatre, and changes in theatre precede general changes in the lives of people. Theatre is obligatory eventually because it resembles life more closely than the other arts do, requiring for its appreciation the use of both eyes and ears, space and time. "An ear alone is not a being." Thus, more and more, we encounter works of art, visual or audible, which are not strictly speaking either paintings or music. In New York City they are called "happenings." Just as shadows no longer destroy paintings, nor ambient sounds music, so environmental activities do not ruin a happening. They rather add to the fun of it. The result, coming to the instance of daily life, is that our lives are not ruined by the interruptions that other people and things continually provide.

I have attempted briefly here to set forth a view of the arts which does not separate them from the rest of life, but rather confuses the difference between Art and Life, just as it diminishes the distinctions between space and time. Many of the ideas involved come from the Orient, particularly China and Japan. However, what with the printing press, the airplane, telegraphy, and nowadays Telstar, the distinctions between Occident and Orient are fast disappearing. We live in one world. Likewise the distinctions between self and other are being forgotten. Throughout the world people cooperate to effect an action. Hearing of anonymity, one can imagine the absence of competition.

Can anyone say how many artists will be born in the next twenty minutes? We are aware of the great changes taking place each instant in the numbers of people on this planet. And we know of the equally great changes in practicality—what, that is, through technology, people are able to do. Great numbers of men will bring about the future works of art. And these will go in more directions than history records. We no longer have to lull ourselves expecting the advent of some one artist who will satisfy all our aesthetic needs. There will rather be an increase in the amount and kinds of art which will be both bewildering and productive of joy.

APPENDIX

A GUIDE FOR CRITICAL ANALYSIS OF A PAINTING

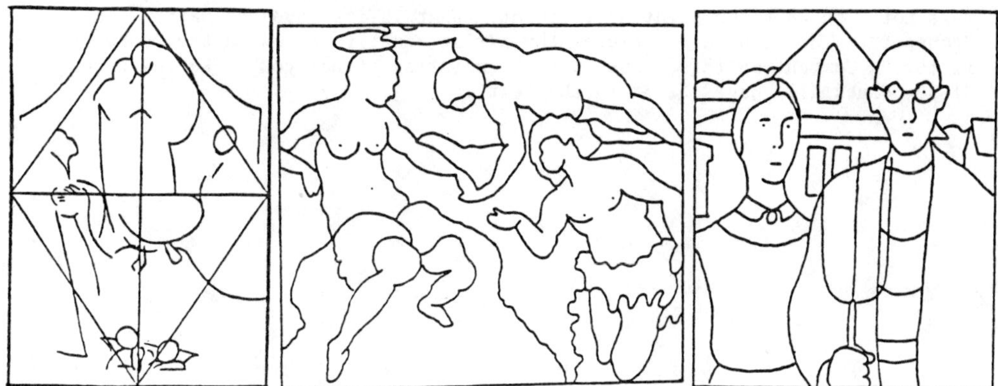

For this analysis you will be assigned or asked to choose on your own a painting to study. It is suggested that you read the Guide through and review the passages in THE HUMANITIES to which you are referred before undertaking the study.

PART ONE

In Part One you will study the painting from several points of view and make informal notes in the spaces provided.

PART TWO

In Part Two you will make a comprehensive statement about the painting and your experiencing of it. This reflective evaluation should be carefully organized as a separate essay. Two thirds of the grade will be based on Part Two.

NAME OF PAINTING ____________________

ARTIST ____________________ DATES ____________________

NAME ____________________ CLASS MEETING TIME ____________________

ADDRESS ____________________ DATE ____________________

PAINTING ANALYSIS NO. __________

PART ONE: Informal notes on the painting.

In Part One you are asked to study the painting from several points of view and to make notes in the spaces provided. Formal sentences are not necessary. You may work through the various points of view in any order you choose. There will probably be more things to note under some headings than others, but make your coverage as complete as possible.

1. Make notes on what the painting is about. What is its "subject matter" <u>and</u> "content"? The "content" includes the artist's attitude toward the "subject matter." Comment on this. How does the painting affect you? (Review pages 31-56, especially pages 32-38 in the text.)

2. What seems to have been the feelings the painter wished to communicate? Explain why you think so. Your own emotional response is valid. "Define" it as best you can. Try also to identify what the painter has done to evoke this response (e.g., in handling of the elements of the visual arts.) That is, submit your own subjective feeling to objective analysis. Have any limitations of purpose, function, size, etc., been imposed on the artist? How have these affected the work? (Review pages 213-237 in the text.)

3. What is the medium? What are the potentials of this medium? How fully did the artist exploit these? Make notes on how the medium seems to have affected the methods of expression? (Review pages 133-161 in the text.)

4. Make notes on the use of the elements in the painting - - things which can be considered separately, such as line, color, use of light and dark, shape, volume, etc. Make notes on the artist's general methods of expression (handling of space, distortion, use of light, interest in textures, volumes of the objects represented, etc.) How are these used in the organization of the painting? (Review pages 309-330 in the text.)

5. Draw here two outlines of the frame of the painting. Be careful to approximate the shape of the painting itself. In the first, sketch in the most important organizing lines. (Do not try to copy the painting.) In the second, shade in the value distribution in the painting. Which type of organization described in the text does the organization in this painting resemble most? (Review pages 309-330 in the text.)

6. Do the characteristics of form, use of elements, or content of the painting lead you to believe that it belongs to a particular geographic area, period, trend, "school"? Does this painting seem typical of this artist's work? (Review pages 21-23, 38-40, 48-56, 235-238, 425-436 in the text and see "Abstract art," "Abstract expressionism," "Cubism," "Romanticism," and "Classicism," in the Glossary.

Note here any sources beyond the text which you have used in studying the painting.

PART TWO: Critical analysis and personal perception.

In Part One you have made informal analytical notes on the painting from various points of view. From your review of these and reflections on them, you are asked in this part to articulate your personal coherent perception of the work. Use any of the ideas from Part One that you think are pertinent, plus additional ideas you have from reflecting on the interrelations of these. Your statement should relate personal response to objective analysis and should be more than a mere repetition of the notes you have made. It should be presented as a well-rounded, well-organized essay.

PART ONE: Answers ranked: 0 - no credit 1 - fair 2 - good 3 - excellent Highest possible score-18	PART TWO: Essay ranked: 0 - no credit 1 - fair (and multiplied 2 - good by 12) 3 - excellent Highest possible score-36	PART ONE + PART TWO for Total Score Highest possible total-54
Score	Score	Total

A GUIDE FOR CRITICAL ANALYSIS OF MUSIC

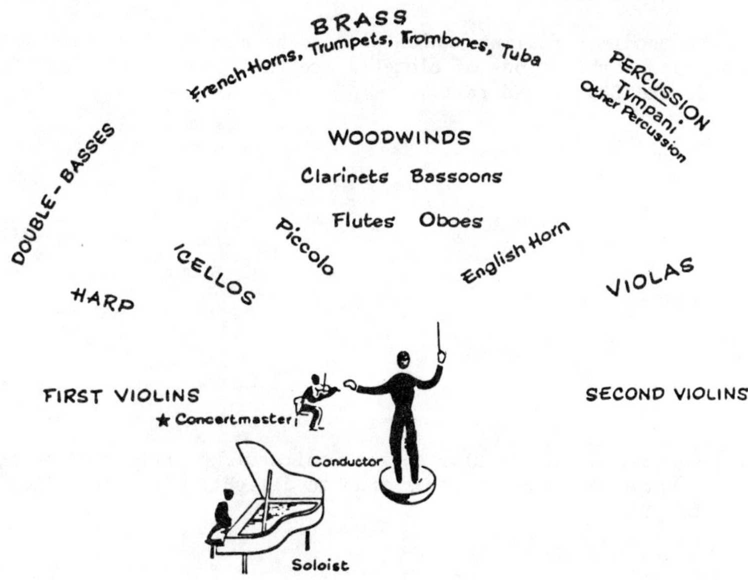

For this analysis you will be assigned or asked to choose on your own a piece of music to listen to and to study. It is suggested that you read the Guide through and review the passages in THE HUMANITIES to which you are referred before undertaking the study.

PART ONE

In Part One you will study the piece from several points of view and make informal notes in the spaces provided.

PART TWO

In Part Two you will make a comprehensive statement about the composition and your experiencing of it. This reflective evaluation should be carefully organized as a separate essay. Two thirds of the grade will be based on Part Two.

NAME OF COMPOSITION ____________________

COMPOSER ____________________

DATE OF COMPOSITION, IF KNOWN ____________________

NAME ____________________ CLASS MEETING TIME ____________

ADDRESS ____________________ CLASS MEETING TIME ____________

MUSIC ANALYSIS NO. ____________

PART ONE: Informal notes on the selection.

In this section you are asked to examine the selection from several points of view and to make notes in the spaces provided. Formal sentences are not necessary, and you may work through the various points of view in any order you choose. There will probably be more things to note under some headings than under others, but you should make your coverage as complete as possible.

1. Make notes on the moods or feelings which seem to be expressed in this work. What musical elements and combinations of elements are used to express them? (Review pages 32-34, 123, and 386 in the text.)

2. Does the piece suggest any particular social, cultural, political or religious values? Does it have any function other than to delight? Explain. (Review pages 91-92 in the text.)

3. What instrument, group of instruments, voice, or combinations of these is used? Make notes on the effect the choice of instruments and/or voices has on the music. (Review pages 162-184 and 389-392 in the text.)

4. Make notes on the elements which can be discussed separately, such as tempo, rhythm, melody, harmony, timbre, dynamics, etc. What relationships or uses of these elements aid in achieving unity and/or variety in the piece? (Review pages 238-271 in the text.)

5. What is the musical form? If it is a traditional form, how strictly does the composer follow it? (Review pages 364-392 in the text.)

6. Are there characteristics of form, use of elements, expressive content which lead you to believe the piece belongs to some particular geographic area, period, trend, school, or composer? (Review pages 430-432 on "classicism" and "romanticism," but see especially pages 429-430 for other suggestions in considering "style."

Note here any sources beyond the text which you have used in studying the piece, e.g., album covers, books, comment by the composer, etc.

PART TWO: Critical analysis and evaluation of your experience in studying the musical selection.

In Part One you have made informal notes on the selection from various points of view. From your reflection on these, you are asked in this part to make a statement about your personal coherent perception of the work. Use any of the ideas from Part One you think are pertinent, plus additional ideas you have from reflection on the interrelation of these. Your statement should relate personal to objective analysis and should be more than a mere repetition of the notes you have made. It should be presented as a well-rounded, well-organized essay.

PART ONE: Answers ranked: 0 - no credit 1 - fair 2 - good 3 - excellent Highest possible score-18	PART TWO: Essay ranked: 0 - no credit 1 - fair (and multiplied 2 - good by 12) 3 - excellent Highest possible score-36	PART ONE + PART TWO for Total Score Highest possible total-54
Score	Score	Total

A GUIDE FOR CRITICAL ANALYSIS OF THEATER - DRAMA

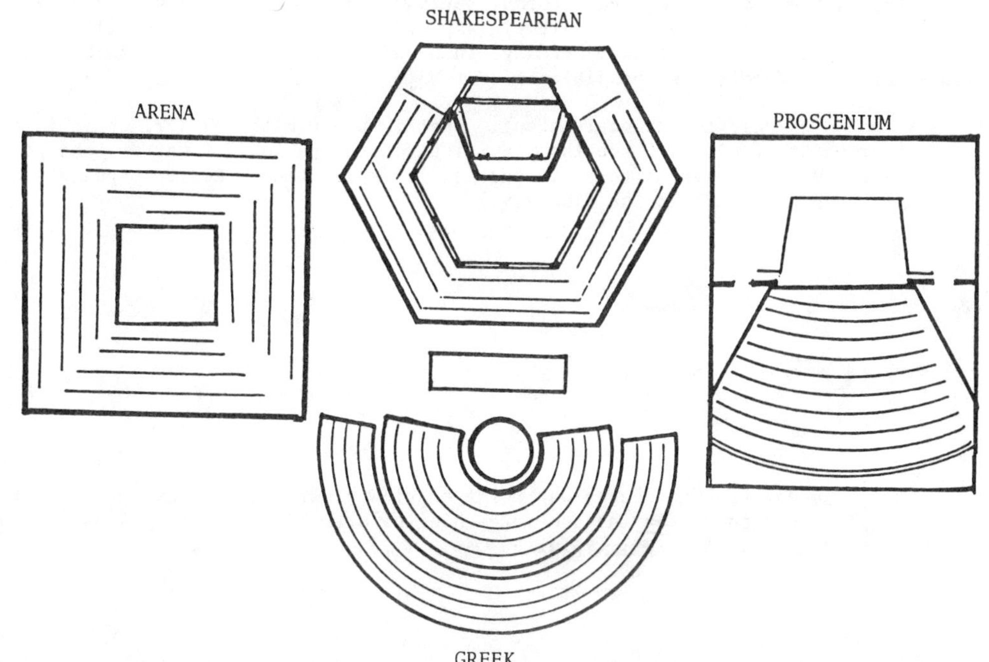

For this analysis you will read a play (drama) and/or see a performance of it (theater) Whichever you do, you are for the analysis to consider drama (the written text) and theater (performed drama) as a combined art, since the playwright is writing for performance and must make the text conform to both the limitations and possibilities of performance. It is suggested that you read this Guide through and review the passages in THE HUMANITIES to which you are referred before undertaking the study.

PART ONE

In Part One you will study the drama and/or production of it from several points of view and make informal notes in the spaces provided.

PART TWO

In Part Two you will be asked to make a comprehensive statement about work and your experiencing of it. This reflective evaluation should be carefully organized as a separate essay. Two thirds of the grade will be based on Part Two.

NAME OF THE PLAY____________________

AUTHOR__________ DATES__________ NATIONALITY__________

DATE OF WRITING OF THE PLAY, IF KNOWN____________________

IF SEEN IN PERFORMANCE: WHEN, BY WHOM?__________ DIRECTOR__________

ATTACH PROGRAM IF POSSIBLE

NAME____________________ CLASS MEETING TIME__________

ADDRESS____________________ DATE__________

THEATER - DRAMA ANALYSIS NO.__________

PART ONE: Informal notes on the play as read and/or seen in performance.

In this section you are asked to examine the play from several points of view and to make notes in the spaces provided. Formal sentences are not necessary, and you may work through the various points of view in any order you choose. There will probably be more things to note under some headings than under others, but you should make your coverage as complete as possible.

1. Make notes on what the drama is about. What is the subject matter? What is the bias or point of view? Since the playwright chose the subject matter, the point of view may be revealed both by it and how it is treated. (Review pages 35-36 in the text and "Absurd" in the Glossary.)

2. Does the author seek to change our point of view about the subject matter of the play? Is the author, for instance, teaching or preaching or making light of what we usually take seriously? Explain.

3. Theatre is a combined art. Identify the mediums used: literature, design (staging, makeup, lighting, deployment of actors, costumes), acting (persons dressed in a particular way, speaking in a particular way and moving in a defined space), music, dance. (Review pages 190-194 in the text and "Frame" and "Combined arts" in the Glossary.)

4. Analyze two or three of the mediums mentioned above and comment on how the elements of each are used to contribute to the play's effectivenes. (Review pages 190-194 in the text.)

5. A drama presents a story or narrative or familiarizes us with a group of characters in a particular set of circumstances. What is the narrative unfolded in this play (the actual chronology of events)? Make notes on the real time sequence of events and on the order in which these have become the "plot" of the play. Are they the same? Why do you suppose the playwright chose this particular order of presentation? (Review pages 398-402 and 407-410 in the text and "Plot" in the Glossary.)

6. The essentials of narrative are exposition, conflict, climax, and denoument. Using a simple diagram like the one below indicate roughly how much of the play is given to each. (Review pages 398-400 in the text and "Exposition" in the Glossary.)

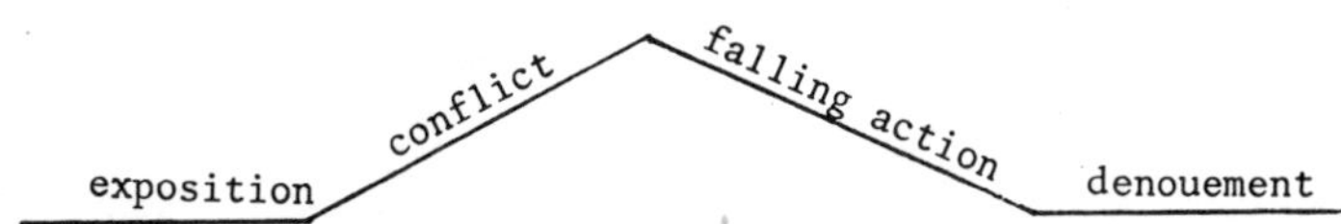

7. Make notes on the style of the drama as written or, if seen in performance, as presented. Have changes been made in the written play to update it, to emphasize or modify the "content" or to adapt it to a particular audience or to particular circumstances of presentation? Comment. (Review pages 35-38 and 435 in the text.) Stage settings and costumes tend to duplicate styles in the arts, running the gamut from realism to pure abstraction, from impressionism to abstract expressionism. (Review pages 38-51 in the text and see "Abstract," "Abstract expressionism," "Impressionism," and "Representational art" in the Glossary.)

Note here any sources you have used in studying the work . . . e.g., text notes, program notes, books (other than the text), articles, etc.

PART TWO: Critical analysis and evaluation of your experience in studying this example of theatre-drama.

In Part One you have made informal notes on the play and/or performance from various points of view. From your reflection on these, you are asked in this part to make a statement about your personal coherent perception of the work. Use any of the ideas from Part One you think are pertinent, plus additional ideas you have from reflection on the interrelations of these. Your statement should relate personal response to objective analysis and should be more than a mere repetition of the notes you have made. It should be presented as a well-rounded, well-organized essay.

PART ONE: Answers ranked: 0 - no credit 1 - fair 2 - good 3 - excellent Highest possible score- 21	PART TWO: Essay ranked: 0 - no credit 1 - fair (and multiplied 2 - good by 14) 3 - excellent Highest possible score- 42	PART ONE + PART TWO for Total Score Highest possible total- 63
Score	Score	Total

A GUIDE FOR CRITICAL ANALYSIS OF DANCE

For this analysis you will watch the performance of a dance. It may be on film, on the stage or in some other setting. It is suggested that you read this Guide through and review the passages in the text to which you are referred before undertaking the analysis.

PART ONE

In Part One you will study the dance from several points of view and make informal notes in the spaces provided.

PART TWO

In Part Two you will make a statement on your concluding perception of the dance after analysis and reflection. This comprehensive statement about the dance and your experiencing of it should be carefully organized as a separate essay. Two thirds of the grade given will be based on Part Two.

TITLE OF THE DANCE________________ PERFORMER(S)________________

WHERE OBSERVED________________ CHOREOGRAPHER AND COMPOSER________________

NAME________________ CLASS MEETING TIME________________

ADDRESS________________ DATE________________

DANCE ANALYSIS NO.________________

PART ONE: Informal notes on the dance.

In Part One you are asked to study and reflect on the dance from several points of view and to make notes in the spaces provided. Formal sentences are not necessary. You may work through the various points of view in any order you choose. There will probably be more things to note under some headings than others, but you should make your coverage as complete as possible.

1. Make notes on the "subject matter" and/or "content-communication" and/or "theme" of the dance (story, depiction of mood, feelings, environment, character study, satiric comment, design in movement, etc.) (Review pages 34 and 194-201 in the text.)

2. Makes notes on the specific use of the separate arts which are combined in dance: music, visual arts (designs in two and three dimensional space), and theater (movement, mime, gesture, costumes.) (Review pages 112, 190, and 416-418 in the text.)

3. Make notes on how the elements of the different arts are used in the dance: lines and volumes in two and three dimensional patterns (for example, bodies in relation to each other, to the frame of the stage, and to the space of the stage), dynamics (tensing-relaxing, falling-recovering, contracting-releasing, strong movements, gentle movements, staccato, etc.), phrasing (even, uneven, improvised, danced as fluid, disconnected, etc.), and rhythm (regular, irregular, strong-weak, simple-complicated, used-ignored, etc.). (Review page 411 in the text.)

4. Make notes on how the elements are used to give form to the piece. Is the form narrative, some musical form, non-repetitive, improvisation, made of contrasting themes, contrapuntal, variations of a theme, or some other? (Organization in dance can be represented in the same way as is organization in music. Review theme and variation (page 368-372), rondo (pages 377-378), suite (page 384), free forms (pages 385-386), contrapuntal (pages 256-261), program music (page 386) in the text.) If the content is narrative, you will want to make notes on how the essential parts of it are handled. (Review pages 398-402 in the text.)

5. Make notes on the general classification of dance to which this dance belongs (ethnic, social, classical ballet, modern, ritualistic, some combination of these.) (Review pages 411-419 in the text.)

6. Make notes on the specific characteristics of this dance within the general category to which it belongs. Do you associate these with some tradition, period, geographic area, choreographer, a particular dancer? (Review pages 194-197 in the text.)

Note here any sources beyond the performance and text which you have used in writing your analysis of the dance.

PART TWO: Critical analysis and personal perception.

In Part One you have made informal analytical notes on the dance from various points of view. From your review of these and reflections on them, you are asked in this part to articulate your personal coherent perception of the work. Use any of the ideas from Part One that you think are pertinent, plus additional ideas you have from reflecting on the interrelations of these. Your statement should relate personal response to objective analysis and should be more than a mere repetition of the notes you have made. It should be presented as a well-rounded, well-organized essay.

PART ONE: Answers ranked: 0 - no credit 1 - fair 2 - good 3 - excellent Highest possible score-18	PART TWO: Essay ranked: 0 - no credit 1 - fair (and multiplied 2 - good by 12) 3 - excellent Highest possible score-36	PART ONE + PART TWO for Total Score Highest possible total-54
Score	Score	Total

A GUIDE FOR CRITICAL ANALYSIS OF MUSICAL THEATER (OPERA, OPERETTA, MUSICAL)

For this analysis you will be assigned or asked to choose on your own an example of musical theater to listen to, to study and perhaps see performed. It is suggested that you read the Guide through and review the passages in THE HUMANITIES to which you are referred before undertaking the study.

PART ONE

In Part One you will study the piece from several points of view and make informal notes in the spaces provided.

PART TWO

In Part Two you will make a comprehensive statement about the composition and your experiencing of it. This reflective evaluation should be carefully organized as a separate essay. Two thirds of the grade will be based on Part Two.

NAME OF WORK ______________________________

COMPOSER ______________ DATES ______________

NATIONALITY ______________

DATE OF COMPOSITION ______________ SOURCE OF THE LIBRETTO ______________

IF SEEN IN PERFORMANCE, WHERE, BY WHOM? ______________

NAME ______________ CLASS MEETING TIME ______________

ADDRESS ______________ DATE ______________

MUSICAL THEATER ANALYSIS NO. ________

PART ONE: Informal notes on the opera, operetta, or musical.

In this section you are asked to examine the work from several points of view and to make notes in the spaces provided. Formal sentences are not necessary, and you may work through the various points of view in any order you choose. There will probably be more things to note under some headings than under others, but you should make your coverage as complete as possible.

1. Early opera used mythological stories as the basis for libretti. Later, nationalistic subject matter was used. Still later, opera was based on literary works, especially those with exotic backgrounds and stories. Some libretti were written expressly for musical dramas. Into which of these categories does the work you are studying fall? Summarize the story briefly and indicate its source. How has the source been modified? (Review pages 124-125, 202-203, and 118-119 in the text.)

2. What values are suggested by or in the work - - e.g., aesthetic, social, cultural, political and/or others? Are there remnants of the aristocratic origins of opera in the work?

3. Operas, operettas, musicals use several mediums, thus are sometimes called "combined arts." In different works the mediums used receive different emphasis and serve different purposes. Make notes on the use of the different mediums in the work you are studying - - the comparative importance of music and story, use of spectacle, inclusion of dance, spoken or sung dialogue, a chorus, etc. Which medium predominates? Explain. (Review pages 389-390 in the text.)

4. Make notes on how the different mediums are used - - i.e., the elements of vocal music, instrumental music, drama, acting, choreography, dancing, scene design and costume design. Are the uses made of different elements characteristic of the period in which the piece was written? How do they contribute to the story? To the total impact of the piece? You may decide the story is a mere vehicle for integrating spectacle, dance, music. If so, the elements of these arts are the important ones to consider. Characterize the music (vocal and instrument), the plot, the setting, design, staging, and the overall result as they are integrated. (Review pages 389-390 in the text.) Make notes on the effect the choice of instruments and/or voices has on the work.

5. Make notes on the organization of the composition. Is narrative the only structural feature? Is it straight forward, sequential, or presented in some other order? How are the other arts used to contribute to the structural unity of the work? Is it through-composed or a compilation of "set pieces" held together by dialogue or recitative? (Review pages 419-420 in the text.)

6. Choose a particular sequence or episode in the work you think effective and explain how the elements of each of the arts used contribute (or do not contribute significantly) to the total effect.

7. In the various periods of history different sets of conventions have characterized operatic style. Note explicitly the conventions in the piece being studied and relate them to the period in which it was written. Some composers developed highly individual conventions of their own which have become hallmarks of their works. Are the conventions in this work associated with any composer or group of composers? (Review pages 389-390 in the text.)

Note here any sources you have used in studying the work - - e.g., program notes, album covers, books (beyond the text), articles, etc.

PART TWO: Critical analysis and evaluation of your experience in studying the opera, operetta or musical.

In Part One you have made informal notes on the work from various points of view. From your reflection on these, you are asked in this part to make a statement about your personal coherent perceptions of the work. Use any of the ideas from Part One you think are pertinent, plus additional ideas you have from reflection on the interrelations of these. Your statement should relate personal response to objective analysis and should be more than a mere repetition of the notes you have made. <u>It should be presented as a well-rounded, well-organized essay</u>.

PART ONE: Answers ranked: 0 - no credit 1 - fair 2 - good 3 - excellent Highest possible score- 21	PART TWO: Essay ranked: 0 - no credit 1 - fair (and multiplied 2 - good by 14) 3 - excellent Highest possible score- 42	PART ONE + PART TWO for Total Score Highest possible total- 63
Score	Score	Total

A GUIDE FOR CRITICAL ANALYSIS OF FILM

The art of seeing films is perhaps one of the most difficult to learn, for the study of film - - in the 20th century that most characteristic, popular, and seemingly ubiquitous of the arts - - creates special problems for the serious viewer. The appropriate subject of study, the film itself, consists of an intangible complex of images and sounds that appear and disappear in an instant. When they have vanished, there is little to consult but words, and as often as not the words are concerned with paraphrasable content, the story or narrative, and the ideas these inspire. And while these subjects hold undeniable importance, they offer only a fragment of the total film experience.

In the study of films, therefore, we place the emphasis on analysis of the visual and temporal structure which carry so much of the expressive content of films and at the same time offer delight in and of themselves. Analysis is not, of course, an end in itself, but a means of expanding awareness.

- - Lincoln F. Johnson

For this analysis you will be assigned or asked to choose on your own an example of film for critical analysis. Because film is a "time art" as well as "a combined art" the complex of appeals to our various senses moves by us so rapidly that it is difficult to reflect at the time on what has produced our responses to it. It is important, therefore, that you see the film being studied at least twice.

You should read the indicated sections in THE HUMANITIES before seeing the film the first time and then review them before seeing it a second time.

PART ONE

In Part One you will study the film from several points of view and make informal notes in the spaces provided.

PART TWO

In Part Two you will make a comprehensive statement about the film and your experiencing of it. This reflective evaluation should be carefully organized as a separate essay. Two thirds of the grade will be based on Part Two.

TITLE OF THE FILM____________________ DIRECTOR____________________

DATE OF FILM, IF KNOWN____________________ WHERE SEEN?____________________

WHEN?____________________

NAME____________________ CLASS MEETING TIME____________________

ADDRESS____________________ DATE____________________

FILM ANALYSIS NO.____________________

4. Film is a "combined art" and therefore has available for use all of the elements of the arts which are integrated in it. We have become so accustomed to responding to the visual and auditory aspects of film as a unified experience that we are not usually conscious of their separate origins nor of the synchronizing and editing which has brought them together in the finished film. Are music and/or natural sounds used as background or to expand the meaning and emotional content of the film? What role do they play? Supportive of mood, place, time, action? Are colors used in any distinctive way? Was the film made "on location" or in a studio? What use is made of lighting? Are there sequences which seem included for their intrinsic merit as art rather than to develop mood, setting, period, or some facet of a character's personality? What is the style of dialogue? How much is conveyed visually? Through sound, speaking? (Review pages 190 and 203-205 in the text.)

5. Make notes here on the structure, the overall organization of the film. Is the organization important in itself, or does it simply provide an occasion for more important material? Is the subject, story, narrative presented sequentially? Is there an exposition, a crisis, a denouement? Is it all middle - - presentation of characters in action? Remember that film more often than literature, opera, ballet or theatre departs from traditional narrative conventions and expectations. (Review pages 420-422 in the text.)

6. Make notes here on two sequences which you thought especially effective uses of the film as art and analyze them in detail. How were elements and organization used to give them meaning beyond "paraphrasable content"? (Review the analysis of Kubrick's film, pages 206-208 in the text.)

7. What was the overall impact of this experience? Did the film leave you with questions? Did it change your mood? Did it challenge you to view your own life or the lives of others differently?

8. Of the many films with which you are familiar, which does this resemble most in style? Do you know other films made by the same director? Do these seem to confirm the "auteur theory" of film criticism? (Review page 204 in the text and "Auteur theory" in the Glossary.)

Note here any sources beyond the text which you have used in studying the film.

PART ONE: Informal notes on the film.

In this section you are asked to examine the film from several points of view and to make notes in the spaces provided. Formal sentences are not necessary, and you may work through the various points of view in any order you choose. There will probably be more things to note under some headings than under others, but you should make your coverage as complete as possible.

1. The opening sections of a film are important. They set the mood, tone, expectations of what is to follow. How does the film begin? How are the title and credits presented? What is the relationship of the title to the film? Is it descriptive, thematic, ambiguous, enigmatic, etc.? Are music or natural sounds used? (See "Establishing shot" in the Glossary.)

2. What is the film about? Remember that the ostensible subject matter, ideas, story may on analysis and reflection emerge as mere skeletons on which the deeper meaning of the film, its "content" is developed. Make notes on both explicit, nominal subject matter and on any less obvious meanings you sense in the film. (Review pages 35-38, 205, 420-422 in the text.)

3. Comment on the medium - - i.e., the camera and sound techniques used to put audio and visual images on film. For example, is there a tendency toward organizing scenes within a "frame"? What methods of transition are used (e.g., fade-in, fade-out, flashbacks, cutting from one speaker to another)? Does the camera act as the eyes of the director or the eyes of a character or characters? Does it record "objective" material, "subjective" interpretation, associations, symbols, etc.? Comment on "aesthetic distance" in the film. (Review pages 203-209 in the text and see "Transitional devices" in the Glossary.)

PART TWO: Critical analysis and evaluation of your experience in studying the film.

In Part One you have made informal notes on the film from various points of view. From your reflection on these, you are asked in this part to make a statement about your personal, coherent perception of the work. Use any of the ideas from Part One you think are pertinent, plus additional ideas you have from reflection on the interrelations of these. Your statement should relate personal response to objective analysis and should be more than a mere repetition of the notes you have made. _It should be presented as a well-rounded, well-organized essay._

(over)

PART ONE: Answers ranked: 0 - no credit 1 - fair 2 - good 3 - excellent Highest possible score- 24	PART TWO: Essay ranked: 0 - no credit 1 - fair (and multiplied 2 - good by 16) 3 - excellent Highest possible score- 48	PART ONE + PART TWO for Total Score Highest possible total- 72
Score	Score	Total

A GUIDE FOR CRITICAL ANALYSIS OF ARCHITECTURE

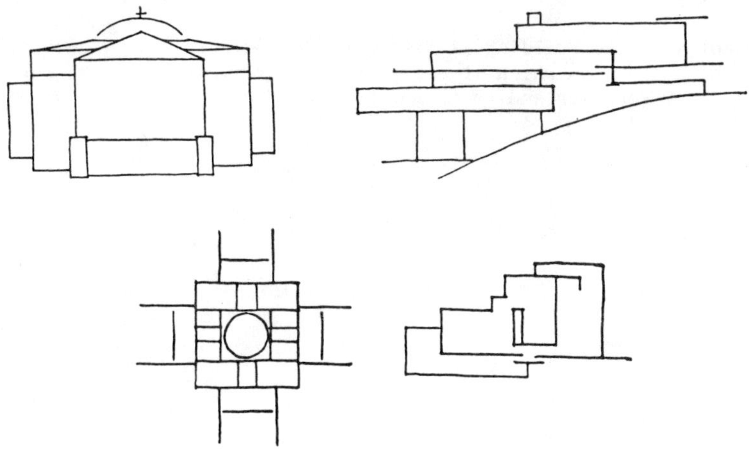

For this analysis you should choose a building you will be able to visit and study. It should be a building of some distinction and one which you will enjoy learning more about. It is suggested that you read this Guide through and review the passages in the text to which you are referred before undertaking the study.

PART ONE

In Part One you will study the building from several points of view and make informal notes in the spaces provided.

PART TWO

In Part Two you will make an over-all critique of the building. This reflective evaluation of the building and of your experiencing of it should be carefully organized as a separate essay. *Two thirds of the grade given will be based on Part Two.*

NAME OF THE BUILDING ______________________________

LOCATION ______________________________

ARCHITECT, IF KNOWN ______________ DATE CONSTRUCTED, IF KNOWN ________

NAME ______________________ CLASS MEETING TIME ______________

ADDRESS ______________________ DATE ______________

ARCHITECTURE ANALYSIS NO. ________

PART ONE: Informal notes on the building.

In Part One you are asked to study the building from several points of view and to make notes in the spaces provided. Formal sentences are not necessary. You may work through the various points of view in any order you choose. There will probably be more things to note under some headings than others, but you should make your coverage as complete as possible.

1. Make notes of what the building is, its purpose, function. How does it reflect values in the culture in which it emerged? (Review pages 32-33 on "Purpose" and pages 97-105 on "Function and Form" in the text.)

2. What seem to have been the "controlling" considerations of the architect? To make it serve a particular function? To make it a public expression of some kind? To make it a different, highly individual architectural creation? Some combination of these? Are the shape, function, decorative, expressive details and relation of parts well integrated? Are there climatic, geographical, period, or social-cultural influences reflected in the building? (Review pages 97-105 and 353-356 in the text.)

3. What are the mediums used? Why do you suppose they were chosen? Have they been used effectively? Explain. (Review pages 133-134 and 353-360 in the text.)

4. Describe the principles of construction used? Were they dictated by the medium? By the function? By the expressive intent? (Review pages 338-360 in the text.)

5. Indicate the characteristics of the building that relate to some particular period, geographic region, social-cultural context, or style of architecture. If you know of other buildings by the same architect or of similar buildings, you may wish to compare this building to them. (Review pages 338-363 - - especially the summary of styles on pages 361-363 - - and pages 431-432 in the text.)

6. Draw here sketches of the building in significant profiles. Include only important visual lines, and decorative, stylistic features. (See sketches of Palladio's Villa Capra and Frank Lloyd Wright's John C. Pew House on the cover of this Guide.) Make a rough sketch of the floor plan if you have access to the interior. In addition, attach a photograph or other picture of the building.

Note here any sources beyond your own observations and the text which you have used in writing your analysis of the building.

PART TWO: Critical analysis and personal perception.

In Part One you have made informal analytical notes on the building from various points of view. From your review of these and reflections on them, you are asked to in Part Two to demonstrate your personal, coherent perception of the building. Use any ideas from Part One that you think pertinent, plus additional ideas you have from reflecting on the interrelations of these. Your statement should relate personal response to objective analysis and should be more than a mere repetition of the notes you have made. <u>It should be presented as a well-rounded, well-organized essay</u>.

PART ONE: Answers ranked: 0 - no credit 1 - fair 2 - good 3 - excellent Highest possible score-18	PART TWO: Essay ranked: 0 - no credit 1 - fair (and multiplied 2 - good by 12) 3 - excellent Highest possible score-36	PART ONE + PART TWO for Total Score Highest possible total-54
Score	Score	Total

INDEX OF READINGS AND ACKNOWLEDGEMENTS

Russell Green, "Five Rocking Chairs". 25
Copyright (c) 1958 by Stephens College. Reprinted from *The Stephens College Bulletin*, January, 1958 by permission of the author and Stephens College.

Lincoln F. Johnson, "The Analysis of Film". 129
From *Film: Space, Time, Light, and Sound* by Lincoln F. Johnson. Copyright (c) 1974 by Holt, Rinehart and Winston. Reprinted by permission of Holt, Rinehart and Winston.

Gyorgy Kepes, "The Universal Language of Art". 6

"The Image as Focused Experience". 206
Copyright (c) 1956 by Gyorgy Kepes. All rights reserved. Reprinted from *The New Landscape*, Paul Theobold and Co., Chicago, by permission of Gyorgy Kepes.

E.S. Miller, "Three Poems". 183

"Grasshoppers". 198
Copyright (c) 1972 by E.S. Miller. Reprinted from his *Selected Poems* in the Open Places Poets Series, Stephens College, Columbia, Missouri, by his permission.

Paul Cezanne's lithograph, *Bathers*, on page 210, is used through the courtesy of The High Museum of Art, Atlanta, Ga.